Life, Laughter, Lessons

LIFE IS FUNNIER THAN FICTION

A MEMOIR BY

FRED PAWLUK

FOREWORD BY CHARLOTTE DIAMOND

Tellwell Talent
www.tellwell.ca

ISBN
978-0-2288-7822-3 (Hardcover)
978-0-2288-7824-7 (Paperback)
978-0-2288-7823-0 (eBook)

FOREWORD

By Charlotte Diamond

Any visit with my friend and author Fred Pawluk is always a laughing and learning experience! His story telling, peppered with spontaneous puns and seasoned with vivid tales of his past adventures, have always captured my attention and imagination. He is truly a talented raconteur along the lines of fellow Canadian Stuart McLean and his popular *Vinyl Cafe*.

We all love a laugh and escape through stories of our youth and the crazy, sometimes foolish, adventures through which we have lived.

Fred's stories trace true events and his memories from the age of five to the present. He recalls stories of working on a Milton, Ontario, dairy farm with the challenges of milking cows in an overcrowded barn ("Blackie the Cow"), travelling with his wife Sue to Thailand and walking an elephant, jungle, path ("Been There, Dung That"), or salmon fishing through the night in the Strait of Juan de Fuca, north of Victoria, British Columbia, with Harry on his gill-net fish boat ("Fishing with Twinkies").

Fred's sense of fun and wit is evident in his over-two-hundred-page-turner tales. He expresses a keen sense of history that reminds us to savour each moment of our lives and record our memorable words of wisdom for future enjoyment.

This book could be on a bedside table for an entertaining read at the end of the day, on the coffee table to share a laugh or spark a conversation, or in your car for a pleasant diversion as you wait for a delayed West Coast Island ferry to arrive! There is laughter and lessons to be learned as this collection of stories takes us through Fred's sometimes problematic adventures.

Enjoy the ride!

Charlotte Diamond CM

Award-winning author, singer, songwriter and recording artist

PREFACE

Retirement was the catalyst.

I never considered writing, let alone writing a memoir, prior to giving up the daily grind. But within one year of having excess time on my hands, memories began to bubble up—not just regular daily occurrences but primarily the humorous and absurd. I came to realize I have had countless experiences along this vein.

For ten years I recorded these incidences in point form. Gradually I fleshed them out into anecdotes of various lengths.

All my accounts are factual with a deliberate attempt to avoid hyperbole. Although the vast majority are from personal experiences, I have included a few stories shared with me by family members and friends.

At no time did I have ambitions to publish a book. The stories were meant to be recorded on my hard drive for family enjoyment. However, as the stories accumulated, I began to share them orally with friends and family. The humorous ones were for the most part appreciated—enough so that I was encouraged by my wife, Sue, to put them into print.

And so, it has come to fruition.

DEDICATION

To all my grandchildren: Felix, Avery, Freddie, Aretha, Andrew, Matthew, Nathan, Sam, Oliver, Bentley, Chrissy, Max, and Emily; sisters Margaret and Caroline.

ACKNOWLEDGEMENTS

To my wife, Sue; daughters, Katie and Emma; parents and friends who contributed stories; Charlotte Diamond, a valued friend; Tamás Revoczi, my computer guru and photographer; Christine Schrum, editorial consultant.

CLAY FIGHT

When I was six years old, our neighbours, the Midgely's, decided to replace the existing house on their property. The process began with the laborious excavation of their basement. They had to do it all by hand since today's mechanical equipment either did not exist or the cost was prohibitive.

The subsequent clay they dug up was shovelled into lofty piles on the immediate perimeter of their excavated basement. The chunks of clay, which hardened over time, proved to be a perfect weapon for eventual clay fights.

The Midgley family consisted of a mother, father and two sons, Bryan and Ardie, who were ten and nine years old, respectively. Bryan and Ardie often took advantage of the fact that they were older than me. And, of course, I was at a distinct disadvantage when it came to a clay fight.

On the day of said "clay fight," Bryan and Ardie were positioned on their side of the property, strategically hidden behind a two- to three-foot pile of clay. I in turn hid behind my pile of clay, kitty-corner from my so-called neighbours.

I can't honestly remember what precipitated the warfare that ensued; it may have been a case of "necessity being the mother of invention." And so, the battle began with clay chunks being flung back and forth, alternated with strategic ducking to avoid any unfortunate hits.

It wasn't long before my father, becoming aware of the ongoing battle, rushed outdoors shouting, "Freddie, stop fighting, you're going to get your teeth knocked out!"

There probably was a momentary lull in the "friendly fight" until my dad retreated inside our house. Then all hell broke loose again with clay being lobbed back and forth as enthusiastically as before . . . until the moment of my misstep when I failed to duck at the identical time a clay chunk arrived.

The chunk hit me squarely in the mouth. The pain was instantaneous. Blood flowed immediately and my two front teeth were dislodged just as quickly.

My immediate cries drew my father outdoors with the comment, "Freddie, I told you. I told you."

My recollection from that moment on is rather vague. I assume I was brought indoors and given medical attention. Where Bryan and Ardie disappeared to, I do not know.

The event was never to be repeated and my friendship with Bryan and Ardie survived for many years thereafter.

FROZEN PANT LEG

Being raised in Northern Ontario in the early 1950s, we experienced cold winter weather identical to that of Winnipeg, Manitoba. My memories of how often I suffered the bitter consequences of the climate are too numerous to mention.

However, there was one occasion in my Grade 2 year that stands out in my mind. Attending Prince Charles Elementary School, Sudbury, Ontario, I was able to zip home for lunch on most days since our home was a short ten-minute run/walk.

On a particularly cold day, shortly after stepping off the school property, I lost control of my bladder and peed my pants. Most of the pee ran down the left side of my pant leg.

Fortunately, no one was accompanying me, and I was able to save face to a certain degree until I got home. In the interim between relieving myself and arriving home, the excessively cold temperature caused my pant leg to freeze solid. I was limping with a stiff leg well before walking in the front door of my home.

Again, fortunately for me, my mother was at home and her empathetic approach helped lighten my load, literally. She directed me to strip down, throw my pants into the washing machine and wash up.

Lunch followed and then I was off to school again feeling much relieved that the experience was behind me.

PEEING DENIAL

Mrs. Armstrong was our Grade 2 teacher. To the best of my memory, she was a compassionate person despite the fact that three individuals, Bob Powers, Kazmir Pabisz and I, were chronic troublemakers in class. On many occasions, she threatened to bring diapers to school to tie us to our respective chairs. Needless to say, our behaviour was wanting.

My main claim to infamy during this school year was when I failed to control my bladder while sitting at my desk. The resulting puddle on the floor drew the attention of a female classmate who immediately reported the situation to our teacher. Mrs. Armstrong recommended that I go to the back room in the class to get cloth rags to soak up my urine.

However, I offered an alternative problem-solving solution by denying that I was responsible for the flood on the floor. Despite the back-and-forth accusations and denials between my female classmate and me, Mrs. Armstrong insisted and finally convinced me to do as she suggested.

I retrieved the cloth rags, sopped up the pee and placed the soaked rags in the back room somewhere.

It is interesting that in recalling this story I can remember all the above-mentioned details but have obliterated all subsequent repercussions from fellow classmates, teachers, and school officials. Needless to say, those present at that particular time must have cracked up. The ensuing story must have been shared on countless occasions, understandably at my expense.

ÑO RESPECT

As a university student in 1968, I was recruited by industry, namely INCO (the International Nickel Company of Canada), for summer employment. And because I was an engineering student, I was assigned to a mechanical maintenance team with the so-called prestige of being "on salary" as opposed to an hourly wage. I was therefore given the opportunity to get ahead in the world.

This mechanical maintenance team consisted of a rigger, welder, mechanic, crane operator, foreman and me, in the capacity of an apprentice. Our assignment was to assist a Swiss technician in the installation of a quarter-million-dollar air compressor at a nickel mine.

Little did I know that my assigned team members would take advantage of my false perception. Over time I became the butt of their practical jokes plus the recipient of one of their time-honoured initiation rites, namely the greasing of my testicles. As someone quick on my feet I did not feel intimidated.

They simply could not catch me.

As for their practical jokes, one of their requests was to collect a "pail of sparks" when the welder cut metal pipe with an acetylene torch. I did not fall for this one. However, I did succumb to a convoluted request to visit the supply shop for "shoreline." This may seem quite naive on my part, but it should be noted that we worked daily with rope and metal slings to hoist heavy equipment by overhead crane.

On my first visit to the supply shop, the clerk looked rather puzzled when I asked for thirty feet of shoreline. He disappeared into the back room, returned, and indicated that he "was out of stock." Upon returning to my workplace empty-handed, the main perpetrator, King Croteau, insisted that the "shoreline" was necessary and that I would need to return to the supply shop. Back I went and confronted the same clerk for thirty feet of shoreline. Again, he disappeared into the backroom, this time returning with only a curious smirk on his face.

Upon my return, empty-handed for the second time, I could now detect the insincerity written on King Croteau's face. I quickly surmised that the "King" in King Croteau represented his supreme ability as a "bullshitter."

As alluded to earlier, I was promised an initiation which took me completely by surprise. I was strong-armed from behind by the welder and held immobile as King Croteau approached with a small pail of axle grease. Helplessly I watched as my pants and underwear were dropped and the grease was applied liberally.

It took several attempts over a forty-eight-hour period to remove all signs of the artwork bestowed upon me.

GET THAT COBRA OFF ME

In 1973, after several months of backpacking through Northern and Southern Europe, my girlfriend and I reached Torremolinos, Costa del Sol, Spain. There we checked into a small cottage accommodation where we met fellow travellers including a young married couple consisting of an American husband and a Venezuelan wife.

Within a matter of days, all four of us decided to travel by bus to Algeciras, across the Strait of Gibraltar into Morocco. From there we took a local bus through the countryside with Fez as our first major destination. This bus was occupied mainly by Moroccan citizens with very few of us foreigners. Consequently, there were many stops, including a roadside visit with a farmer and his freshly butchered cow. The bus occupants eagerly purchased various cuts of the slain animal and brought them on board to be deposited in an overhead storage rack where the blood then dripped onto the seated areas below.

We arrived in Fez, booked into a hotel, and remained together for only one day with the promise to renew acquaintances in Torremolinos.

Our Moroccan stay lasted nine days with dysentery precipitating our early return to Spain. After two of three days, our married-couple friends returned with the following death-defying story. Visiting the medina of an interior Moroccan city, they were attracted to a market gathering. Once closer they realised a snake charmer was entertaining the crowd. Being the curious tourists that they were, they edged in as close as possible, camera in hand. When the snake charmer realized he had a captive audience of two foreign tourists, he immediately took the cobra and began to wrap it around the Venezuelan's neck. Of course, her husband wanted to maximize the opportunity by recording the event photographically. At the same time, his wife, experiencing excruciating terror, screamed blue murder. She pleaded with her husband to pay the snake charmer whatever he wanted to remove the cobra.

It proved to be a delightful story with the benefit of me not having had to experience it personally.

LAUGHING FIDDLER

In 1973 and 1974, I volunteered as the coordinator/artistic director for the Northern Lights Folk Festival Boreal. This annual outdoor event took place on the shores of Ramsey Lake in Sudbury, Ontario. Three days of music hosted simultaneously on three stages drew ten thousand spectators on average. The site, a beautiful redevelopment for Canada's Centennial year in 1967, was appropriately named Centennial Park.

As a violin/fiddle aficionado I made an extraordinary effort to promote a high level of fiddle performances for the festival.

On opening day, on the main outdoor amphitheatre stage, I arranged a fiddle workshop featuring the reigning Northern Ontario fiddle champion, Johnny Bruneau, plus Don Mandle, Richard Mende, and Jean Carignan. Jean was considered the best fiddler in North America. As an indication of Jean's reputation, he had just performed four days previously on Parliament Hill as part of the Canada Day festivities.

The format of the workshop required each musician to perform on a rotational basis until a full hour was used up. I took in the performances from one side of the stage savouring not only the musicianship but the audience's reaction.

As the hour concluded all four musicians vacated the stage and walked along the side towards the backstage area. It was along the side that I observed Johnny Bruneau laughing out loud. This intrigued me enough to approach him. "Why are you laughing?" I asked.

"That's the best fiddler I've ever heard," he replied, pointing to Jean Carignan. "You didn't need me at all."

TOPLESS DANCER

My role with the Northern Lights Folk Festival Boreal placed me at the centre of the storm in the positive sense of excitement, stimulation, and rewards.

During my rounds on a Sunday morning on a festival weekend, I was approached by one of our volunteers regarding a problem on the main stage. It was explained to me that a topless woman was dancing on stage while a group of musicians was performing. This not only proved to be a distraction for the musicians but created a dilemma for the audience as children were in attendance with their parents. The festival was an outdoor family affair.

Obviously, something had to be done. I rushed over to the stage. Fortunately, the topless dancer was not to be seen. In short order, we learned that her brother had managed to bundle her off. Apparently, drugs were the catalyst for the lack of inhibition in her dancing.

This episode turned out to be one of many during my two-year tenure.

BURLESQUE REQUEST

Before I was involved, Mayor Grace Hartman had been responsible for the Northern Lights Folk Festival Boreal. She had moved a distance away after leaving office but wanted to return for the festival in 1974. She contacted me by phone to thank our organization and promised to attend. At seventy-one years of age, she announced that she would be hitchhiking to the event. I was honoured and amused.

As we were preparing on site, a volunteer caught up with me explaining that a gentleman wished to talk to me. The volunteer wasn't apprised of the nature of the man's concern. I was ushered to the main stage area and introduced.

The gentleman praised the event. "I really like what you're doing here." He further added, "I would love to have my girls dance on this stage."

Curiously, I asked, "What girls and what dancing are you talking about?"

"I own the local burlesque and I think my girls could do a really good show!" he replied.

The conversation concluded with me stating, "This is a family affair, and I don't think your girls would work. But thank you for asking."

DADDY'S LOST

As a retail store manager in a major shopping mall, I witnessed the comings and goings of countless patrons.

On one occasion, standing at my store entrance a mother and daughter passed me by. Being close enough I overheard the mother's comment, "We need to find Daddy. He's lost."

Being privy to this exchange made me chuckle.

VOMITING ON THE TAXI DRIVER

A rumour was related to me that a friend, Rocky Rochefort, had an unfortunate accident falling down a staircase at a Sunday household party. Details were sketchy until a month later when I crossed paths with Rocky himself.

Of course, I was concerned about his health and very curious about the nature of his accident. Rocky was more than agreeable to share the circumstances. He explained that he had been attending an afternoon party at the home of friends we were mutually acquainted with. Why I wasn't invited, I do not know.

Considering the context of the time, both alcohol and marijuana were essential ingredients at the festivity.

At some point in the process of trying to navigate a descent into the basement from the main floor, Rocky took a tumble and somersaulted down the staircase.

Seeing that he was now lying inert at the bottom of the stairs, other party goers immediately rushed to his aid. Someone checked his pulse. There was absolutely no sign of one, so 911 was called. Fortunately, Rocky revived prior to the ambulance's arrival. However, the ambulance attendants advised Rocky to go to the hospital for a closer check-up.

Once Rocky was given a favourable diagnosis, he decided to return to the party. What else would one do? A taxi was called and Rocky jumped into the front seat of the cab and proceeded to the party house. Upon arrival, he reached over to his left to pay the taxi fare and simultaneously felt ill, vomiting into the driver's lap.

Rocky related that he felt terrible for the driver but could only tip him with his remaining finances which amounted to twenty-five cents.

BLACK SCALP

Spending my teenage summers working on farms in Manitoba, I quickly came to realize that hard labour, bordering on exploitation, was an essential ingredient for this type of employment.

On Aunty Pauline and Uncle Joe's farm, work consisted of haying, herding the cattle, feeding the pigs, tilling the soil, and spotting for the crop duster, mixed with a generous portion of horseplay with my closest cousin in age, Jimmy.

With all the hard labour, most of which took place outdoors, accumulating dirt on my person was unavoidable. Compounding the situation was the fact my aunt and uncle were financially dirt poor. As a result, both a bathtub and shower were non-existent on their farm.

Unbeknownst to me, dirt, mainly from working the fields while riding the open-air tractor, had been gathering in my hair. Not just any dirt. It was black, very black prairie soil.

After one particular stretch of one month of uninterrupted outdoor field work with no opportunity to bathe, I was transferred to my baba's house in the nearest prairie town, Arborg, Manitoba. Ironically, Baba had never had interior plumbing—no shower, no bathtub.

But Baba must have realized my predicament and convinced me to at least wash my hair. Water was hand pumped, heated on the kitchen wood stove and poured into a basin outdoors.

Parting my hair, coal black would best describe the colour of my scalp. The first washing produced water equally black in colour. A second washing created an improved result—grey only.

To this day I treasure the black scalp as a proud farming experience, one that no city-slicker kid would ever experience let alone treasure.

FIVE ITALIAN COPS

In 1971, my girlfriend, Helene, was attending the University of Strasbourg in France. I decided this was a perfect opportunity to visit Europe for the first time. I timed my trip to coincide with Helene's early school spring break in March. We rented a vehicle in Strasbourg and included Rome in our itinerary as our southernmost destination.

The trip south was largely uneventful until we reached the stretch of highway between Pisa and Rome. Somewhere along that main thoroughfare, in broad daylight, I became involved in an accident where another vehicle sideswiped ours . . . or was it where I sideswiped the other vehicle? Remember, history is an agreed set of lies.

No injuries resulted. Damage was minimal.

The driver of the other vehicle spoke only Italian, and between Helene and I, only French and English. Therefore, a communication gap existed.

In short order, Italian Policia arrived. Whether there was one or two I can't remember. A discussion transpired between the Italian driver and the police, but we were excluded due to the language barrier.

Time passed and another Italian police officer arrived. Or was that two more? Another lengthy conversation in Italian ensued. Helene and I were mystified as to what was taking place and why we were being delayed. We had supplied all paperwork, including insurance, to the Policia but nothing was being resolved. Frustration and impatience were setting in. We couldn't understand what was happening. A communication breakdown best described the situation.

Time was passing, three hours to be exact, when a fifth police officer arrived.

The appearance of the fifth cop brought on visions of the "Keystone Cops," especially with their highly animated and passionate Italian conversations.

The whole situation was about to be resolved as cop number five spoke French, albeit with a wonderful Italian accent, very amusing to observe.

We quickly learned that the officers were concerned with the validity of our auto insurance. This final intervention proved to solve the dilemma.

Finally, after three and a half hours and five Italian cops we were finally on our way, exhausted and amused.

PRACTICAL TEQUILA JOKE

Most of us know the traditional custom involved in drinking shots of tequila: wet your wrist, salt the same wrist, lick the salt from the wrist, shoot back the tequila, and as quickly as possible suck on a wedge of lemon to kill the taste of the tequila poison just consumed.

Well, Tom Murphy, a friend and fellow employee, offered to host the above social procedure in his apartment prior to a night out at the movies.

Gary joined us to make a threesome for the evening meeting at Tom's. I was soon to discover just how much of a practical joker Tom was.

As we gathered in the kitchen, standing beside the fridge, Tom provided us with the required tequila shooting accessories of salt and tequila shot glass but delayed the lemon wedges. Once the tequila was poured into each of our glasses, we followed due process and licked our wrists, salted the same wrists, licked the salt, and shot back the tequila. The lemons were delivered into our free hands at the last moment. We then completed the ritual by biting into the lemon.

Now if you are familiar with the sensation of biting into a lemon under similar circumstances, you will know that the lemon offers tremendous sensory and psychological relief. But to my excruciating surprise, my lemon had been previously frozen. The contrast between the expectation and the non-performance of the lemon effect was devastating. No words could describe the psychological let-down.

Uncontrolled laughter followed on Tom's part with me cursing him for as long as I could manage. I was furious with having been deceived.

Gary was spared as a recipient of Tom's deception. To this day I can't recall if Gary had been let in on the joke in advance or not.

HERD OF ELEPHANTS

Although Sudbury, Ontario, was home beginning in 1947 when my parents emigrated eastward, Manitoba was still considered a place to return to. Both my parents had been born and raised there in the Ukrainian community of the Interlake. Their families remained there with very few venturing afar permanently. As a result, my parents returned on an annual or semi-annual basis to visit family and friends.

The Canadian Pacific Railway (CPR) passenger train "The Canadian" provided the round-trip transportation initially, with me as the eldest and in subsequent years with my siblings Margaret, Caroline, and Michael. As young children raised in a city environment, exposure to the rural setting especially farm animals was uniquely exciting.

On one westward trip, consisting of Mom, me and my two sisters, we were enjoying the wonderful rural scenery through a remote area of Ontario. The train line meandered through and alongside farm after farm.

As we passed open pasture with cattle grazing, Caroline, age four, blurted out, "Mommy, Mommy, look at the herd of elephants." Thunderous laughter immediately followed, and a minor correction was made hopefully to benefit my sister.

ALZHEIMER'S ACCUSATION

In mid-conversation with my daughter Katie in 1992, I temporarily lost my train of thought. She immediately commented, "Dad, you've got Alzheimer's."

As a response, I just let it go. No defence, no excuse.

Approximately a month later, I happened to phone home. Katie answered. "Katie guess what, I don't have Alzheimer's!" I announced.

"Why, did you go and see a doctor?" she replied.

"No," I said. "I just remembered that you owe me money."

My answer was met with dead silence.

To this day Katie has never again accused me of having Alzheimer's and she has never repaid her debt to me.

Lesson learned. If you are ever accused of having cognitive deterioration, counter with, "Don't you owe me money?"

SMUGGLING GERMAN LUGERS

My father served with the Winnipeg Rifles, eventually fighting overseas during the Second World War. He shared few wartime stories with us as children. This situation changed, however, once we reached adulthood.

He was notably talkative and confided several previously unheard stories on a trip that he shared with me, my wife, and our first born in 1977. We were on a return road trip from Sudbury to visit family in Manitoba.

One of his accounts dealt with his return to Canada at the end of the war. Dad travelled on the *Queen Mary* which had been converted into a troop ship. Twenty-four hours prior to arriving in Canada, an announcement was broadcast on board: "No German arms are to be smuggled into Canada. If caught you will be court marshalled."

My father already had one German Luger in his possession. He was dismayed in witnessing fellow soldiers throwing weapons overboard to the point that he intercepted some of them. In total he managed to acquire five Lugers, eventually smuggling all of them successfully into Canada.

When I asked, "What did you do with them?" he indicated that he distributed them to friends and family—in one case to a friend who claimed that he wanted to "shoot his wife." I can't remember if I questioned his rationale under the circumstances, but I did ask if he knew what happened. He did not.

A LOADED LUGER

One of the German Lugers my father smuggled into Canada following the end of WWII was given to his brother John who farmed in Manitoba. During that trip from Sudbury with my father in 1977, we eventually visited Uncle John, who was still farming there.

Shortly after our arrival, we gathered in the farmyard yard directly in front of his home. It was Uncle John, my father, my wife, our six-month-old daughter, me, and John's adult son Walter.

Recalling the fact that my father had given Uncle John a Luger, I asked him if he still had the revolver. "Yes," he exclaimed as he quickly disappeared into the basement of his house.

He returned in short order proudly displaying the weapon. It was immediately passed around including within proximity of my daughter. When it reached my cousin Walter, Walter directed the question to his father, "Is it loaded?"

"Yes," came the reply.

The rest of us gasped in shock.

Walter immediately tore a strip off his father, simultaneously unloading the chamber of the handgun.

Thinking about that day and its potential for disaster still gives me the shivers.

CHARGING BISON

Another story Dad shared on that road trip was about an event that occurred upon his return to Manitoba post-WWII.

Shortly after returning to Winnipeg, and before dating my mother, my father escorted a girlfriend to the Winnipeg Zoo. At the time, the Winnipeg Zoo was a significant tourist attraction in part due to its connection with "Winnie the Pooh." A. A. Milne's "Winnie the Pooh" character was inspired by a real-life bear named Winnie, short for Winnipeg, who had been given to the London Zoo by Captain Harry Colebourn of Winnipeg, Manitoba.

When they reached the bison compound, one animal was standing alongside the fence. My father, a farm boy, decided to demonstrate his comfort level with animals. As he reached through the fencing, he was able to not only touch the bison's nose but decided to give it a flick with his finger.

This instantaneously angered the huge animal.

Dad recalled, "The bison took one step back and then charged the fence. If it weren't for the double fencing, I would have been dead."

When he looked behind him his girlfriend lay stretched out on the ground, passed out from shock. This probably explains why that relationship didn't last.

If it hadn't been for the double fence, I would never have been eventually fathered by this man.

SCARY CARROTS

Grandchildren are a treasure. With twelve and counting my wife and I have had countless erudite and amusing experiences. One of these experiences was generated by Matthew, who was three years old at the time.

During a family gathering at our home, I asked Matthew's mother for permission to take him out to our vegetable garden to pull some carrots.

Once approval was given, Matthew was willing and away we went hand in hand to the carrot patch. I asked him if he would like to pull a carrot. "Oh no," he replied demurely.

It was obvious to me that this was not a comfort zone for Matthew. He probably had never experienced a vegetable garden. So, I held his hand as I chose a carrot, grabbed its green top and gently tugged it out of the ground.

As it popped out of the soil Matthew lunged back in obvious fear.

He was startled by what appeared: a carrot. Still holding his hand, we proceeded to the garden hose to remove the clinging dirt. I then asked Matthew if he would like to have a bite. He declined. I took a bite to reassure him that it was all right. There was still no desire on his part to give it a try.

"Would you like to try pulling another carrot?" I asked.

He nodded in the affirmative. Off we went to the garden again, hand in hand.

We located a suitable carrot once again and I repeated the earlier procedure. "Matthew, would you like to pull a carrot?"

"No," came the reply.

Out came an orange veggie a second time. His reaction this time was more subdued, not as startled. Again, we traipsed over to the water tap. After washing the carrot, I took a bite and offered the same opportunity to my young companion to no avail.

We repeated the entire process a third time with identical results.

It was time to go indoors and try a different tact. I cut one clean carrot into small pieces and offered them to Matthew. To my amazement, he readily accepted and ate a carrot stick. It now had an appearance of familiarity.

The whole episode was discreetly related to his mother, a teacher, who found the story delightful. It was a very rewarding experience for me.

THREE BAGGER

Singing in a Ukrainian choir for over nineteen years proved to be an enjoyable cultural experience in my life. The mixed choir rehearsed and performed between September and the end

of May. For the most part on yearly basis live performances usually took place at our Vancouver Cultural Hall. However, from time to time were invited to perform elsewhere.

On one occasion we were invited to join other cultural groups for a Sunday afternoon festival at a Russian Hall.

Although dressing rooms were available backstage, the number of performing dancing groups and choirs outnumbered the available change rooms.

Consequently, our choir was assigned the furnace room to change into our traditional Ukrainian costumes. As we entered this facility prior to our performance one of the female choir members voiced her concern about the situation. Audrey was obviously intimidated to partially disrobe in the presence of men.

I, being the closest to her, attempted to reassure her that everything would be all right. "I will put a paper bag over my head in order not to see you," I suggested. "And I will give you a paper bag to put over your head in order to not see me."

Then I made a final offer, "I will put a third bag over my imagination to prevent me from visualizing you undressed."

Audrey looked at me in disbelief but had no alternative solution.

AN ATTEMPT AT FLATTERY

As I sat in a hairdresser's chair having my hair cut, my hairstylist commented, "You look like Steve McQueen." I instantly broke into laughter. Despite her good intention, the thought of looking like someone that was dead seemed ludicrous to me.

WHAT DO YOU SPEAK?

In late 1968 I was living in Montreal. Working for Canadian Copper Refiners in East Montreal but living in the centre of the city required me to commute daily Monday through Friday.

Working at an industrial site necessitated the wearing of work clothes. So, I typically travelled each way in what could be considered tattered clothes, especially contrasted to the stylish Montreal dress code.

Standing on a congested street corner waiting for a bus at the end of a busy Friday workday, I spied a derelict approaching me. My initial reaction was "Oh, oh, here comes trouble."

Sure enough, he confronted me, smelling of beer, with the request in French, *"Avez-vous vingt-cinq cents pour l'autobus?"*

Being cognisant of his odour and the fact that a tavern was situated around the corner, I replied in English, "I don't speak French."

He countered in perfect English, "Do you have twenty-five cents for the bus?"

Somewhat taken aback, I blurted out defensively, *"Je ne parle pas anglais."*

My new friend was flabbergasted at my retort, placed his hands on his hips, looked me up and down and uttered the comment, "So, what do you speak?"

Recognizing the futility of hustling me for money, he moved on to two older ladies nearby. I overheard the same pecuniary request made to them, this time with success. Just as quickly he disappeared around the corner, returning in less than five minutes—long enough to quaff a glass of twenty-five-cent ale.

Once again, he approached me but not to solicit me this time. My appearance and my earlier encounter with him probably convinced him that he and I were in the same destitute situation.

This time he offered the advice, "Watch me. I will show you how it's done." He disappeared into the bus crowd, and I disappeared, deciding to walk home.

BLACKIE THE COW

Farming is in my blood. Although not a farmer per se, I acquired a love for this lifestyle working most of my teenage summers on Manitoba farms from the early to mid-sixties.

Consequently, when an opportunity arose in 1976 to work on a very successful dairy farm, I along with my wife, jumped at the chance.

The picture-perfect postcard operation at "Plumbroke Farm" was owned and operated by my wife's Uncle Craig.

Typically, his forty to forty-four Friesian-Holstein cows were milked on a twice-daily basis. On an excessively hot and humid day in the summer of 1978, Kai, the herdsman, Johnny, Craig's son, and I occupied ourselves with haying. The three of us managed to produce and store a thousand bales of hay in the mow of the barn. We were pushed to our physical limits under the extreme weather conditions.

Then came the afternoon milking. Once the milkers were ushered into the barn, we quickly realized that the body heat emanating from the cows in combination with the existing conditions created an unbearable situation. We promptly removed our shirts with only work pants and boots remaining.

As a modern dairy operation, milking machines, an overhead milk line, and a refrigerated tank storage system were utilized. In addition to the mechanization process, each cow still required manual stripping of the remaining two to three pounds of milk. Simply crouching alongside each cow at the back end, hand massaging the utter and teats stimulated the residual milk into the milking machine.

With ten minutes and four or five cows to go to completion, I positioned myself beside a cow opposite the box stall in which Blackie stood. In a crouched position, as if sitting on a stool, my back faced Blackie, a mere metre away. She also happened to have her rear end facing me. We were back-to-back.

Amid this situation, Blackie began to empty her bowels. A combination of urine and manure poured out rather excessively.

Now if you have ever experienced the sight of a cow coughing at the same time as discharging you will know that its contents will shoot out like a projectile. Being cognisant of this fact and our proximity to each other I thought to myself, "Whatever you do, Blackie, don't cough."

My worst fear materialized within seconds. Blackie began coughing.

Not surprisingly, Blackie's by-product was propelled over the box stall railing onto the upper part of my back and slid directly into the crevice of my pants. The physical sensation was revolting. I was beyond disgusted. Immediately, I bellowed out a string of expletives simultaneously wishing to shoot Blackie on the spot despite my non-violent philosophy.

Both Kai and Johnny, situated within metres of the event, spontaneously broke into uncontrollable hysterics. So much so that they literally rolled in the aisle covered in manure.

As I stomped out of the barn I blurted out, "It's all yours. I'm out of here." More laughter ensued from my milking cohorts.

The walk to the farmhouse was a mere thirty seconds, whereupon I stripped off all my remaining clothing outside the front door. My pants, underwear, socks, and boots were completely saturated. I can't recall a more pressing need for a bath than on that occasion.

For some time afterwards, my embarrassing predicament made the rounds with family and friends. I became the butt of many jokes.

ÑOW I CAN DIE

When my fiancée (my first one) and I announced our impending marriage to my parents, my father clasped his hands together and offered, "And now I can die." It was a reassuring moment in our lives.

A TRULY CANADIAN PUN

One of the satisfactions of managing and then owning and operating my own business was the relationships I developed with my employees. With very few exceptions these relationships proved to be rewarding.

My approach was to create a positive work environment that was mutually beneficial. Coffee breaks and lunches were meant to be a shared, social affair. As a rule, conversation acted as a positive lubricant in the workplace dynamics.

On one occasion a valued and rather gregarious employee by the name of Ken shared an experience that he had had the previous weekend.

Ken related that he had patronized the newest Canadian Tire store close to where he lived. Expecting the usual specialized Canadian Tire departments of automotive, hardware, etc. proved to be extremely disappointing for Ken. What accelerated his disenchantment was the excessive size of its clothing department. Ken remarked emphatically, "I will never shop there again."

After patiently listening to his rant, a perfect opportunity opened for me to comment. "Ken, didn't you know that Canadian Tire had opened a new division called Canadian Attire?"

In typical fashion, the pun was met with groans.

PREMATURE APPREHENSION

The standard requirement upon entering a foreign country is to pass through customs. One must declare all goods that may be deemed restricted and possibly be subject to an inspection. This was no different for me on the occasion of landing at London's Heathrow Airport en route from Amsterdam.

As I proceeded towards a customs officer, I presented my carry-on sports bag for inspection. Prior to leaving the Dutch capital, I had purchased a wooden hash pipe for a souvenir. I had no apprehension about its illegality. It had never been used for its intended purpose, namely smoking drugs.

When the officer unzipped my bag, he immediately discovered the hash pipe. It sat prominently on top at eighteen inches in length. His reaction was something to behold. I'm sure that he envisioned a drug bust. Excitedly he raised the pipe, giving it a microscopic examination, turning it every which way. In addition, he brought the unit to his nose, sniffing for any tell-tale residue. To his disappointment all indicators of illicit drugs proved negative.

Nevertheless, I received a five-minute lecture on the negative effects of drugs and drug use. I then continued my way.

DONKEY RIDING

Travel is one of the best forms of education in my opinion.

One of my most treasured travel memories was living on the island of Rhodes, Greece, in the late winter/spring of 1973–74. My girlfriend Suzanne and I spent two and a half months primarily in a resort/fishing village occupied only by local Greeks and a dozen foreigners like us, more accurately described as hippies.

Without knowing the actual Greek namesake, we nicknamed the location Hiraki.

During our stay there, the Greek population consisted of an elderly couple nicknamed Grandpa and Grandma, their fisherman son, Andreus, and one other fisherman for a total of four.

Once the weather warmed up in March more outdoor activity was engaged. This included assembling a makeshift taverna on the stone patio surrounding the water's shoreline.

On one occasion, Grandpa, Grandma and the two fishermen were joined by most of us, the hippies. Retsina, the drink of choice, was consumed in liberal quantities by all, eventually causing our level of civility to disintegrate. Grandpa, for one, became quite enamoured with a very attractive young Danish girl seated beside him. His behaviour did not go unnoticed by his wife. It was sometime later that I learned the consequence of his amorous advances.

It was on the second day following the outdoor drinking session that I noticed Grandma was no longer to be seen. With my curiosity aroused, I sought her son Andreus to solve the mystery.

"Where is Grandma?" I asked him.

Andreus replied, "My mother was not happy with Dad's behaviour, and she left town on their donkey."

The following day Grandma returned to Hiraki, donkey riding.

MISTAKEN IDENTITY

The outdoor Hiraki drinking session not only incriminated Grandpa but nearly terminated my relationship with my girlfriend, Suzanne.

I admit that the consumption of retsina that afternoon contributed to a rapid deterioration in my ability to recognize my immediate surroundings.

For the longest time, Suzanne sat to my immediate right as we drank around the table. I did remember her excusing herself to return to our hut.

In her absence, one of the Danish girls sat down beside me. I either did not notice or my inebriated condition prevented me from doing so.

I had been carrying on a conversation to my left until I decided to return my interest to my right. Assuming Suzanne was still beside me, I placed my right hand on what I thought was my girlfriend's thigh.

At that very instant Suzanne returned to catch me with my hand on another woman's body. A verbal barrage of condemnation precipitated.

I think I slithered back to our living quarters in a severe state of drunkenness and amid persistent criticism from my partner for my perceived misdemeanour.

The next twenty-four hours consisted of a severe case of vomiting and my determined denial of any intentional wrongdoing. "I thought it was you sitting beside me," was my constant refrain.

All was forgiven before the end of the next day and retsina has never touched my lips ever since—a span of forty-nine years and counting.

HAMMER THAT CAKE

Birthdays are great occasions for families to get together. They are filled with opportunities to reminisce, catch up on new developments and engage in a lot of laughter.

This was no different when we celebrated my wife's birthday in January 2011. The gathering took place at our home with Sue's four-adult offspring, their significant others and a handful of grandkids. Dinner was a potluck affair to be followed by a birthday cake festivity.

As usual, the activities centred in the kitchen and adjoining family room areas. Toys were located in the children's play section at the end of the family room farthest from the kitchen.

It was here that three-year-old Sammy and I were playing with a variety of toys when the birthday cake procession wound its way from the kitchen into the family room where Sue was seated. The cake was placed on a low coffee table.

The lit candles and the singing of "Happy Birthday" drew the immediate response of the grandkids including Sammy. They rushed over to help Grandma blow out the candles on the cake. As the final photos were being taken, Sammy spontaneously raised a hand with a plastic toy hammer and proceeded to whack the birthday cake.

We were all dumbfounded. He managed two good swings before we were able to intervene and prevent Sammy from continuing his birthday cake rampage. Words cannot adequately describe the nervous laughter that was generated by Sammy's action. However, "laughing ourselves silly" will have to suffice.

It is highly doubtful that a more memorable conclusion to a birthday celebration will ever occur in our family again.

THEY DON'T KNOW

Mrs. Skehor was a senior who befriended me in the eighties. We belonged to a Ukrainian organization in which we had mutual friends. Unfortunately, several of her contemporaries were dying off due to old age.

She voiced her concern to me one day: "I miss Rosie, I miss Marta. They don't know what I'm doing!"

Naturally, I cracked up.

CAULIFLOWER DAN

Suzanne and I arrived in the port of Rhodes, Rhodes Island, Greece, by ferry in late January 1973. There we were met by Mama Nina aggressively promoting her *pensione* as a place to stay. She impressed me as an honest grandmotherly type and so we followed her to her home for an overnight stay. Our eventual destination was to be Lindos, Greece.

We were given a ground-floor sleeping accommodation—two cots onto which we could spread our sleeping bags. Sometime during the first evening, we literally crossed paths with another tenant who was residing upstairs.

My initial impression of this individual was not favourable. He appeared dishevelled, unkempt, unshaven, and possibly drunk. A spitting image of Ichabod Crane, he was tall, dark, and gangly.

We retired for the night; but by the next day, we realized that the traffic on the ground floor was too disruptive for our liking. Nina agreed to move us upstairs for night number two.

It was there that we became better acquainted with the individual from the previous day. Returning from a brief outing we were met on the first floor by Dan. We discovered him in a state of panic due to an accident upstairs.

He had been boiling a pot of beets and cauliflower over a single-burner gas stove. The pot had fallen over and spilled its contents on the floor. Dan was pleading for the use of our gas burner thinking that his burner was no longer functional.

When we met him upstairs, Dan was in the process of scooping up the beets, cauliflower and all manner of floor dirt, hair, etc. into his cooking pot.

It was despicable.

Did I mention that he was inebriated as well?

Once this project was completed, Dan descended to the ground floor, refilled the pot with water and returned upstairs. He resumed cooking, this time with our gas burner set on the floor.

As we waited for the contents to boil, I asked, "Why beets and cauliflower?"

Dan replied, "I need them to counteract sclerosis of the liver."

This belief flabbergasted me. It didn't seem credible. It became readily evident to me that "Cauliflower Dan" was a deserving nickname. And so, it has stuck to this day.

In the interim, the water began to boil over the edge of the pot. We had previously pleaded with Dan that he had filled it too full. As the boiling water was spilling over, I attempted to grab the handle of the pot so that the excess water could be poured off. Simultaneously Dan lunged to prevent me from interfering, almost causing a repeat spill.

Acknowledging this dangerous situation, I desisted from trying to help. Dan continued in his drunken way.

MORE CAULIFLOWER DAN

Lindos, Greece, was our main destination when we planned our 1973 European trip. A friend, Morgan Davis, had spoken of it so highly that we were sold on it as a place to visit. He described it as an unbelievably picturesque setting—beautiful, whitewashed buildings crowning an acropolis.

After a handful of days spent at Mama Nina's pensione in Rhodes, we decided to rent scooters and investigate the treasures of Lindos. It proved to be an exquisite and rewarding experience. Seeing is believing.

On our return, we decided, on a whim, to go slightly off-road. The attraction was a small fishing/summer resort community of twenty to thirty huts which came to be known as Hiraki Beach. It was located approximately twelve kilometres from Lindos.

To our surprise, we ran into Cauliflower Dan. In a brief conversation, he convinced us to relocate to Hiraki. Somehow, we managed to negotiate in a matter of minutes, rental accommodation for eight hundred drachmas (thirty dollars) per month—a steal by Canadian standards.

Once settled into our new premises we quickly established friendships with all the foreigners, mostly hippies. Our social activities were quite vibrant with any excuse for a party.

Inexpensive wine, for as little as three to four drachmas (twelve and a half cents) and ouzo at fourteen drachmas (fifty cents) per bottle, made life rather utopian—a veritable alcoholic's paradise.

Suzanne and I were very fortunate in that we had rented what could be considered the luxury hut in town. A two-element hotplate and a radio were the envy of others. No one else had these benefits. As a result, our hut became the mecca for social gatherings. Communal meals were prepared there. The radio became a magnet for our community. It culminated in a birthday celebration for Cauliflower Dan that we hosted. We had a full house with wine and retsina flowing readily. It was Dan's forty-seventh birthday, or so we thought.

During the party, a pseudo-girlfriend of Dan's asked to see proof of his age. Dan complied by searching his wallet and removing suitable documentation. When the document was read out loud it was discovered that he was forty-five years old, not forty-seven.

In his drunken stupor, Dan whooped for joy, claiming that this two-year grace would delay the effects of the sclerosis of his liver—even more reason to celebrate and drink.

Eventually, everyone except Dan vacated our home to attend a makeshift taverna elsewhere in Hiraki. When Suzanne and I returned we found him passed out on a couch with a broken bottle of wine splattered on the concrete floor. Glass slivers and wine were strewn everywhere. Once the mess was cleaned up, we retired for the night.

The following morning, we confronted Dan as to what had happened the previous evening.

"I was conducting music on the radio with my bottle as a baton," he replied, "and it fell out of my hand."

Cauliflower Dan turned out to be an incorrigible alcoholic.

EVEN MORE CAULIFLOWER DAN

It seemed that no matter where we travelled on the island of Rhodes, Cauliflower Dan would appear. This was no different than on a Sunday morning in March when Suzanne and I decided to hitchhike into Lindos. Sightseeing and grocery shopping were on our agenda.

We meandered through the narrow cobblestoned lanes, popping our heads into any of the open retail doorways. Passing by a taverna at eleven thirty in the morning, surprised that it was open, we nevertheless peeked inside.

Sure enough, there was Cauliflower Dan seated at a table by himself imbibing in one of his favourite liquid refreshments. Upon seeing us, he beckoned us to join him.

We politely deferred to a later time, wanting to complete our fruit and vegetable shopping.

When we finally returned an hour later Dan had already been joined by two or three other Hiraki colleagues. Room at the table was made for us. And of course, beer, the refreshment of choice for the day, was ordered and shared.

By this time Dan had a head start and was feeling no inhibition. Both the jukebox and the sizable open dance floor beckoned him to demonstrate his dancing skills. Remember this predated *Dirty Dancing*. John Travolta did not have anything on Dan.

Once the coins were inserted into the jukebox, Dan went solo.

As a gaunt-looking six-foot-plus male, and ever the epitome of Ichabod Crane in appearance, he sleazed across the floor in giant strides, turning ever so slowly. At the same time, he kept a wary eye for any reaction he was generating from us, the onlookers.

The taverna was empty of any Greek patrons except for the proprietor until the moment a young Greek appeared in the doorway entrance.

He cast an eye around the room, quickly catching the presence of Cauliflower Dan now seated again at our table. With arms wide open he yelled "Dan" and rushed over to renew an old friendship. They had met one month previously.

Within seconds we were introduced, but before he actually sat down to join us, he excitedly pulled out his wallet. After fumbling briefly, he retrieved a piece of paper. Unfolding it, he exclaimed, "Dan gave this me. Dan gave this me."

It was a cheque issued by Dan to this young Greek for exactly one million dollars. This was ludicrous—completely improbable. Dan didn't have that kind of money. We laughed ourselves silly.

More beer was ordered, more beer was consumed, and more money was put in the jukebox.

Both Dan and the young Greek provided uninhibited demonstrations on the dance floor albeit in contrasting styles. Dan's style, reminiscent of an ice dancer, consisted of long flowing circles executed in slow motion. He was in his glory, totally drunk and totally lost in his creativity. We as onlookers were unable to contain our laughter.

As for the Greek, we were mesmerized. He began dancing, balancing successive chairs with his teeth. It eventually culminated with him balancing a small table in a similar fashion. What entertainment!

For the grand finale, the young Greek hoisted Cauliflower Dan from just above his knees into the air. With his arms outstretched and towering well above the shorter Greek, Dan repeatedly sang out the words, "I am Jesus Christ. I am Jesus Christ."

It was unavoidable, we continued to laugh ourselves silly. How we ever got ourselves back to Hiraki, I do not know.

PADDLING IN CIRCLES/LAKE LOUISE

On our migrating trip from Ontario to British Columbia in August 1978, my then-wife and I were inspired by the Lake Louise spectacle. This was in direct contrast to the state of our marriage at the time. We were simply incompatible and hadn't yet realized the full extent of the situation.

However, it did manifest itself in Lake Louise when we agreed to rent a canoe and attempt to paddle the lake.

Once we finalized the rental process, we donned our PFDs, grabbed our paddles, and headed down to the lakeshore. As we were about to enter the canoe, my wife announced that she was taking the stern because she had grown up learning to paddle at a summer recreational/union camp that her father had directed.

My ego was being challenged in the situation. I was just as adamant thinking that as a male I should be the stern paddler, of course, the one in control. My argument fell on deaf ears. Knowing the "anarchist" nature in my wife, I conceded. But not without an ulterior motive. I was about to sabotage the whole affair.

Once we entered the canoe without capsizing, our paddle began: I miserable in the bow and my wife contentedly in the stern.

Having greater upper body strength, I began to paddle furiously. Despite my wife's pleas and paddling expertise, she was unable to compensate for my uncooperative behaviour. We paddled perfect donuts.

The entire romantic Lake Louise paddling session lasted mere minutes.

And so, we continued on our way West, excitedly anticipating our future in la-la land together.

VILLAGE VEGETARIAN

Driving into the parking lot of a newly constructed shopping centre I noticed a storefront sign, "Opening Soon. Your Village Vegetarian." This was music to my ears. One month later, I discovered my error. The actual business name was "Your Village Veterinarian." To say I was disappointed would be an understatement.

MANITOBA MOSQUITOS

My teenage summers were spent to a large extent working on Manitoba farms owned and operated by aunts and uncles. I worked mostly on my Aunt Pauline's farm located in the Sylvan district approximately 170 kilometres north of Winnipeg.

Not only was Manitoba known for its infestation of mosquitos during the good weather months, but the Sylvan area was alternatively known as the "Land of the Swamp" as confirmed by a history book documenting this geographical location.

On one summer night in 1961 or 1962, my cousin Jimmy, upon hearing the howling of wolves, decided to check on the cattle that were grazing some distance from the farmhouse.

Jimmy grabbed a rifle, inserted some shells and off he went into the darkness of night. I and Jimmy's younger brother, Patrick, who was six or seven years old at the time, followed in hot pursuit looking and listening for wolves.

From the moment we stepped outside, swarms of mosquitos terrorized me. My t-shirt offered absolutely no protection from these blood-thirsty parasites.

During the full hour of our scouting excursion, I complained relentlessly in direct contrast to Jimmy and Patrick. Not once did they complain. Despite my doubts, they didn't appear to have been attacked by the mosquitos. I found this difficult to believe considering my dilemma.

Once we returned to the trailer in which we slept, I stripped off my t-shirt and had Patrick count the mosquito bites on my back only. They totalled fifty-three.

The confirmed combined mosquito bite count for both of my cousins equalled zero. Why? Why? Why? The difference continues to haunt me.

SCARED SHITLESS

Jim Gulay was my closest cousin during my growing-up years for several reasons. Not only were we six months apart in age, but we also spent the better part of four summers working together on his parents' Manitoba farm.

Despite the proximity of our ages, there were significant differences: Jim was a farm boy, I was a city slicker; he was brazening in nature, I was shy and retiring; he was quite stocky, I was slight.

This contrast in physical build gave me the impression that Jim could take on the world and not be intimidated by anyone or any circumstance. My perception proved to be wrong, remarkably wrong.

On a glorious summer evening, a male friend of my aunt and uncle paid a visit to the family farm. The adults socialized indoors while Jim and I kept ourselves preoccupied outdoors. As the evening wore on darkness gradually descended.

At dusk, the two of us moved indoors to keep the adults company. Finally, the guest excused himself to return home.

Shortly after, Jim and I decided to retire for the evening. Our sleeping quarters were located in a small trailer approximately fifty metres from the farmhouse, a mere twenty-second walk.

My cousin led the way with me following just one metre behind. As we approached a pumphouse, located halfway, the guest, who had been lying in wait, lunged out from behind the structure, emitting the loudest "boo" imaginable.

I witnessed Jim's legs shoot out in front of him as gravity simultaneously brought him to the ground. There he was sitting perfectly and totally defenceless.

Both I and the perpetrator burst into laughter.

Jim was not amused.

So much for the perception of having a bodyguard for a cousin or a cousin for a bodyguard in a time of need.

TARRED X 2

Cousin Jim may have startled easily, but he was certainly strong. In one instance, I was walking across the farmyard followed by Jim. Coming from behind and for no apparent reason, Jim locked one arm around my neck. At the same time, he lathered my head with a handful of gooey roofing tar.

His strength rendered me defenceless. He had adequate time to spread the tar thoroughly in my hair.

Once released, I was able to vent my disgust at this unprovoked attack. It was inconceivable that he would have done this.

The real fury came soon after when his mother, my aunt Pauline, discovered the situation. Jim was thoroughly reprimanded for his idiotic behaviour.

That night my pillow slip suffered the consequences of a tarred head of hair.

By the following morning, I plotted my revenge. But first, where was the tar?

I spent much of the day trying to source Jim's supply in as discrete a fashion as possible. Sure enough, I eventually found it.

I waited for the perfect opportunity. With a handful of tar, I attacked, smearing as much as I could into his scalp. It was a glorious sensation of retribution.

When this second act was discovered later by Aunt Pauline all hell broke loose. "How stupid can both of you be?" was her sentiment. "Freddie, wait till your mother arrives in two days. Will she be mad!"

The drying and hardening process with the tar in our hair was quite rapid. With both of us suffering identically, we began to work cooperatively in finding a solution.

I can't remember in what order, but we tried gasoline, kerosene and wood ash with minimal success. As the tar progressively hardened over time it became more difficult to achieve any success.

When my mother arrived, the condemnation renewed. "How could you be so stupid?" was her refrain.

Finally, Jim and I discovered the ultimate solution—butter. We kneaded the homemade farm butter into our hair and scalp. It required constant massaging between thumb and forefinger to soften the hardened tar.

In total, it took us seven days to remove all remnants of our idiotic behaviour.

PANIC, PANIC, PANIC

Aunt Pauline and Uncle Joe were heading into town one morning. Fisher Branch was at least a thirty-minute drive from their farm, so Cousin Jim and I estimated our maximum window of opportunity to be two hours to avoid detection.

At the first sign of Jim's parents disappearing down the country road in a cloud of dust, Jim sprang into action. The goal: visit a girl a five-minute drive in the opposite direction.

First, we had to transfer a battery from one of the tractors into a rundown '49 Ford sitting idly in the farmyard. Once accomplished, we jumped inside for the ride to our destination.

No problem. We arrived in good time. After spending thirty minutes trying to woo his love we headed back. I glanced at the speedometer, which indicated seventy-five miles per hour, when Jim slammed on the brakes for no apparent reason.

His excuse, ducks were swimming in the ditch alongside the road. He got out, picked up a few stones and threw them in the direction of his intended victims. Thankfully without success.

We both jumped into the car again and Jim slammed the gas pedal to the floor.

A mere few seconds later we realized that a front tire had gone flat. Jim now demonstrated the first sign of panic.

He detached the battery from the Ford and began a slow run back to the farmyard. His intent was to get the tractor going, return to the car, and tow the car home.

As the crow flies, the four-hundred-metre distance to the farmyard required crossing three or four wood rail fences and the interim fields. At first, Jim tried to scale each fence with the battery in hand, but batteries are weighty objects.

Once back, Jim returned the battery to the tractor, grabbed a length of chain, and off we went. The old Ford had to be towed back home before his dad and mom arrived.

We hooked up the car, and Jim positioned the tractor alongside the ditch on the opposite side of the road from the car. As he attempted to accelerate, the tractor began to sink into the soft bank and water.

The tractor was now stuck. Our panic increased exponentially. Jim detached the battery once again and began his second attempt at returning the battery in hand.

At the first fence, he plopped the battery on top. As he began his climb the battery fell onto the ground. I couldn't resist laughing at the futility of the situation.

He scaled the remaining fences with my assistance. I held the battery on top while Jim climbed over. Again, I couldn't resist the hilarity of the situation. With Jim occasionally falling from a fence, his level of panic intensified.

When we entered the farmyard this second time my cousin hooked up the battery to another tractor. We drove the second tractor back and hooked it up to the first one stuck in the ditch. Jim managed to pull it out, and with me in the seat of the disabled one, we headed back in tow.

The first tractor was returned to its original parking spot. This way no one would suspect anything.

With time of the essence, off we went to now tow in the '49 Ford. This was met with success and all vehicles were positioned as previously. The battery was also returned to its original tractor.

Jim's demeanour changed radically from extreme panic to total relief. All was achieved before his parents returned.

However, the game was discovered the next morning when Uncle Joe came knocking on our trailer door. "Jim," he shouted, "what did you do to the tractor?"

"What do mean?" was Jim's innocent response.

"The tractor won't start. What did you do?"

Jim's father discovered water in the engine block of the first tractor. The ghost was up. Jim had to confess the whole affair.

MANURE PILE

Farms are the perfect environment for animals as I discovered, not only for the traditional productive species but for household domestic varieties as well, namely cats and dogs.

These household pets, abandoned by their city-dwelling owners, regularly found their way onto our Southern Ontario farm. Ready access to food and freedom were the primary attractions. And it wasn't just strays that benefitted.

Prior to going on a two-week vacation, my aunt Julia asked if I wouldn't mind taking care of her dog on the farm. I agreed. Shortly after the dog was delivered and its owner disappeared, the dog began to wail uncontrollably. Fearing the dog might run away, I tethered it to a metal stake not far from the farmhouse.

Its forlorn behaviour lasted for thirty-six hours after which I released it from its imprisonment. She now had the run of the farm. Her sense of freedom was undeniable, most notably when she discovered the manure pile.

This three- to four-metre hill of bovine waste product was the result of the mechanical barn cleaning system. The never-ending supply of cow manure was transferred daily from the milking parlour to the outdoors.

Fresh and steaming, this by-product mound became a mecca for our visitor.

Over the remainder of her two-week stay, she spent an inordinate amount of time sniffing, digging, and rolling in her playground of choice. Of course, with the territory came the aroma. She reeked of organic matter.

On the day of Aunt Julia's return, her dog was easily located—on top of her castle. When called by her owner, the dog was remarkable in her reaction.

She failed to respond. She was in her glory, completely a free spirit and enjoying the fruit of her labour.

It required considerable effort to entice the dog to re-join her owner and enter the vehicle. And I'm sure it took an equal effort on the part of my aunt to endure her dog's body odour on the return home.

It was remarkable having witnessed a major shift in an animal's demeanour from a timid, whining specimen to an assertive, independent one.

TALKING TO MYSELF

Caught talking to myself by a complete stranger, the man asked, "What did you say?"

"I was just talking to myself," I replied.

"I hope you're having an intelligent conversation," came his response.

JESUS LOOK-ALIKE

I was a product of the times in the early seventies. By the time I travelled to Europe in 1973 I had grown a beard and let my hair grow midway down my back.

We had just landed by Turkish ship in the Port of Naples. Knowing that our stay would last from early morning to late evening, we wanted to make the most of our stopover.

Remembering a wartime story of my father's, I suggested a trip to Pompeii for the day. So off we went to the Naples train station. Once the tickets were purchased, we entered a coach, chose our window seats, and waited.

The train tracks were located below the level of the station platform such that in our seated positions we could barely see above the platform. From the outside only our heads were visible.

During this time before our departure, I noticed a group of young boys walk by, stop, look in, and crouch down directly opposite me. They pressed their noses against the window looking quite perplexed. I couldn't understand what was so concerning.

Once they began making the sign of the cross, I realized the nature of their interest. They took me for a Jesus look-alike. We laughed out loud. It wasn't the first time that had happened. I had been called "Little Jesus" a few times by townspeople in Greece.

ÑAPLES TRAFFIC-CIRCLE CIRCUS

Having returned from our train trip to Pompeii, we still had time to shop for food and sightsee in Naples. We headed up the hillside away from the port.

As we made our climb, the port including our vessel became smaller and smaller to the eye. At the same time, dusk was falling. Street and retail business lights filled the air that had been vacated by the sun.

We eventually reversed our direction deciding it was essential we return to our ship before its departure. The glittering lights of the port appeared to be at least two kilometres away. Our pace picked up as we descended.

Within a kilometre of the port, we began hearing an unrecognizable sound emanating from the direction in which we were heading. Our curiosity was aroused. It took some time before we realized the source: car horns. Evening rush hour traffic was in full progress.

The closer we got the louder the din. Vehicles were bumper to bumper with drivers continually leaning on their horns. Once we arrived at the heart of the traffic congestion all we could do was stand back and split our guts.

The backup was due not only to the number of vehicles merging but also due to the traffic cop who was attempting to regulate the flow. He was utilizing his whistle to its fullest potential: frequently and loudly.

What made the scene completely farcical was the simultaneous participation of a taxi passenger. His cab was located in a line-up of approximately fifteen cars from the police officer. With his window open, this passenger stood on the rear seat, body almost completely upright outside the vehicle, blowing a whistle identical to the one the cop was using.

For every whistle blow from the police officer came a shrill blow from the passenger. Total chaos ensued. The conflicting duelling whistles confused the drivers.

Standing on the sidewalk across from the whistling passenger, we and all the other observers laughed harder with each whistle blow.

No other serendipitous experience I have had has ever matched this in terms of farce.

POMPEII LIZARDS

Our trip to Pompeii was uneventful as far as I recall. However, Pompeii's impressive archaeological site made up for it. Its visual offerings and historical data made the visit very rewarding and educational.

While travelling for months as backpackers, exhaustion would set in from time to time. On this occasion, we placed our backpacks on an open grassy area to lie down for a rest. It didn't take long for my girlfriend and me to fall asleep in the midday Pompeii sun.

I can remember waking up surrounded by three or four lizards. At first, I was startled but was then quickly absorbed in thought as a memory of a story my father had shared with me years earlier flooded my mind.

He too had been in Pompeii. But his visit took place in the early stage of WWII. As part of the Canadian military, my dad was first sent to fight in Italy. Passing through Pompeii they were required to overnight.

Sleeping took place in a foxhole. He woke up in the middle of the night, surrounded by lizards—identical to the situation I experienced some thirty-three years later. The coincidence was unbelievable. These lizards were attracted to us for our body warmth.

It was an amazingly serendipitous experience to have the same thing happen to me as to my father so many years apart.

PEAS IN MY TOES

Dave Tolonen, aka Bucky, aka Sunnyside Slim, was one of those iconic characters who will never be duplicated. "Not a serious bone in his body" best describes him.

I first met him as a customer in the music store I managed. We bonded over our mutual love for music. What solidified our friendship was the eventual realization that we were neighbours, living on the outskirts of Sudbury, Ontario.

Bucky was also the epitome of a party animal back in the early seventies. Alcohol and marijuana were dear to his lifestyle as well as mine at the time. And as neighbours, we partied often at my place.

Bucky would usually drive over even though our properties bordered each other. I remember two occasions in which he made attempts to drive home following an evening of debauchery. In very short order, there would be a knock at my door with Bucky asking to use the phone to call for a tow truck. He drove into a swampy pond on one occasion and shot off the road into a ditch on another. Keep in mind that his home was only four hundred metres away.

This sets the stage for a rendezvous we had in Toronto in the very early spring of 1972. We travelled there separately but planned to meet at the El Mocambo night club. After an evening of music and drinking, we hailed a cab over to his hotel where we met his friend.

Soon after, Bucky pleaded, "I'm hungry. Let's order pizza." Although the three of us were inebriated, I was the one that placed the order by phone. The time was one thirty in the morning. Both Bucky and his friend either passed out or fell asleep.

I patiently waited for the pizza delivery, but the process was agonizingly long. Finally, around three o'clock in the morning, the delivery arrived. I paid. The other two could not be roused. Being hungry I devoured a fair share and fell asleep.

At some point during the night, I was awakened by footsteps going to the bathroom followed by the sounds of vomiting in the bathtub.

After falling back to sleep again, my next awakening came around seven o'clock in the morning. Someone had made their way to the bathroom and into the bathtub. Shortly after the shower had begun to run, Bucky could be heard shouting, "What's these peas doing in my toes?"

What he didn't realize was that he had gotten up in the middle of the night and vomited in the tub. And this is what Bucky stepped into when attempting a shower. What I came to realize was that peas must have been part of a meal he had the previous evening.

Recounting Bucky's antics to his countless friends and family, I made sure the expression "What's these peas doing in my toes?" and the associated story were never forgotten.

BUCKY'S LUMP

On a snowy Sunday winter morning in 1972, I decided to walk over to visit my friend Bucky. As I approached, I noticed that he was shovelling his driveway.

More importantly, there were two very unusual differences that I observed. Firstly, Bucky's beloved Chevrolet was not sitting in the driveway, and secondly, he was wearing a toque. Both variations immediately aroused my curiosity.

Bucky was never without his car, and he never wore head coverings.

"Where is your car, Bucky?" I asked.

"I had an accident last night," he replied rather dejectedly. "I was driving along Ramsey Lake Road when I ran into the front end of a grader. I hit the front tire and my car was totalled."

"Any injuries?" I asked.

He removed his toque, exposing a lump on his forehead the size of a hardball. "I hit my head on the steering wheel."

Both he and I laughed at his predicament. The lump garnered the same reaction that a third eye would have on a cyclops.

Of course, the story made the rounds at Bucky's expense.

Now scroll ahead to the day of his second marriage in 1980. The reception was attended by a sizable number of guests, including me. Once the pre-dinner formalities were done, guests were allowed to acknowledge the bride and groom. I took my turn when appropriate.

Having prepared in advance, I presented a wrapped gift to the groom, insisting that it be opened at that very moment.

As Bucky began to unwrap the present, I explained the story behind the contents.

Once the sizable "Tonka Toy Road Grader" was revealed everyone was in stitches.

To compensate for this bit of frivolity I did contribute a serious gift to the bride and groom.

WHAT IRONY

Sue moved into an older house back in 1996. Four years later she had the house torn down and a new one built. This property backed onto the ocean, specifically the Georgia Strait. A human-made dyke partitioned the two. It provided a recreational path for runners, cyclists, and walkers.

Within two years I offered to build an Allan Block wall. This metre-and-a-half-high barrier was meant to secure Sue's vegetable garden from erosion. During my labour, a passer-by stopped to talk to me. "That looks like hard work," she offered. "You're doing a great job. I have been walking on this dyke for a long time," she continued. "The previous owner never looked after this property."

I had difficulty containing myself from laughing out loud. As soon as she went on her way, I rushed to share the story with my wife—the past and present owner. What irony.

FIRST LSD TRIP

During the summer of 1969, my employment in Sudbury, Ontario, was interrupted by an Inco strike. With time on our hands, my friend Grant and I decided to head south.

We jumped in my Volkswagen bug, eventually visiting friends and family in Toronto, Hamilton, Windsor, Detroit, and Rochester.

While in Toronto, friends convinced us to meet them at a Blindfaith evening concert at the old Varsity Stadium. This was to be our first experience with a major rock band.

We paid our five-dollar admission and made attempts to find our friend Brian but with no success. It wasn't until well into the concert that Brian finally located us.

He offered us a tab of acid each and we accepted. This was to be our first LSD trip. "How long will it take?" we asked.

"About half an hour," was the reply.

After Brian disappeared into the crowd, Grant and I continued enjoying the concert. We waited patiently for the LSD effect to kick in. Thirty minutes passed with no apparent results.

When the concert concluded, still no sensation. A full hour must have passed. We tried to find Brian to question our situation. No luck. So, we decided to return to our sleeping arrangement at the home of Grant's brother.

While driving, Grant and I checked in on each other's condition. Still no luck.

After popping into a fast-food outlet, the LSD took effect. My head began to spin. My surroundings began to visually warp. It was a most unusual mind-altering experience. Completely novel. Both Grant and I were experiencing the onset of an acid high.

Once again, we jumped into my bug and headed down the busy retail-lined streets. We were increasingly mesmerized by the passing scenery of bright lights.

I couldn't believe what I was seeing and experiencing. Our minds were blown away.

All was well until we realized the nature of our destination. Grant's brother was a cop. He worked for the Toronto Police Service.

Paranoia set in instantaneously. "Are we going to be caught?" crossed our minds. Despite this temporary mental setback, we proceeded with our plans.

We arrived at his brother's home with everyone asleep. What a relief that we didn't need to interact with anyone in our condition, especially a cop.

Still fearing we would be found out, we quietly entered a bedroom vacated for us by one of the children. The room was decorated for a boy. As a result, I was captivated by some of the décor, most notably the Mickey Mouse wall clock. To use the vernacular of the times, everything was mind-blowing.

Once we put out the lights, the visual stimuli were replaced by mind games. Finally, an hour or two later sleep supplanted uncontrollable giggling fits alternating with periods of deep introspection.

To our relief, we awakened in the morning to an empty house. We had no need to explain our previous night's activities.

In retrospect, this first LSD trip was very positive, entertaining, and extremely enlightening.

SPAGHETTI WAR

During the same summer of my temporary unemployment in 1969, five friends and I planned a three-day getaway to a mutual friend's camp. A camp, in Northern Ontario vernacular, is the equivalent of a cottage or cabin elsewhere.

Getting to the camp required an hour drive south of Sudbury. We travelled there in separate vehicles. Prior to departure, adequate quantities of grocery and beer supplies were purchased.

The rustic camp was located on the shore of a lake with a separate outdoor sauna situated on the dock. The owners were of Finnish descent, so the camp and sauna were of authentic design and build. It was a wonderful place to be. We could jump or dive directly from the dock into the lake.

The most memorable event that took place during our stay revolved around the preparation, consumption, and aftermath of one meal.

Spaghetti was the main course—but not just a reasonable quantity of spaghetti. Sitting in the kitchen, I observed a large, galvanized pail filled with water being heated on the wood-fired stove. While the water was coming to a boil, many large cans of spaghetti sauce were emptied into one the largest cast iron frying pans I had ever seen.

The level of the spaghetti sauce was kept just below the top edge. Once it reached its boiling point the sauce began to bubble over onto the stove. Two boxes of spaghetti, possibly four pounds worth, were dumped into the galvanized pail when it came to a boil. Once cooked, the spaghetti was drained, and the sauce was added to the pail. The combined quantity was massive. Just imagine a very large metal pail brimming with pasta and sauce.

We sat down at the kitchen table across from the stove, anticipating a feast. Our dress code was quite casual - swimsuits only.

We served ourselves. I can remember the heaping quantities on each plate—four inches high may be an underestimation. Combined with the ongoing beer consumption, I remember that all six of us could not finish our meals.

The dinner disintegrated into a full-fledged food fight on the adjoining dock. Spaghetti and sauce were heaved at each other with vengeance knowing that our source for cleansing was just below us.

With our bodies splattered in noodles and red sauce, we took turns diving into the lake. The resulting water could easily have been nicknamed the "Red Sea."

MISCHIEVOUS MIME

One of the acts in the 1973 Northern Lights Folk Festival was Cedric Smith. Originally with "Perth County Conspiracy Does Not Exist," he proved to be a very appealing performer. Consequently, we brought him back to perform in the fall.

When Cedric returned a mime accompanied him. The act consisted of Cedric on guitar, singing or reciting poetry. The mime simultaneously acted out the words or meanings.

A local television station got wind of their presence in town and invited them to appear on an entertainment program being broadcast live. I escorted them to the TV station. While the performance took place, I spent time in the reception area.

Immediately following their portion of the program, I witnessed the phone ringing off the hook at the reception desk. Many of the callers were complaining about the performance. They were not only offended by Cedric's satirical content but also, and even more so, by the appearance and actions of the mime. Being white-faced and silent was apparently not acceptable to the Sudbury viewing audience.

Following this gig, the three of us decided to visit the nearest hotel to quench ourselves with a glass or two of beer.

While sitting, drinking, and conversing, I noticed a familiar face passing through the lounge. I knew him as a regular but had never previously talked with him. As he passed our table looking in our direction, he stopped dead in his tracks.

The white face of the mime seemed to irritate him. Approaching us he immediately wanted to engage in a conversation with our friend. But the mime, playing his role dutifully, refused to utter a word. This infuriated the passer-by.

He became more and more belligerent as the mime continued to remain silent.

It didn't take long before a challenge was made to fight. By this time, the scene instigated by this individual had alerted hotel staff. To our satisfaction, he was gently removed from the premises.

In retrospect, it was an amazing experience witnessing how easily people became intimidated by the presence of a mime.

SEX CHANGE

Weddings, as we all know, are perfect opportunities for families to gather and enjoy each other's company. This was no different in the late summer of 1980.

It was a Manitoba wedding, so my three-and-a-half-year-old daughter and I made the trip from British Columbia, leaving my wife behind to manage our business.

Arriving in Winnipeg we were offered accommodation with Aunt Millie.

By the second day, other family members arrived, including my mother and sisters. We congregated that evening for some pre-wedding celebrating.

My daughter, Katie, participated until it was bedtime. We had been given the use of a bedroom to ourselves with a mattress on the floor.

The sun hadn't set yet at eight thirty on that August evening. So, it was a chore getting her to fall asleep. Aggravating the situation was the laughter and conversation emanating from other parts of the house.

I lay down beside Katie, closed my eyes and remained completely silent.

The strategy was to get her to fall asleep as quickly as possible. I wanted to get back to the party.

Katie was having no part of this. She fidgeted and talked away. I remained resolute and refused to react. My eyes were closed. Five, ten, fifteen minutes passed and still no change. Except Katie began gently stroking and pulling my beard.

This continued for some time until I lost my patience. "Katie," I said, "what are you doing?"

Her response utterly flabbergasted me. "I'm going to cut off your beard and cut off your penis and make you into a lady."

That destroyed my pretension of being asleep. I cracked up at her precocious comment. I couldn't believe what I had heard, although I was aware that she had been exposed to naked male children. We had taught her proper names for body parts.

Once Katie fell asleep, I rushed back to the gathering to relate the episode that had just taken place. I'm not sure if they appreciated my candidness.

MASTER OF HYPERBOLE

George, my girlfriend Suzanne's brother-in-law, was a natural-born entertainer. Whether he was aware of it, I'm not sure. His modus operandi consisted of one exaggeration after another.

As a human being, he was perfectly delightful to be around. Laughter, laughter, and more laughter were the usual reactions to his antics.

One adventure with George began with an early morning visit to his home in preparation for the great fishing expedition he had promised.

He was asleep when Suzanne and I arrived. Once awakened and dressed George proceeded directly to the fridge, at which point he consumed a can of Pepsi. This was breakfast.

This simple act was hilarious for me. I had heard the Northern Ontario urban myth that French Canadians drank Pepsi for breakfast. Sure enough, George confirmed the legend.

Whether the sugar high was the cause or not, George was pumped up for the fishing trip. And I mean pumped up! He— not me or his brother-in-law—was going to catch the biggest fish imaginable. Whitefish Lake was going to be his and only his for catching fish.

George's small aluminum boat and trailer had already been hooked up to his vehicle. We picked up his brother-in-law en-route to the fishing ground one hour away.

The entire trip was dominated by George bragging about his fishing prowess, past, present, and future. This was going to be the day when he would show us how it was done.

Upon arrival, we put the boat in the water and away we went to his secret fishing hole where the fish were guaranteed. Again, George insisted he would be the prime beneficiary for he was "born to fish."

Our rods must have been in the water for sixty minutes with absolutely no bites. George was beside himself. Excuses abounded. This was most unusual. It had never happened to him before.

"I can't believe it," he kept repeating. Then, with an alternative plan, he sprang into action. "Let's go over to the other end of the lake and visit friends," suggested George as he reversed the boat's direction. During the twenty- to thirty-minute jaunt I kept my line in the water.

Sure enough, I got a bite and pulled in a whitefish. George went into a fit of disbelief.

"How could this happen?" he uttered disdainfully. "Why would a fish hook onto your line when I'm the fisherman?" he continued.

George was the consummate actor.

There was no letting up until we noticed smoke wafting from the shoreline ahead. As we approached it became apparent that the smoke was coming from the cabin of George's friend. Smoke was visibly streaming out the windows facing the water.

The boat's small outboard motor did not match our haste to get to the scene of the emergency. George was becoming quite agitated.

When we finally pulled into shore, he jumped onto the cabin's deck and opened the door into a smoke-filled kitchen. The oven was the source of the smoke. More specifically it was a roast.

George, a firefighter by profession, leapt into action. He pulled out the blackened remains and heaved the golf-ball-sized lump into the lake.

George saved the day. This offered him the perfect opportunity to play the hero role. And as a consummate actor and a master of hyperbole, he went into overdrive.

If it weren't for George, the cabin would have burned down.

When the owners arrived a short while after, George described the entire spectacle, replete with his heroic contribution. Repeatedly he emphasized his invaluable efforts.

The remainder of that day paled in comparison. I can't recall ever meeting anyone since that compares with George and his antics.

INVISIBLE POLICE OFFICER

Driving along a main thoroughfare on a busy Saturday afternoon I had two passengers accompanying me in the front seat: my girlfriend was on the far side with her seven-year-old niece between us.

I was returning to my workplace, a retail business, in the company vehicle. The station wagon exterior was covered in the company's logo.

As I was driving and conversing with my girlfriend, the niece suddenly blurted out, "There's a police officer."

When I looked back in the rear-view mirror, there he was, an officer, standing in the middle of the road shaking his fist in my direction. I had been oblivious to him standing on the roadside, attempting to flag me down.

I recognized him as a cop who had a reputation for being very officious. This was someone who meant business.

What was I to do, pull over or keep going? I needed to make a split-second decision.

I kept going, rationalizing that it was too late and that he couldn't catch me. Five minutes after returning to work the phone rang. Another staff person answered the phone and then passed it on to me. It was the cop. He had traced me by the information provided on my company vehicle.

"Were you the guy driving the station wagon?" he asked.

"Yes," I replied.

"You better watch out. I'll get you the next time," he warned.

Fortunately for me, it never happened.

FOUND OUT

As a painting contractor, I experienced several interesting and unique situations over a lengthy career. Employee-employer relationships, customer relations, and financial survival generated a fair share of these circumstances. Safety on the job site was another one.

Working on ladders required the utmost attention. Proper training was a prerequisite. I had the good fortune of being trained properly during my apprenticeship. In turn, I made it a point to instil safety consciousness in my painters. Nonetheless, there were exceptions to the rules. And I was at fault on an occasion or two.

It was pure irony to be discovered for a safety violation by someone at the other end of a phone. And not just any old person . . .

My cell phone rang while I was straddling a twenty-four-foot extension ladder near its peak to paint the exterior of a house. Fumbling to retrieve my phone, located in a special pocket compartment in my painter's pants, I managed to answer in time.

However, I was unable to identify the male caller. He was a stranger. His conversation lasted for at least forty-five seconds. I listened intently and got the gist of it. He needed a painting estimate and was providing me with many details about the project, but it was impossible for me to digest all the information without writing it down.

Finally, I interrupted him, explaining that I was at the top of a ladder.

"I suppose you're hanging onto the phone with one hand and a rung with the other hand?" replied the caller. "You're speaking to the president and CEO of WorkSafeBC.

I was dumbfounded. What an ironic and embarrassing situation.

In defence, I replied, "My van is close by, and I need to get down from my ladder so I can write down all the information."

He patiently waited as I climbed down, walked to my van, and retrieved pen and paper. He provided all the details, and a meeting was arranged for a later date.

The call from the president/CEO wasn't as serendipitous as it appeared. I had previously painted for the chief financial officer of WorkSafeBC, and it was he who referred me to his superior.

When all was said and done, I did not get the job.

BLASTED SKUNKS

My mother's brother Tony was the black sheep of the family. This fact became evident to me as I matured as a teenager. In conjunction with stories of his past misdemeanours, I gained further insight into his character when he passed through Sudbury on his cross-Canada adventures.

My parents were renting a new house built by our landlord. It was located at the front of the property with an older one-room shack left standing at the rear. The landlord had built an addition to the shack in order to raise pigeons as a food source. The land between the two buildings had been converted into a vegetable garden. A wooden walkway through the centre of the garden connected the shack to the front of the property.

Over time a family of skunks, attracted to the pigeons, moved into the crawl space under the shack. This became a perfect location for them for both shelter and food, namely the pigeons.

Now here is where Uncle Tony became a player.

On one of his visits, he discovered the skunks in residence. I remember his animated expression when he announced, "I'll get them."

Unbeknownst to me, he had checked with city police about the firearm regulations as they pertained to wildlife on private property. He was told that as long as it didn't impinge on neighbours, he could eliminate the skunks. The green light was all Uncle Tony needed.

As I was returning home from school a day or two later, I could smell the strong scent of a skunk. It permeated a three or four-block radius. I immediately suspected what had happened. The skunks were dead, and Uncle Tony was the perpetrator.

Sure enough, this is exactly what had happened.

I was told that the mother skunk, with two offspring trailing behind her, was walking on the wooden walkway through the garden. Uncle Tony had been lying in wait. At the first opportunity, he blasted all three with my father's twelve-gauge shotgun.

By the time I arrived, the skunk remains had been buried. But the scent lingered for a full twenty-four hours.

For Uncle Tony, the affair was worn like a badge of honour.

GARLIC BREATH EXTRAORDINAIRE

Identifying my uncle Tony as a black sheep is not an exaggeration. I found him to be quite wild and at times crazy. Unconventional might be a more generous term. And going under an alias was his modus operandi to avoid police scrutiny. For good reasons.

Uncle Tony was visiting us at fall harvest time. When he was helping us gather vegetables from our garden, he discovered that we had garlic growing. He showed an extraordinary interest in the herb.

With approval from my mother, he pulled out a few fresh garlic bulbs before dinner. Sometime between dinner and bedtime, Uncle Tony peeled and cleaned a bulb. Separating the cloves, he popped them into his mouth one by one, chewing each clove well before swallowing.

Being in the same room, I could see he took great delight in the process. I was also acutely conscious of the odour being emitted. It was foul.

When it came to bedtime, Uncle Tony was assigned the extra bed, kitty-corner from me in my bedroom.

Thinking nothing of the situation I retired for the night.

The shock hit me first thing in the morning. I awoke with the most severe case of garlic breath. While sleeping, Uncle Tony had been exhaling the garlic odour and I had been inhaling the same. The garlic odour was intense.

As a teenager, I was acutely aware of the negative consequences of having this horrendous affliction. I decided that I was not going to school that day. My classmates would ridicule me unmercifully.

I pleaded with my mother to let me stay home. But with no success. Off to school I went.

I can't honestly remember the consequences if any. It must have been a case of successful camouflaging—keeping my mouth shut—or the known mental ploy of eliminating negative experiences from one's memory bank.

ÑONE TO THE ÑUNS

During a 1971 European trip, my girlfriend and I included a visit to Rome.

The Vatican was one of our sightseeing destinations. We happened to arrive on the steps of St. Peter's Basilica quite early in the morning, well before the large crowds arrived.

We approached the front entrance with its extensive series of doors. A large contingent of nuns was spread out, seemingly there to greet visitors. However, we quickly realized their purpose: to collect money. I was startled when one came running towards me and shoved a large metal collection plate into my chest.

The initial pain caused by the force of the jolt and the audacity of the nun's actions were enough to convince me to donate not one lira.

I walked away satisfied in not having given.

BELLA BELLA

Kayaking, specifically ocean kayaking, became a serious interest and hobby for me from the mid-nineties into the early 2000s.

I was involved in eight wonderful trips ranging from an overnighter to ten days. Daughters or stepsons or Sue, my wife-to-be, accompanied me on these adventures.

They are all memorable, but the Bella Bella excursion with Sue was rife with humorous episodes. This round-trip paddle lasted ten days from start to finish.

Bella Bella is a very remote community on an island situated off the far northwest coast of British Columbia. Once ocean-bound, we did not cross paths with any other humans, just a small cruise ship.

On the fifth day, we met another couple kayaking. We overnighted on the same island and engaged in conversation.

When we related our experience with the passing cruise ship, the male pointed out a missed opportunity. "You should have shouted, 'Throw all your chocolates overboard!'"

His suggestion was taken under good advice should another similar opportunity arise.

Each evening we pulled into shore, unloaded, set up our tent, prepared dinner and retired for the night. One of these dinners incorporated some dehydrated precooked beans given to us by a friend.

Both Sue and I experienced the potency of beans as we had never experienced them before. The frequency and quantity of the beans' gaseous effect gave me the impression that the tent was levitating with us in it.

Our paddle continued the following day. By late afternoon we pulled into a sizable, sheltered bay where a party of eight to ten kayakers were overnighting. We discovered that they were invertebrate scientists from the University of Victoria.

In a casual conversation with two of them, we learned that they had spent time in Central America. One related an experience where she was housed in a hut on stilts above a waterway. When she awoke in the morning, she realized that her personal sanitation had fallen directly into the water. She seemed sincerely aghast at the situation.

I recognized the irony and pointed out, "No different than Victoria." It was a well-known fact that the City of Victoria did not have any sewage treatment. Their sewage was pumped directly into the ocean.

Our Victoria acquaintance did not appreciate my reminder, especially with her science background.

As we continued our journey the following day, the intense heat of the sun convinced us to pull into shore. We disembarked and dove into the water to cool off. We were desperate. However, our desperation quickly turned from seeking the cooling effect of water to seeking relief from its freezing effect.

The water we had immersed ourselves in was glacier fed. It took less than thirty seconds of exposure for my testicles to signal a need for an emergency exit.

IDIOTIC DRINKING

We were young, foolish, and heavily into drinking. Those were the years immediately following high school. Bob and I were late starters. It was a novel experience. We tried everything: vodka, bourbon, Black Russians, Rusty Nails. We made the rounds whether it was Sudbury, Toronto or otherwise.

After going our separate ways for our post-secondary education, I at Waterloo and Bob in Toronto, we occasionally rendezvoused.

When he made his way to Waterloo for a visit, we renewed our old drinking habits. Off we went. The bars in and around the university were our destination. We hopped from one to another drinking as much hard liquor as we could, trying to not duplicate drinks. "Variety, the spice of life" was our motto.

We had utterly no consideration for the consequences of drinking and driving in those days. It was a case of complete irresponsibility, regretfully so.

When we finally returned to my rented basement room, Bob lay down immediately, or was it passed out? Before I had a chance to do the same, Bob revived himself and rushed to my bathroom in apparent desperation.

He didn't quite make it. He vomited violently against the closed door. The vomit slid down the face of the door into a puddle of liquid and solids. Bob returned to his bed and collapsed for the night.

In the meantime, I went over to investigate the scene of Bob's mishap. It wasn't a pretty sight. The accompanying smell was disgusting.

Realizing that I was responsible for the rental accommodation, I began to clean up the vomit. In the process, the offensive nature of what I was doing caused me to throw up. Now there was double the workload and double the unpleasantness.

The next morning Bob and I reviewed the previous night's activity, whatever we were able to recall. We could not remember the return trip to my place.

In retrospect, it was a pathetic reflection of our character.

SHEEPSKIN COAT

While hitchhiking through France in 1973 we were picked up by a cockney lorry driver. Not only was he magnanimous and offered us a ride but he took the time to educate us. We learned about the origins of the term "cockney" and various aspects of English society.

He explained the nature of his regular truck route: London to Turkey and back.

A gorgeous sheepskin coat was brought out to show. This Turkish handicraft was a product he arranged by trade on each trip. In exchange, our genial host provided porn magazines.

We couldn't believe our ears. It didn't amount to fair trading as far as we were concerned.

PASTIES NOT PASTRIES

During the winter of 1968–69 Bob, my friend and drinking partner, and I habitually travelled five or six nights a week to a hotel on the outskirts of Sudbury. The difference in the locale is the only rationale I can think of for this daily twelve-mile trek. Not very intelligent, was it?

There was no outstanding attraction. Bob and I just did it. On the other hand, it could have been the nightly lounge entertainment. This didn't seem to exist in Sudbury itself. Another possible draw could have been the French-Canadian clientele that frequented the hotel. It was a different culture, a breath of fresh air perhaps.

The lounge entertainment which changed on a weekly or bi-weekly basis was not exceptional. However, during one two-week stint, the house band was fronted by a stripper.

Again, there was nothing exceptional until the final set of the final night of the two-week engagement. The lounge was packed with a very drunk and boisterous crowd, Bob and I included.

We were seated strategically in the centre of the room, directly in front and three tables away from the stage.

On the very last performance of the evening, the stripper surprised the audience by first removing one of her pasties and teasing the patrons. She practised throwing her sequin-decorated nipple cap in various directions. The intoxicated male customers clamoured for her attention.

"Throw it to me, throw it to me," was the frequent refrain.

This included my friend Bob. He hooted and hollered. Sure enough, the pastie was heaved in his direction. He caught it with his outstretched hand. Instantaneously, the prize was proudly displayed to all in the room. Bob was in his glory. The equivalent of a gladiator displaying his kill.

But the drama did not end there.

The stripper continued her dance routine, finally removing her second pastie. She repeated the same teasing procedure, but this time the excitement intensified exponentially.

Men were now on their feet almost hysterical for her favour. One stood to my immediate left. Alcohol had gotten the best of him. He was drunk.

The stripper finally released her cache in his direction. His arms were raised in the air parallel to each other in anticipation. He was about to catch the pastie with both hands as if he were clapping.

At the precise moment that the pastie was to enter his grasp, I reached up with my left arm and inserted my hand between his two.

It was pure luck. The object of our desire fell into my hand. I clasped it and in one swift motion, transferred it to my right hand. This was immediately followed by me pretending that the pastie had fallen on the floor.

My drunken competitor fell for the hoax. He dropped to the floor in search of his elusive prize. While he was desperately crawling on all fours, I revealed the pastie to everyone else.

Everyone in the vicinity became giddy with laughter. It was a classic case of irony at its funniest.

The unsuccessful gentleman left empty-handed while Bob and I departed with one pastie each.

Mine remained in my coat pocket for three or four days. It was quickly discarded when I realized that my mother might find it accidentally. I was still living at home.

POLICE DISCOVERY X 2

I can't quite remember the year that has been designated as the "Summer of Love." Was it 1967? If that's the case, I missed it.

I know for a fact I was late to mature. My peers were ahead of the curve compared to me. They knew things that I didn't know. They did things that I didn't do.

However, that didn't prevent me from playing catch-up, specifically in the realm of love.

Lena, an Italian beauty caught my eye in the summer of 1971. I fell madly in love—and I mean madly—with no rhyme or reason for the intensity.

My amorous advances were often met with her comment, "You're a dirty old man." This comment was always dispensed lovingly.

We maximized our romantic endeavours during our summer fling. It ended with Lena going off to college.

On one of our dates that summer, we decided to go to an evening movie. Although seats were still available, we chose the option of standing at the rear of the theatre. There we necked the entire evening. I can remember leaving the premises totally content without any concept of what the movie was about. Another passionate occurrence involved a night-time rendezvous at a secluded area known as Moonlight Beach. How is that for a romantic location?

We were comfortably ensconced in the company station wagon with the seats conveniently folded down. In the midst of our amorous tryst, a set of car lights approached. We covered ourselves as best as possible. The red roof dome gave it away.

It was the Sudbury police. The squad car pulled within five metres of us.

An officer stepped out. Flashlight in hand, he advanced towards us, directing his beam into the interior of the station wagon. When he realized the situation, he kindly reversed his course without saying a word.

Lena and I were quite intimidated during the encounter but relieved by the time the police car disappeared out of sight.

You would think that this would have been the end of it. But it wasn't. Our little secret was revealed.

Three days later one of my fellow employees confronted me at work asking, "Was that you in the station wagon the other night?"

My first thought was, "How did Tom know?" I wasn't about to manufacture a feeble alibi. I was aware that he had previously been a member of the Sudbury Police Department.

"Yes," was my reply. "How did you find out?"

Tom explained the investigating officer was a friend of his. He had contacted Tom, knowing that he worked for the company that advertised itself on the station wagon.

By process of elimination, it wasn't Tom or the owner but me. So much for confidentiality.

COLON VS. SEMI-COLON

New York is a fascinating city. I have had the privilege of visiting it many times since one of my daughters, Katie, defected there in 2000.

I don't use the expression "defected" loosely. She disappeared for a month before the family learned of her intention to move. It was done on the sly.

One of my visits took place in 2010. Katie had been married and was now a mother of two boys ages five and three.

Having previously been introduced to a wonderful Italian restaurant in Times Square, I decided to treat my family.

Due to work schedules, we compromised. It became a late lunch or an early dinner.

As usual, the meal was fantastic. Carmine's offered traditional family-sized dishes. The beverage selection was great, and the service was incomparable. Children were treated royally. We left, totally content in the late afternoon.

At the suggestion of my son-in-law Charles, we decided to take a stroll through Times Square, whereupon we came across a sizable street display.

The exhibit was sponsored by the American Medical Association. It was meant to educate the public about colon cancer. The presentation consisted of a replica of a human colon. The inflatable mock-up measured approximately three metres in diameter and ten metres in length. What made it remarkable were the flesh tones. It looked very realistic.

The colon reproduction was meant to be entered and walked through.

Unfortunately, no access was permitted. It was being closed for the day. Not only was it surrounded by a steel fence enclosure, but the air was also being released. It was collapsing. Realizing the opportunity, I turned to my daughter and son-in-law and remarked, "This is the first time I've witnessed a colon becoming a semi-colon."

The reaction to my pun was no different than most. They groaned while deliberately resisting detectable laughter.

WHERE ARE YOU FROM?

As a stereo salesman in the early seventies, I was baffled by an experience that proved to be quite funny.

A young customer engaged me in a conversation regarding stereo equipment. His accent was instantly recognizable. It was a southern drawl. There was no doubt in my mind. But I wasn't sure which southern state to attribute it to.

Once the business talk ended my curiosity got the best of me. "Where are you from?" I asked.

"Sturgeon Falls," came the reply. His answer completely floored me.

I burst out laughing. "How can that be?" I asked. "You have a southern US accent."

"That's where I live," he explained.

The irony was profound. Here was a man with a southern pedigree living in a community that was ninety-five percent French Canadian. Sturgeon Falls, forty-five miles east of Sudbury was a town that I was familiar with. French was the prevalent language spoken there.

WRONG NOTE

The NYC subway system is a godsend. It enables anyone and everyone to manipulate the vastness of Greater New York City. And it happens to be the sole means of transportation for my daughter and family. As residents of Williamsburg, Brooklyn, most of their daily activities originate in Manhattan. Work, school, shopping, and social activities necessitate underground travel.

On one of my visits, Katie bundled up the two boys, and we headed for the nearest Brooklyn subway station. After negotiating the crowded train, only standing room remained.

At the next stop, two young musicians entered and stood near us. The female carried a cased cello on her back. The male balanced an upright double bass.

As the train continued its journey, a jerking side-to-side motion developed. With us standing, balancing became difficult. It eventually caused me to bump into the double bass and its owner simultaneously.

My daughter, who is a classical violinist, was obviously concerned and chastised me for the collision.

Defensively I responded, "What's wrong Katie, did you think I was going to hit a wrong note?"

The two young musicians laughed, acknowledging appreciation for my humour. My daughter wasn't amused. She demonstrated a characteristic she had developed many years earlier. Katie deliberately avoided laughing at her father's jokes.

"Why do fathers always try to be funny with their daughters?" was a comment she had made in the past.

Her sentiment still hasn't deterred me from trying.

OVERWHELMED FIREFIGHTERS

Working on the dairy farm, a typical post-breakfast chore for me was a short trip to feed the heifers. From late fall to early spring these animals were housed in a second barn located at the far end of the L-shaped farm.

The trip required a drive on the paved road from our farmhouse. It usually took ten minutes each way.

While feeding these young cattle in the barn, an emergency vehicle siren could be heard in the vicinity. It seemed to be travelling from east to west just north of my location. The siren sound stopped shortly after.

I stepped outside to check its location. It was a fire truck attending a house fire less than a kilometre away. Smoke was drifting from the top floor of a farmhouse.

No less than five minutes later I was back on the road returning home. I decided to stop in as I was passing by the scene of the fire.

One pumper truck and a handful of volunteer firefighters were preparing to fight the blaze. Two residents had already been awakened and safely removed.

I learned that the pumper truck had only five hundred gallons of water on board.

Being a rural locale, no fire hydrant was nearby. The firefighters were concerned about running out of water. As I was familiar with the property, I informed them that there was a pond just to the west of the house. A half metre of snow was camouflaging its existence.

They quickly went into snow-clearing-and-ice-chopping mode. Their firefighting axes were a handy asset. But with the ice equal in thickness to the snow, the volunteers' energy waned quite quickly. Two alternated on the axe while two others were at the ready with a water pump. They needed a hole in the ice large enough and deep enough to reach the water level.

I could see the firefighters simply did not have the physical stamina to succeed. It reminded me of the Keystone Cops. After every two or three swings, the axe would be passed to the next man.

I offered to take over. With my farm-work conditioning, I was able to complete the ice hole in a minute or two.

In the meantime, the house fire was being doused with water from the five-hundred-gallon pumper truck reserve.

Time was of the essence. More water would be required: the sooner the better.

The crew at the pond were desperately trying to start the gas engine on the water pump. One would pull the cord, one would play with the throttle and choke levers, and a third would troubleshoot with instructions.

Déjà vu. Another scene reminiscent of the Keystone cops. Exhaustion set in quickly after three or four pulls on the cord. Then there would be a switch. It was also evident that these volunteers were not familiar with the pump's operation.

Recognizing the incompetence, I offered to assume the cord-pulling duties. I was able to pull seven or eight times in succession until the engine finally started. The water started pumping. The volunteers were relieved to know that they now had a reliable water source.

I can't remember if I was thanked or not. It didn't matter. I left satisfied knowing that the fire would be extinguished.

On the following Wednesday, I read the newspaper account of the Sunday fire. The house was saved with only minor damage. There was no mention of the dynamics that took place during the event.

I could only chuckle to myself.

HILARIOUS STANDOFF

Our senior high school basketball team played out-of-town exhibition games from time to time. Our coach arranged for one such game in the late fall of 1966. We were to travel to North Bay, Ontario, seventy miles from our Sudbury home.

The trip there and the game itself were uneventful. This contrasted with the return journey.

The team players travelled in two vehicles: the coach's and mine.

Before leaving North Bay, we made plans to meet midway to Sudbury at a specific restaurant in Sturgeon Falls.

Arriving in Sturgeon Falls at eleven o'clock on a Saturday night proved to be quite an eye-opening experience—notably for seventeen- to eighteen-year-old males.

As we pulled into the restaurant parking lot we were met with an outdoor disturbance. It was confusing at first to understand what was going on.

Curious, we parked our vehicles and approached what seemed to be the centre of activity. A sizable crowd surrounded two male antagonists. They were in the midst of a physical fight. But this was not your typical fisticuffs.

One man, the larger one, hovered above the smaller one who was kneeling on the parking lot pavement. The smaller fighter's head was being clenched by his adversary. To compensate, the testicles of the larger man were being yanked by the smaller rival.

Rousing laughter permeated the air.

Every time the towering man raised his arm in an attempt to hit the other, his opponent gave a two-handed wring of his family jewels. This paralyzed the larger man's ability to follow through with a threatening swing.

Each repetition of this process brought howls of laughter.

A constant barrage of offensive words between the two added to the farce.

We were witnessing a hilarious standoff in which neither competitor could gain an advantage.

The police had been mentioned numerous times, but none had arrived before we decided to jump into our vehicles and head home.

I doubt I will ever witness a similar performance again.

YELLOW SNOW

After-school basketball practice generally kept us busy until six o'clock in the evening. During the winter months, we would head home in the dark.

This walk took twenty to thirty minutes as a rule. It also required us to pass the CPR Station which was at the midpoint of our return. The Canadian Pacific Railway's renowned passenger train would rest here for an hour whether going east or west.

Passengers could disembark if they so chose. Sightseeing, exercise, or a glass of beer were some of the options. The last option could be found at the Ledo Hotel conveniently located right across the street.

Following one of our winter basketball practices, two fellow members and I were making our way home. As we approached the Ledo Hotel, we became aware of someone shouting nearby. As we proceeded, the vocal outburst became clearer. A man was exclaiming, "Wait for me, wait for me!"

He was standing on the sidewalk facing the Ledo Hotel. In fact, he was urinating in public against the building cladding.

As he continued relieving himself, his call of "Wait for me, wait for me!" was intensified. Simultaneously the man shook his unoccupied fist in the air, directing it at the train moving in a westerly course.

We quickly realized his dilemma. The gentleman had vacated his train during its one-hour stopover. He popped in for a beer across the street but overstayed. Having a full bladder complicated matters. He ended up missing his ride.

As we walked past the forlorn drunk, a patch of yellow snow became evident. Although we empathized with the fellow, we couldn't resist the comedic episode.

A lifetime of entertaining memories was provided in just that five-minute encounter.

GIGANTIC GROCERY STORE

During Expo 86, nine million visitors passed through the USSR Pavilion.

At the time I managed the gift and souvenir boutique. As a result, I came into contact with countless tourists and customers.

One of these tourists, a man with a southern US drawl, caught my attention. He seemed to be curious about a monstrous building next to the Expo site.

He was describing BC Place Stadium. This structure, with an immense pillow-like-looking roof, had a capacity for fifty-five thousand people.

Each side of the stadium had a digital readout sign mounted on top of a very tall metal post. "Safeway" the sponsor for the signage was mounted in large print at the pinnacle.

Based on this scenario, the American visitor shared his observation with me. In a slowly drawn-out drawl, he remarked, "We have Safeways in the States but not that big!"

His statement was incredulous to my ears. Was he serious or not?

I tried to detect if he was being sincere or simply pulling my leg. As best as I could determine, he was serious.

DRUNK SERVING A DRUNK

Extended vacation periods during one's school career can become boring. It can be a struggle to keep busy and entertained.

This was the situation that three friends and I found ourselves in as teenagers. It took place between Christmas and New Year's 1963.

Playing poker ran its course one evening. We needed a change. The solution was to head down to the Red and White, a greasy spoon restaurant on the periphery of the rundown part of Sudbury.

After entering the establishment, we chose a corner booth. From this location, we could observe all the goings on. It was a quiet night with very few customers.

One staff person, a male, was working behind the counter. The counter ran the full width of the room. Permanent swivel stools lined one side of the counter. The kitchen itself stood on the other side. A rather large stove, featuring a flat griddle, was separated from the counter by one arm's length.

Once seated, we detected that the chef/waiter was drunk. He carried on his duties but in a slow, deliberate, and halting manner.

Our eyes were glued to him. His antics were amusing to us.

It became even more entertaining when a drunk customer entered. This person meandered over to the counter and dropped onto one of the stools. He sat directly across from the stove. There he proceeded to interact with the chef, each man in a varying degree of drunkenness.

From our vantage point, we could hear the discussion clearly despite the slurring. The customer ordered a chicken dinner, and the chef went into action. Pre-cooked vegetables were poured onto the griddle from a bowl. A scoop of mashed potatoes received the same treatment. And lastly, a chicken leg was thrown on.

With his trusty spatula, the cook played with the first two items, flipping them over and over. The chicken leg was tossed from side to side with a flick of his wrist.

We, in our booth, were completely captivated by the ongoing antics. There was very little verbal communication between the two despite their intoxicated condition.

When the meal appeared to finally be ready, as in reheated, the cook placed the mashed potatoes and vegetables on a plate. He turned from the stove to the counter and served the customer with the comment, "The chicken isn't ready."

As the customer dug into his partial dinner, the chef flipped the chicken leg on the griddle one last time.

At the appropriate moment, the chef grabbed the chicken leg from the griddle and swung it in a 180-degree trajectory overhead to the counter and onto the plate.

The customer did not blink an eye. The cook could have cared less. And we let out a long and boisterous guffaw.

It was a once-in-a-lifetime experience.

TOO MUCH MEATLOAF

"Canada is Hockey." This paraphrases "Canada is Snow" by Gilles Vigneault.

The connection between meatloaf and hockey seems far-fetched, but there is a link, albeit not one that should be replicated.

In the winter of 1974–75, Sunday night pickup hockey was part of my ritual. Our players' abilities ranged from post-university competitive to past non-competitive. I was in the past-non-competitive range.

Prior to one of these hockey outings, I decided to prepare a pre-game dinner, including meatloaf. Being a bachelor at the time the meal didn't require any formality or sharing. The meatloaf was all mine.

When all was prepared, I sat down for my meal. The aroma of the meatloaf was especially appealing. After one slice I decided to go for a second. My appetite still wasn't satiated. I carved another slice out of the loaf pan. I couldn't stop myself. In total, I must have consumed five or six slices equal to two-thirds of the entire meatloaf.

What was especially appealing was the fat content. The bottom of each slice was soaked in its juices.

With the meal completed, off I went to meet the gang at the hockey rink.

Once there, I changed into my hockey gear and briefly warmed up on the ice. I sat on the bench for the first shift. Then came my turn.

Anyone that has ever played the game of hockey knows that you give it your all. It was no different for me. I skated my heart out for my three- to four-minute shift.

As I was heading to the bench for the exchange of lines, the fat content began to well up in my system. I could sense an excessive amount of odorous gas exhaling from my body through my nostrils and mouth. The sensation was absolutely sickening.

I was doubled over by the time I reached the bench. I arrived just in time to belch a tremendous amount of fat-scented gas in conjunction with major vomit.

It was unavoidable. I had no control. My embarrassment was secondary in intensity to my discomfort.

When I finally overcame the symptoms, I had missed at least one or two shifts. My recovery was successful after that. I continued to play albeit with a little less gusto.

Eating an excessive quantity of meatloaf in combination with a strenuous hockey game was a tortuous experience not to be repeated.

Never try it!

HILARIOUS SCHOOL STRAPPING

Corporal punishment was still allowed during my elementary school days. It happened to me several times over a number of years.

What could I attribute it to? In most cases, I can't remember the specific reasons. Misbehaviour in some form or other would have sufficed. I was an energetic, fidgety child.

Come to think of it, there were situations where a classmate would set you up as the fall guy. You would take the rap even though you were innocent.

In Grade 6, I was reprimanded twice with a strap. Miss Barlow was our teacher. She had previously been my teacher in Grade 4, but I can't recall any punishment levied in my direction then.

Miss Barlow was not necessarily a mean individual. But when we pushed her too far, she was forced to apply discipline. This came in the form of a rubber strap, approximately two feet long and two inches wide. It could deliver a painful result if enough force was applied.

The standard procedure for Miss Barlow was to yell at the mischievous student, "Get out! Into the hall!" Everyone knew that meant the strap was about to be used.

When the culprit was me, I opened the door to the hallway and stood outside apprehensively until Miss Barlow arrived. She had me stand facing her alongside the hallway wall, my arms and hands outstretched with palms up. Five swings of the strap were her usual quota.

But what made the whole affair hilarious was the fact that she was notorious for missing on two or three of her attempts.

The misses resulted in her either hitting her thigh or grazing the wall.

Trying to prevent my laughter became the most demanding part of the process. I didn't want to demonstrate any outward sign of amusement for fear of vengeful retaliation. But I was laughing inwardly.

Once the strapping session was over, I would march back into the classroom followed by Miss. Barlow.

As I returned to my chair I was met with whispers, "How many times did she miss?"

It was a classic case of one's reputation preceding her.

FIGHTING FROZEN SALMON

The following anecdote is rather tragic with a humorous component. The scene that I'm about to describe was comical to observe but the circumstance was a sad reflection of a broken relationship.

First a little preamble.

Steveston was once known as the largest salmon fishing community in British Columbia. With this culture in mind, it wasn't surprising to come across a couple walking along a major thoroughfare fighting over a salmon.

I just happened to be driving by when I noticed a drunk middle-aged twosome. Slowing down, I had the opportunity to better comprehend the situation.

They were arguing over a full-sized salmon. It was being hugged possessively by the woman. At the same time, the male kept grabbing at her possession. It became a tug-of-war. Loud and foul language was used as they continued their journey.

They pleaded with each other solely for the ownership of the fish. Eventually, the male halted his pursuit. The tearful female proceeded with the salmon clutched to her breast.

SADISTIC STRAPPING

Miss Meritt, our Grade 8 history teacher, was a different kettle of fish compared to Miss Barlow when it came to discipline.

During our final year at Prince Charles Public School, a new system was introduced. Rather than having one teacher instructing us in all subjects, a rotation of four teachers assumed the role.

Our Grade 8 class would move from room to room throughout each day. History was the final daily lesson. Miss Meritt taught this subject.

Bob Powers and I had been the best of school friends going back to Grade 2. For this class, Bob sat immediately behind me. I sat in the first chair in the row closest to the windowed wall. We were located closest to Miss Meritt's desk but two rows over.

She had a perfect view of the entire classroom, including Bob and me.

Miss Meritt began class one day by sitting on her desk facing the class and reading aloud from a textbook. As she was reading, I received a tap on the shoulder from Bob. I turned around.

Bob whispered, "Pass me your eraser." I complied and reached behind to transfer the eraser. At that very moment, Miss Meritt looked up and caught us in our brief exchange.

"Bob, Fred, if I catch you doing that again you'll stay after school for the strap!"

I can remember thinking, "We did nothing wrong. What is her problem?"

She resumed her routine.

It couldn't have been more than a minute later when I received a second tap on my shoulder. I turned around.

Bob whispered, "Here is your eraser" as he passed it to me.

Sure enough, Miss Meritt raised her head to catch us in the act again. "Bob, Fred, stay in after class for the strap."

Instantaneously, the adrenalin began to rush through me. What accelerated that process was my knowledge of her reputation. Miss Meritt had once strapped the school bully and made him cry.

I was dreading the outcome as never before. It was the exact opposite of the situation with Miss Barlow.

Class ended. Bob, I and Miss Meritt were the only ones remaining.

I can't remember who was first, Bob or me. But I remember that it was five whacks on each outstretched palm.

For a petite woman, Miss Meritt put every ounce of effort into each swing. The pain intensified with each hit. She didn't miss as Miss Barlow did.

There was no humour in the situation. It was torturous.

After ten straps my palms were red and swollen.

To this day I can't understand why she was so sadistic. It couldn't have been our minor misdemeanour. All I can speculate is that she must have had personal issues.

READ ME PLAYBOY

During the summer of 1969, I was employed at the sizable nickel smelter in Copper Cliff, Ontario. Booming demand for this metal required a round-the-clock operation with a workforce of two thousand per shift for a total of six thousand workers.

Workers were drawn from all parts of Canada and the world. Newfies and draft dodgers were quite prevalent. One Newfie, Norm, really impressed me, chiefly for his strength. He stood at about five feet ten inches but probably weighed in at 225 pounds. He was solid muscle.

On numerous occasions, I worked side by side with him.

I can remember a sizable steel ball that required moving on the shop floor. I'm not even sure if anyone else attempted the task. But when Norm leaned into it, the job looked effortless. I knew that it was an impossible undertaking for most others let alone me.

One of the permanent job assignments required two-man teams to watch over the input end of six nickel furnaces. When large pots, filled with molten rock and metal, delivered their contents into the furnace via a chute, the furnace door had to be raised manually.

From time to time, the furnace opening would become clogged with chunks of rock that had not been melted in the molten slurry. As a team, both members would first use a water hose to cool down the clogged red-hot material. When sufficiently cooled, one person would hold a six-foot pointed metal bar and the other would swing a sledgehammer. Many attempts would be required to dislodge the obstruction.

More than often, I held the bar for others as they swung the sledgehammer. No one swung it harder than Norm. And I trusted no one more than Norm despite the fact he was cross-eyed.

I had also learned that he was illiterate. He had only a Grade 4 education. He signed cheques with a simple scribble. Then he would pass the cheque to a friend to cash it for him.

But his illiteracy was most prominent one day when I witnessed the following scenario.

I came upon Norm leaning up against a friend who had an open magazine. To my discovery the magazine was Playboy. As I approached, the comment I overheard from Norm was, "Read it to me."

I couldn't contain my laughter. The irony of the situation was remarkable. When did the reading requirement supplant the eye-candy content in *Playboy* magazine?

TWO JAMAICANS

The summer of 1966 was my first real employment as a student—meaning real wages.

A copper refinery was my job site. It consisted of several departments including the tank house. Approximately twelve acid-filled tanks occupied the sizable floor area. At a depth of four feet, each tank was equivalent to half a basketball court.

With the acid heated to 140 degrees Fahrenheit and summer temperatures reaching 90 degrees Fahrenheit, the coolest place in the tank house was measured at 112 degrees Fahrenheit. Sweating was a constant dilemma, so we were required to wear head sweatbands. We also needed salt tablets and water rehydration every fifteen minutes.

There seemed to be a regular turnover of employees that summer. For a brief time, I was partnered with two Jamaicans. These men were given employment as a secondary occupation to their primary role as semi-professional soccer players.

Working with these individuals proved to be an eye-opening experience at my age. Their love of life was demonstrated in their casual approach to everything. When they conversed with each other in their Jamaican dialect no one could understand them, but their sense of humour was contagious.

On one particular occasion, our shift boss assigned me, another Caucasian, and the two Jamaicans to clear up a floor area in an adjacent building. This required us to move materials around to free up space.

No sooner had the instructions been given when the non-Jamaican member rushed over to a particularly sizable and heavy-looking metal object. He proceeded to squat, attempting to move it by wrapping his arms around it.

Noticing his dilemma, one of the Jamaicans immediately sprinted off to an adjoining room. Mystified, I asked the other Jamaican, "Where did he go?"

"I don't know," came the reply.

In the meantime, the white guy was struggling miserably in his endeavour.

The departed Jamaican reappeared just as quickly as he had disappeared. He was now carrying a galvanized pail. He rushed over to the labouring white guy and placed the pail directly under his rear end. He pointed at him, simultaneously blurting out, "He's going to shit himself! He's going to shit himself!"

We couldn't contain our laughter.

JAMAICAN HOUSE PARTY #1

Jamaicans love their music, reggae. I love music as well.

Music was the bond that brought the Jamaican community of Sudbury, Ontario, together with me. As the manager of a music store many Jamaicans frequented, I became acquainted with some of the men.

One was Barrington Scott. Once I was befriended by Barrington the doors opened to others.

Now as you can imagine, Jamaicans did not take kindly to the Northern Ontarian winters. The only reason they made the North their home was the readily available employment.

To compensate for the harsh winter conditions, their weekend indoor parties were habitual.

The first party I attended took place in the dead of winter on a Saturday night. Not quite the reminiscent Sudbury Saturday Night party of Stompin Tom Connors fame, it took place in the home of a Jamaican couple. The dancing and partying were contained to the basement rec room with food served on the main floor.

Rum was the drink of choice and gigantic spliffs were the smoke preference. Needless to say, the above lubricants certainly kept the attendees in wonderful spirits. All inhibitions seemed to evaporate.

When the call came down that food was being served, we joined the march upstairs.

A traditional Jamaican meal was provided. A line was formed leading to the kitchen stove where the host and hostess dispensed a stew from an oversized pot.

As the only non-Jamaicans, my girlfriend and I were curious as to what exactly was in the stew.

"What kind of stew is this?" I asked as we were given our bowls. The reply was unintelligible to my ears for two reasons: the Jamaican dialect and my drunken, stoned state.

We proceeded to a table, sat down, and began consuming our stew. All the Jamaicans around the table seemed to be relishing the delicacy enthusiastically. I quite enjoyed my initial spoonfuls but still was not sure what we were eating.

Again, I asked, "What kind of stew is this?" Once more I received an answer that I couldn't comprehend for the same reasons.

I was determined to find out what was exactly in the stew. I repeated my question, and the same refrain was offered. To my ears, it came out as "cookadabool."

Finally, it donned on me. "Do you mean cock of the bull?" I asked.

"Ya, mon, it make you strong!" The reply was accentuated with an arm motion indicating power.

I politely put down my spoon. It had been quite appetizing prior to knowing its content, but I couldn't stomach the thought of the actual primary ingredient.

JAMAICAN HOUSE PARTY #2

Summer was much more conducive to partying for my Jamaican friends. Heat was what they treasured.

I had the privilege to be invited to the same Jamaican home for a summer version of the previous winter's party.

Again, the bulk of the socializing took place in the basement rec room with one essential difference: we could open the doors and spread outside.

Being a particularly hot and humid evening, the outdoors became our main forum for the party. Of course, we imbibed the same refreshments and ganja as we did in the winter version. Jamaican hospitality was not to be refused.

Amongst those attending was a Black Canadian from Nova Scotia. He became our chief source of entertainment, keeping us in stitches with his stories, incessant talking and outgoing personality. I'm sure the stimulants he consumed enhanced his behaviour.

From time to time his performance was interrupted by complaints of mosquitoes bothering him. He would stand up from his sitting position, scratch his bottom, and grumble about being bitten.

Sudbury summers are notorious for their mosquito infestations, so we took it for granted that our friend was being harassed. However, no one else seemed to be suffering the same dilemma.

He continued mesmerizing us with his banter while complaining about mosquito attacks periodically. This was accompanied by him raising himself from his seated position to scratch his rear end.

This scenario furthered the hilarity. We, the audience, couldn't comprehend his complaints. No one else was being pestered.

Finally, our friend stood up to investigate the source of his problem. He had been sitting on a wooden pallet while the rest of us were sitting on a rock surface.

The sharp end of a nail was detected projecting ever so slightly out of the plank. This discovery initiated a roar of laughter.

I can remember this episode being one of the funniest situations that I have witnessed.

TOUPEE OR NOT TO TOUPEE

I was reunited with one of my childhood neighbours, Ardie, in my early adulthood. Three to four years older than me, Ardie was already married by then. In late 1969, he opened a retail business. By the early part of 1970, he hired me part-time as a university student.

Later that year I became a minor partner/employee. Because our friendship had been established for quite some time there was a great deal of trust between us.

Although Ardie was an exceptionally bright, highly motivated, and sociable individual he suffered from a case of premature balding. I was never aware of him being self-conscious but as it turned out, he was.

One Friday evening during business hours, Ardie and his wife disappeared. I was left to manage the store. They were to return before closing. When they did return, Ardie entered the store wearing a toupee. My reaction was instantaneous and unavoidable. I burst out laughing. It was such an unexpected shock to see the drastic change in someone so well-known to me.

I regretted my action. But the damage was done. Ardie never wore that toupee again.

WEDDING NIGHT

While working for INCO at its nickel smelter in 1969, a five-month strike occurred. Prior to the strike, one of our fellow employees had plans to marry later in the summer.

It was unfortunate but a group of two or three peers harassed this employee on an ongoing basis. They took advantage of his demeanour as a "mama's boy." I witnessed the group's behaviour towards him on several occasions.

I felt sorry for him. Despite his unmanly nature, I had learned that he already owned a house at age twenty-seven. Something to be respected.

This group especially pestered him regarding his approaching marriage. They tried to pry as much information as possible about his fiancée and their sexual relationship.

Fortunately, the strike put a temporary end to the situation.

Yet, when we returned to work in December the offending group continued their ways. They were especially interested in whether the wedding had taken place.

I happened to be present when the following conversation ensued.

"Did you get married?" they asked.

"Yes," came the reply.

"Did you make love to your wife on your wedding night?"

"No," was the response.

"What, you didn't make love on your wedding night?"

"I was too afraid to ask."

"Did you make love the next night?"

"Yes. I asked her and she said yes."

The entire conversational exchange brought howls of laughter from the perpetrators.

I was amused but again felt empathy for the victim whom I considered a decent person.

HORSEPLAY

During my employment in 1969, there was some horseplay but only in the absence of supervision. Young men or better still immature adults were the usual perpetrators.

The graveyard shift, midnight to eight o'clock in the morning, provided the best opportunity for these antics. During what was considered the lunch hour, from four o'clock to four thirty in the morning, we would gather in the lunchroom. As a rule, we ate meals quickly to allow us time to lay down our heads for a brief sleep.

On occasion, an employee would be wearing a brand-new flannel shirt. If they happened to put down their head for a short rest, someone would set a flame to the excess fluff on the backside. Once ignited, "Fire!" was shouted as loudly as possible.

The victim of this practical joke would be awakened in a state of panic. Fortunately, the lack of sufficient flannel material would prevent any serious outcomes.

A similar practical joke was played on those who read newspapers in the lunchroom. If someone unfolded the entire paper in front of themselves a person on the reverse side would apply a flame. In short order, the paper would catch fire and the shocked reader would be forced to abandon it.

The horseplay commonly incorporated the use of water. The workplace had an abundance of catwalks, and this offered a perfect opportunity to take advantage of pouring as much as five gallons of water onto any unsuspecting person below.

I witnessed such attempts on several occasions and was a victim of them as well.

During favourable weather in the summer, we would eat outdoors. The location happened to be directly under a catwalk six stories above. Unsuspecting individuals or risk-takers would be taken advantage of. Aided by gravity, the water from this height would come crashing down. The quantity and tremendous force of the water literally drenched all in a ten-foot diameter.

On another occasion I and others witnessed three fellow employees rush down a staircase to the outdoors carrying a five-gallon pail of water. At the bottom, one member climbed onto a six-foot ledge. The intent as far as I could deduce was to pour water over the next person to come down the staircase.

The fellow on the ledge asked for the water pail to be passed up to him. His two accomplices struggled to lift it up to him. Once handed over, the pail was immediately turned upside down onto one of the collaborators.

The obvious deceit infuriated the recipient to no end. He was spitting mad. As observers, we howled consequently.

In another occurrence, I was the unfortunate victim.

As a two-person team on the graveyard shift, we would alternate breaks. On one particular winter shift, we took turns resting by curling up in a wheelbarrow positioned in the narrow corridor between two industrial furnaces.

My partner had first dibs for a twenty- to thirty-minute period. Then it was my turn.

I fell quickly asleep. Shortly after, I was shockingly awakened by a drenching from a cascading waterfall from a catwalk above. The water not only soaked my exposed side but my backside as well. This was due to the wheelbarrow filling up.

I was able to catch a glimpse of the fleeing suspect but was unable to distinguish who it might have been. I surmised that it had to be my partner. He was the only one who knew where I was resting.

I returned to the worksite and my work partner, trying to assess his guilt. No luck. But I was convinced it was him. I plotted my revenge. The next day I managed to dump five gallons of water from a catwalk at a different location.

Whether he was guilty or not was irrelevant. I was satisfied.

CAMPING DEBAUCHERY

Camping became a regular occurrence for me and a hardcore group of five or six friends between 1970 and 1971. We camped in the summer when the night-time temperatures were advantageous, but the mosquito population was at its worst.

On one occasion, we had reserved two campsites about forty-five miles south of Sudbury for a Saturday and Sunday. Some friends were able to travel early on the first day, but due to my employment, I couldn't arrive until later in the evening.

I can't remember what food we brought. It was secondary to the tequila and marijuana that we consumed.

As the evening wore on, we progressively became more and more incapacitated. A bonfire became the centre of attraction. It mesmerized us. We kept feeding it with whatever burnable material we could find. In addition, we gathered branches to insert in the fire to create glowing tips. These we waved around in the dark producing light shows. Our creative juices were flowing. The unfortunate aspect was that these branches had a short life span. They constantly required replenishing.

It must have been around one o'clock in the morning when our supply of branches was exhausted.

Don, aka Beaver, offered to harvest more. He quickly disappeared into the darkness while we continued stoking the bonfire. It wasn't long before we heard a rustling sound coming from a distance.

The rustling noise continued for what seemed a lengthy period. My curiosity was aroused. I probably had forgotten that Beaver was on a mission.

Sure enough, Beaver reappeared. To our surprise, he was dragging a seven- to eight-foot tree that he had uprooted. Proudly, Beaver announced, "I have enough branches for everybody for the whole night!" We couldn't believe the outcome.

We eventually retired or passed out for the night.

We paid for our decadence the following morning. I remember being awakened by a faint call from the other nearby tent. "Wa-ah, wa-ah," was all that I could make out. It was repeated several times. Unable to distinguish the words, I crawled out of my tent and headed in the direction of Brian, aka Big Bird.

He kept up his plea, "Wa-ah, wa-ah." Reaching his tent, I could see Big Bird through the mosquito netting. He was now standing looking totally emaciated. One eye was completely shut from blackfly bites and the other was barely pried open. I assumed the cause was the combination of stimulants consumed.

"What do you want, Big Bird?" I asked.

"Wa-ah, wa-ah," was his reply.

Finally, I recognized the meaning of his plea. He wanted water. He was severely dehydrated.

I quickly retrieved some water for Big Bird. He was a sorrowful sight. It took an additional hour for him to exit his tent and open both eyes successfully.

I never again participated in such a display of camping debauchery.

U-BOAT SINKING

I had the good fortune to work with King Croteau at INCO in the summer of 1968. A member of the mechanical maintenance team, he was also a foremost storyteller, thus earning his nickname. I was assigned to this crew as an engineering university student.

Although all five members of the team were welcoming, King Croteau was by far the most gregarious. His reputation preceded him when it came to making the rounds on the job site at Frood Mine. He was stopped constantly with requests to share an anecdote.

In most cases, lengthy farfetched stories were shared with those eager to listen.

I can remember a joint errand that took a full sixty minutes. It normally would have taken five minutes each way. The difference in time was filled with his hilarious anecdotes and boisterous laughter.

I use the word anecdote rather loosely. It was more a case of pure bullshit-hyperbole at its upper limit but was ultimately entertaining.

His most impressive account dealt with his so-called WWII experience.

As an underage sixteen-year-old, King Croteau enlisted in the Royal Canadian Navy. He was assigned to a patrol boat in the North Atlantic. Supply vessels required protection from German U-boats.

Once his age was discovered, King was made a cabin boy. His claim to fame came when a U-boat periscope was spotted between his patrol boat and the supply vessels. The patrol boat pulled alongside the U-boat and dropped King overboard by rope with a can of green paint. He painted the periscope lens green.

With the departing of the patrol boat, the U-boat kept raising itself in the water thinking that the periscope was still submerged.

Eventually, the U-boat climbed completely out of the water exposing itself to aircraft. The submarine was eventually shot down with anti-aircraft guns.

With all his hyperbole, I enjoyed his storytelling ability.

DIGITAL DAMAGE

Our two-year-old daughter, Katie, had developed a unique habit. As she held her security blanket, Katie would pull off fluff and tuck it into her right nostril. Then she used her right-hand index finger bent at the second knuckle to pack the fluff further.

No amount of discouragement prevented her from persisting until an accidental situation cured her.

That instrumental finger became jammed in a closing swing door. It required medical attention but didn't suffer a serious breakage. Once this digit healed, Katie never returned to her former habit.

QUART BEERS

In the summer of 1970, I found myself in Montreal with three friends, Don, Grant, and Brent, who made the trek with me from Sudbury. We planned to visit two Montrealer's who had been fellow students at Laurentian University.

Our ulterior motive was to exploit the liberal Quebec drinking laws and attempt to ingratiate ourselves with the fashionable Montreal girls. We succeeded in the former but not the latter.

As it was a long weekend, we managed to fit in several activities. One was a tour of the basilica on Mont Royal where Brother André's heart was embalmed in a glass jar. The interior hallways of the church were lined with discarded crutches and wheelchairs. These were attributed to the miracles performed by Brother André.

As we wound our way through the labyrinth of rooms and hallways, Don, a non-practising Catholic was being hassled by one of our Montreal friends. In a deliberate attempt to annoy Don, he began sprinkling him with holy water. Under constant pursuit, Don kept fleeing through the various corridors. It was a race. And this race became a complete farce considering the context in which we found ourselves. This was a sacred building and here were twenty-four-year-old adults running crazily about.

The following day, Sunday, we decided to take advantage of pubs open for business. Compared to Ontario laws, this was a novelty.

Our source for quenching our thirst was located on the famous Crescent Street in Montreal.

I can remember entering the pub at four o'clock in the afternoon and sitting down with my three fellow Sudburians for our first quart of beer. Quarts did not exist in Ontario. So, this furthered the appeal for us.

We obviously savoured the situation very much because we kept consuming quart after quart. There was no apparent need to do otherwise. Time passed quite effortlessly, especially as we progressively became inebriated. Now, one quart was the equivalent of two and a half regular bottles of beer. By the time we had exhausted our financial resources, it was eleven o'clock in the evening. I had drunk eleven quarts with two others and the fourth friend had drunk twelve quarts. We were plastered.

Exiting the pub, we jumped into my Volkswagen bug and headed in the direction of our accommodation in South Montreal. After passing through a tunnel, we came upon a fast-food restaurant. Realizing our hunger, we made a pit stop.

With absolutely no money between us, we managed to beg for enough cash from strangers to satisfy all our hungry appetites.

We continued to our friends' home without any unpleasant incident.

Reflecting on our previous day's drinking escapade the next morning, we agreed that collectively we could remember very little.

On further reflection the whole affair with driving while drinking was unbelievably foolish. We were very fortunate not to have suffered any tragic consequences.

AUSTRALIA 1770

Travelling north from Brisbane, Australia, Sue and I veered off the main highway when something of interest caught our attention. As a rule, my wife and I were attracted to the coast, so potential sites for ocean swims and seafood were our primary motivational factors.

It was April 2013. We were travelling by campervan. As I did the driving, Sue handled the navigation.

She was very meticulous about referencing maps and travel books. I was consulted on a going basis to determine what may be of interest. As a result, I had explicit confidence in her ability despite an occasional difference in preference.

As we were driving along this stretch of highway, Sue read historical references to some of the approaching towns. One town was known for its 1770 discovery by Captain Cook. She gave me the details of his voyage to this area way back in time. It sounded quite intriguing.

"So where are we going?" I asked.

Sue replied, "Seventeen Seventy."

"But I know the history. You just read it to me. Where is our next stop?"

"Seventeen Seventy," she repeated.

I couldn't understand the logic of the conversation. Obviously confused but more importantly frustrated, I pursued the issue. "You have read the historical account! I understand the 1770 date of discovery! But where exactly is our next destination?"

Once again Sue answered, "Seventeen Seventy."

This response was enough to convince me it constituted sufficient grounds for divorce. What was going on? By this stage, the conversation was quite heated.

Finally, the whole issue was resolved when Sue stated emphatically, "Seventeen Seventy is the name of the town as well as the date of its discovery!"

Only then did I realize the dilemma. The tension evaporated instantaneously with an extended session of laughter.

When we emailed this travel account to our adult children shortly after, they responded with great amusement.

ADULT EMBARRASSMENTS

In the late 1990s, two family gatherings on my mother's side took place. Both were organized in Manitoba. The first was in Winnipeg and the second was just north of Gimli on the shores of Lake Winnipeg.

This side of the family was quite close and extensive; my mother originally had eleven siblings. Although some had passed away, the gathering was still sizable.

Various activities were organized during the two-day event, including perogy- and watermelon-eating contests.

Numerous males and a few females took up the challenge.

For the perogy challenge, the odds-on favourite was my cousin Jim. As a heavyweight farm boy, he appeared unbeatable. But I wasn't going to let this deter me. The same applied to Katie, my twenty-year-old daughter who was participating.

My reputation as a big eater had to be protected. I was determined to win the contest.

My strategy was to dispense with the sour cream, thus reducing the additional quantity to be consumed. There was a two-minute time limit.

When we were given the go, I tried to pack one perogy after the other down my throat. My strategy quickly backfired. I began to gag. Without the sour cream, I didn't have enough lubrication. When the two-minute limit expired, neither Jim nor I was the victor. It was Katie, my daughter.

That was embarrassment number one. Especially when she rubbed salt in my wound.

When it came to the watermelon-eating contest, the rules varied slightly. No hands were allowed. The two-minute limit was still in place.

I was determined that neither Jim nor Katie would defeat me. Unfortunately, my determination did not match my ability. Once again, my daughter took first prize.

That was embarrassment number two. Katie repeated the gloating as in the first contest. Onto embarrassment number three.

One of the attendees was a long-lost former aunt. Aunt Luddie had been divorced for many decades from my uncle Bill. They had emigrated to the USA back in the late fifties. I remembered the exact year in which I had last seen her. It was 1960, in Niagara Falls, New York. I would have been twelve at that time.

Notwithstanding this fact, Aunt Luddie had a different interpretation of our last encounter.

When we were reintroduced at this family reunion, her immediate comment was, "The last time I saw you I held you up in front of me and you peed on me!" With others present, especially my daughter Katie, I was taken aback. How humiliating. How do you respond to a comment out of the blue like that?

I didn't.

492 MORRIS STREET

From six months of age until age thirteen, 492 Morris Street was my family's home address.

In the early years, we resided in quite an older rental house with eight hundred square feet or less of living space. I can recall only two events from that time, both somewhat traumatic.

In the first case, a cigarette lighter had been given to me during an evening house party/gathering. It belonged to my father. I had asked him for it, and he gave it to me, whereupon I snuck into a closet to experiment with my newfound toy.

I may have been three or four at the time.

The closet door was a simple cloth curtain hanging down from a rod. Once ignited the lighter set the curtain on fire. Flames erupted but nearby adults quickly extinguished them.

My mother immediately chastised my father for his irresponsible act. I can't recall any personal scolding, and I suffered no fire-related effects.

The second off-putting event around that time evolved out of an innocent game my mother was playing with me. I was being chased by my mom around the dining/kitchen area. As I was backing up trying to escape her grasp, I fell into a closet and onto an empty glass milk bottle. Until this point, we were both laughing. Unluckily the bottle broke, and a shard of glass entered my buttock. I screamed in pain. Blood poured out. My mother quickly bundled me up, grabbed the next bus and whisked me to a medical clinic. Even with stitches, the scar remains to this day. If requested, proof of it will not be provided at this stage in my life.

Around the early 1950s, our landlord began to build a newer house at the front of the property. We remained living in the older house behind it. During the construction phase, this site became an intriguing playground.

My most memorable event was crawling backward through an open window into the basement. Unbeknownst to me, an open five-gallon pail of oily liquid tar sat below me. As both my legs entered the container, I can remember the sensation being disquieting. Fear of the consequences immediately crossed my mind. My saving grace was the fact that the pail was half full. I was only up to my knees in the gooey mess.

Once the new house was completed it became our home. During this period of early childhood, I can remember a repeated predicament that I got myself into.

To corral me, my parents placed me in a leather halter with a length of cord. During the summer months, I was tethered to a wooden fence. Not wanting to be confined, I would try to escape by crawling under the fence. I would then get stuck and squeal like a pig.

My parents would rush over to free me, but I would still be left tethered. Resenting this captivity, I would repeat my earlier escape attempt, become entrapped, and squeal for attention again.

Another attempt by my parents to contain me was to enclose me in the kitchen with an ironing board as a barrier. It was meant to prevent me from coming through an open doorway. On one occasion, the ironing board collapsed and pinned me to the floor. Again, I screamed relentlessly, causing my parents to rush to my rescue.

It's surprising I still remember these episodes. And that I have survived to tell them.

SUCCESSFUL ERECTION

When working on the farm, we would spend five to seven hours a day on chores related to the milking of cows, so the radio always provided news and entertainment while we worked in the barn.

Our morning routine would begin at 4:50 a.m. Feeding and milking took us to 7:45 a.m. Breakfast followed, and we would return to the barn by 8:30 a.m. to clean the milking equipment and manure and tend to the calves and any animal health issues.

The entire time the radio kept our minds occupied. Because I had the lowest seniority, the choice of stations was assigned to others. For all intents and purposes, the dial was locked on a very conservative Toronto station, CFBR. I couldn't stand it.

However, one program caught my ear. A long-time host conducted the regular morning program. It was live on air. He decided to call a friend who farmed north of Toronto.

The first question asked was "What are you doing today?"

"I'm erecting a storage shed," came the reply. A brief discussion revolved around this project. Other topics were touched on during the short ten-minute interview. When it came to signing off, the well-intentioned radio host closed with, "I hope you have a successful erection."

Dead air immediately followed. We in the barn burst into laughter having heard this major unintended Freudian slip.

At the time I'm sure the radio personality, his friend, and the entire listening audience spent a moment erupting in laughter.

HOFBRÄUHAUS

When I travelled Europe for the first time in 1971, my girlfriend and I were making our way north from Venice in a rental vehicle.

We had heard of the famous Hofbräuhaus in Munich, Germany, so this became our goal for the day. There were no lengthy stops for sightseeing along the route, so we could reach Munich before the end of the day.

We succeeded by pulling into the parking area surrounding the beer hall around nine thirty in the evening. Once parked we entered to discover a wild scene, at least to our Canadian experience. The place was hopping. The noise was deafening. Beer was being dispensed by servers in vast quantities in from half-litre to two-litre steins. The oompah band was in full performance. Traditional German clothing gave it an air of authenticity. It was a Saturday night.

Once seated with a beer in hand, we surveyed the scene more acutely. It appeared that at least two thousand people were present. The age range seemed to be eight to eighty. The whole experience was exhilarating. We were having fun.

It didn't take long to acclimatize. We ordered and consumed one stein after another until the last call was made at twenty minutes to midnight. This seemed very incongruous with the existing situation. Why would the Hofbräuhaus shut down at midnight when the roof was being raised in such a festive atmosphere?

We confronted our waitress when she came by to take our final order.

"Why are you closing so early, especially on a Saturday night?" we asked.

"Tomorrow is Easter Sunday, that's why."

Although this seemed like a reasonable policy, it still seemed highly unusual to us. We were under the impression that European drinking regulations were quite liberal. So why let an event the next day influence what takes place the evening before.

We were dumbfounded when our waitress answered our next question: "What time do you open tomorrow?"

Eight o'clock in the morning," she responded. It brought an immediate burst of laughter from us.

It seemed inconceivable that they would respect Easter by closing at a decent hour the night before but then open at an ungodly hour on the day that should be respected.

UNIVERSITY CONFLICT

My university year 1969–70 was quite tumultuous in Ontario. A series of confrontations took place on several campuses. The strikes pit faculty and students against university administrators.

It probably was no different than most disputes. Power and control were the contentious factors.

I was affected as a student enrolled at Laurentian University, Sudbury, Ontario. The situation came to a head in January 1970. Tensions were running quite high. The situation had reached an impasse. It required a resolution.

Finally, the board of governors granted a joint meeting with the faculty. Reluctantly, they also allowed students access to the gathering but with no voice. As a concerned student, I decided to attend. I felt it was history in the making.

The boardroom consisted of a large oval table surrounded by at least sixteen chairs. Each chair was occupied by a governor. To my eye, each member had notable status and credentials in the community of Northern Ontario. These were the powers that be.

The remainder of the room was standing room only. It appeared that faculty and students were in equal numbers. Collectively they outnumbered the governors by a ratio of six to one. I sensed that the governors were quite uncomfortable with the scenario. Their authority was probably being challenged for the first time. The atmosphere was extremely tense.

Once the meeting was called to order, the chair read out the riot act. Conditions were placed on the number of faculty speakers allowed to speak. Students were denied participation. Disruptions were not to be tolerated.

Despite these rules, it didn't take long for the formality to dissipate. Statements made by various governors were found to be unacceptable by the other participants. Vocal interjections quickly followed. The chair was forced to rule all uncalled-for comments as "out of order."

As the meeting deteriorated, tensions rose proportionally. When a student spokesperson attempted to comment, he was pounced upon by the chair. Students reacted by raising their voices in anger.

The governors attempted to continue their deliberations. Challenges would interrupt their proceedings.

With the support of sheer numbers, the student spokesperson was given the floor by the chair. His extremely articulate comments were very impressive to my ear. When he concluded his contribution, the room erupted in resounding applause. The governors were silent.

The ovation lasted at least a minute. Approximately halfway into the process one governor stood up and remained silent as he surveyed the scene. When the clapping finally ended this governor commented, "I didn't expect to get an ovation like that!"

His calculated attempt at humour brought the house down. Absolutely everyone guffawed. Laughter was loud and long.

As a consequence, the tension dissolved instantaneously. The meeting progressed with issues being resolved. The strike ended shortly thereafter.

It was a valuable lesson in how humour can neutralize adversarial situations.

MAJOR PAINT SPILL

Over the years many interesting characters posing as painters came through my painting business. Situations arose that were both rewarding and not so gratifying. Some were hilarious and some were tragic.

One second-generation painter, Walter, made my life quite interesting. As a recovering alcoholic he had invited me to an Alcoholics Anonymous meeting to celebrate his seventh birthday. His addiction seemed to be well-managed. However, Walter compensated with dependencies on cigarettes, candy, and lottery tickets.

Notwithstanding these weaknesses, he was intellectually bright. Reading was his favourite pastime during coffee breaks and lunches. He was also a political junkie.

As a result, the workplace could be a stimulating environment with Walter around. It was especially noteworthy on one occasion when a sizeable paint spill occurred.

Walter and I were completing an exterior house repaint. He was on one side of the house, I on the other. Everything looked rosy as we were within two hours of completing the project.

With the afternoon coffee break due, I crossed over to Walter's side to notify him to stop working. What I quickly discovered was a major paint accident.

Walter had stepped off a short step ladder onto a corner of a full tray of paint.

The paint tray had flipped into the air and landed upside down. The white paint contrasted against everything else, making the scene look quite dreadful.

There was paint on the concrete sidewalk, dripping off a four-foot bush, sliding down a wall.

But what was remarkably hilarious was the paint running down Walter's bare legs into his socks and shoes. He was wearing shorts.

The only saving grace was that the paint was latex. It could be washed down immediately with the nearby water hose. I suggested this to Walter adding, "When you're finished the clean-up just come and get me and we'll start our break."

Fifteen minutes later he joined me. We sat down inside the garage. For some unknown reason, Walter began to reminisce about his college days. "I would really like to go back to college and take up writing," he commented.

He went on at length about this newfound ambition. It made sense to me considering his love of reading. After about five minutes of his wishful conversation, I injected the following comment: "But, Walter, I thought that you wanted to keep your foot in the painting business!"

Although I found it to be an uproarious statement, Walter was significantly less enthused.

BUY ME A DRINK

For the better part of thirty-five years, I have belonged to the Association of United Ukrainian Canadians. This organization holds a convention every three years. The conference location can vary from one city to another.

Representatives are chosen by the local branches to attend.

In 1991 I was chosen to represent Richmond, British Columbia, and I travelled to Toronto for the event. Shortly after arriving, I met a Vancouver delegate, Stella Moroz.

We knew each other quite well since we sang in the same Ukrainian choir. I knew her as quite a comical individual. She was a fun person to be around despite her twenty years plus in seniority.

Stella's first comment to me was, "Will you buy me a drink later in the hospitality suite?"

"Of course," I replied.

A brief evening business session was followed by a social in the hospitality suite. When Stella was spotted, I approached her with, "Let me buy you a drink."

"No thank you," she answered. "Maybe tomorrow."

Over the next three days, there were two more evening sessions to socialize.

On both of those occasions, I repeated my offer to Stella, "Can I buy you a drink?" She again declined.

I just felt obligated to live up to her initial request.

At the conclusion of the convention, we were transported to Pearson Airport to catch a flight back to Vancouver. Sure enough, Stella was on the same flight.

While waiting for our departure, I turned to Stella and made my last offer. "Stella, since this is our last opportunity for a drink, can I buy you one?"

Unsurprisingly, "No thank you," was her response. I felt I had been duped by her the entire weekend.

Upon arrival at the Vancouver Airport, Stella was met by her husband, Ed. I knew Ed quite well too. With me by her side, Stella's first comment to Ed was, "Fred tried to get me drunk the whole weekend!"

I was flabbergasted. How could Stella interpret it in such a deceptive manner? Although I recognized her attempt at jesting, I tried in vain to defend myself.

"Stella," I said, "you asked me if I would buy you a drink. You were the instigator." It was a lost cause. Luckily, Ed had a good sense of humour. He understood his wife's ulterior motive. To get me in trouble.

$4.95 VS. $1,795.00

When my wife and I pulled into the Tsawwassen Ferry Terminal we discovered that there was a one-ferry wait. That gave Sue and I one and a half hours—adequate time to visit the newly renovated retail area there.

Meandering through the premises we noticed a wide variety of shops ranging from coffee to high-end art sales.

Spotting a gelato location, I walked up to a mother and two children holding ice cream cones. I asked, "How much did they cost?"

"Four ninety-five," was the answer.

I turned to my wife, stating, "That's ridiculous. I used to pay six cents for a triple scoop of ice cream back in the sixties." Finding the price offensive, we walked away.

Continuing our exploration of the retail location we came across an impressive First Nations art shop. A gorgeous-looking wooden circular piece was on display in a glass enclosure. "Birds Surrounding the Eclipse" described the work.

We were attracted to its unbelievable beauty. After viewing it up close, we asked, "How much?"

"Seventeen hundred ninety-five dollars plus tax," came the reply.

We countered, "Can you reduce the price?"

The saleswoman politely replied, "No I can't. I don't have enough of a markup."

Sue looked at me and I at her trying to read each other's minds. Without more than a moment's hesitation, we agreed to purchase it.

Not only were we ecstatic about our decision but we reflected on the irony of the situation. We had just rejected the purchase of $4.95 ice cream cones because of the perceived inflated price but unquestionably acquired a non-essential item for $1,795.00 plus tax.

So much for rational decision-making on our part.

SIX-CENT ICE CREAM

During my high school days, walking was my main means of transportation. It was about a thirty-minute walk to school.

Winters were torturous at times. I can remember my head of hair freezing with its excessive Brylcreem content. I defied the slogan, "A little dab will do you."

Summer was a different story. My walking pace was more relaxed. There was no need to quickly get out of the cold.

My favourite stop on my return home from school was Orange Grocery. This corner convenience store was family owned and operated by the Orange family.

It was always best to time an ice cream purchase when Mr. Orange was manning the store. A one-scoop ice cream cone was advertised at four cents, two scoops at six cents, but Mr. Orange liberally made a one-scooper a two scooper. A two-scooper became a three-scooper.

It wasn't just the quantity added, it was the way it was applied. Mr. Orange took great care and pride in sculpting the ice cream to reach its eventual size. It was as if he were creating a piece of art.

Patience became a virtue while waiting for Mr. Orange's performance.

It seemed that the longer you waited the larger the proportion. No one to my knowledge ever objected, certainly not I.

With cone in hand, the remainder of the walk was always incidental. I know for a fact that after consuming an Orange three scooper my appetite for dinner was substantially reduced. No complaints.

DRAMATIC NOT TRAUMATIC STRESS

Visiting my daughter Emma in Stratford, Ontario, is always a great pleasure. Firstly, Emma is a delightful human being. Not only is that my own assessment, but I constantly see the respect she commands from acquaintances, friends, and family.

In addition, I benefit from her employment with the Stratford Festival. Access to performances is often provided at no charge. My love for Shakespeare and live theatre is fulfilled.

In the summer of 2013, my two sisters and one nephew met us in Stratford for three or four days. It was a glorious opportunity for a family reunion. Food was the highlight. Not only is my son-in-law a chef but both of my sisters are also food connoisseurs and avid cooks.

Most dinners were feasts. The principle "people are happiest at mealtime" was confirmed multiple times.

Taking a tour of Emma's workplace was another benefit. It was located directly across from the Festival Theatre, within fifty metres. The park surrounding these facilities offered a perfect opportunity for an Emma-led tour.

Copious photos and videos were taken. Laughter lubricated the family walk-about. As we passed a number of large metal garbage bins, I noticed the attractive artwork. These receptacles not only were brightly painted but included Stratford's slogan "Dramatically Yours."

This struck a chord in me. How appropriate for a town dependent on the writings of such a famous bard to generate a creative motto.

My thought process went a little further when I asked Emma, "What happens when these trash bins are emptied? Do they suffer "post-dramatic-stress disorder"?

By the intensity of the groans, I could decipher that my attempt at punning was intolerable to Emma, my sisters, and my nephew.

STRAWBERRY MASSACRE

Since it was strawberry season, my wife decided to take our daughter and head out to a "pick your own" farm. At the time Katie was a half year in age, so she was transported in a car seat.

I bid them adieu as they drove away from the dairy farm on which I worked and on which we lived. While they were away, I continued to carry on my chores working within sight of the long driveway leading from the farmhouse out onto the highway.

It was sometime later that I observed our family car returning with my wife and daughter. Being a first-time father, I was eager to join them. By the time I reached them, Katie had been removed from the vehicle and placed on the ground, still seated in her car seat.

When I finally was able to view my daughter, I instantaneously panicked. Katie appeared to be covered in blood: her face, her hands, her clothing. I confronted my wife in an accusatory tone, "What happened to her? Was there an accident?"

My wife quickly reassured me that the red stains were due to strawberries and not any misfortune.

As it turned out our daughter had been placed on the ground between the strawberry rows while my wife picked. In the process, Katie was able to reach the ripened red fruit. In turn, it was smashed in her hands and onto her face and clothing in her attempt to feed herself.

As a result, her appearance created an initial horrific impression, sending me into a momentary devastated state of mind.

TWIG IN MY SWIMSUIT

Ocean kayaking was a passion for Sue and me for several years. We made five extensive trips of seven days or greater off the West Coast of British Columbia.

Three of these voyages took place in Clayoquot Sound. This area located on the West Coast of Vancouver Island incorporates the town of Tofino as its hub. The natural beauty of this coastal region is spectacular.

One of the most desirable destinations from Tofino was Hot Springs Cove. It required a minimum of two days of paddling in ideal weather conditions.

On one of these trips, we were socked in by fog on day two. After forty-eight hours of this thick blanket, we were forced to abort our journey. On another attempt, we managed to succeed. Although the actual hot-spring site was open to the public, overnight stays were not allowed. We tented in a bay located east and a thirty-minute paddle away. Again, we were forced to abort this expedition on day six after being deluged with rain for three solid days.

Our most successful experience was the middle one of the three excursions. Again, we camped in the same bay across from the hot springs. The weather was glorious.

During the day we would make an obligatory trip to savour the benefit of the natural heat provided by the outdoor springs. But most of the day consisted of us lying on the sandy beach sunning ourselves.

Since the island's location was extremely remote, we had no other company on the rather sizable bay. Anyone approaching would require a boat and would be heard in advance.

In an uncharacteristic fashion, Sue and I decided to sun ourselves in the nude on one of the days. The magnificent conditions inspired us.

Lathering up with sunscreen was essential considering our risky endeavour. Once done we simply vegetated on our backs. The heat of the sun was a treasured resource.

With my eyes closed and possibly sleeping at the time, I thought I detected a splashing sound. Sitting upright instantaneously with eyes opened, I noticed a pair of kayakers paddling into our bay. In a hushed tone, I immediately alerted Sue.

She woke up as well.

Fortunately, the intruders were approximately thirty metres from us and were not aware of our presence. Nonetheless, we jumped into panic mode. We reached for our swimsuits. It was vital to cover ourselves as quickly as possible.

I grabbed my Speedo and managed to slide it onto myself while sitting in the sand. Having succeeded, I shockingly realized that there was a foreign object inside the suit. It was about four inches in length and protruded from the front.

"What the hell is this?" I exclaimed. Sue looked at me in my distressed state.

As I disrobed the truth was revealed. A forked twig, a half inch in diameter had become lodged in my Speedo as I had tried to cover myself.

Once the source of my distress was discovered both Sue and I cracked up. Our laughter couldn't be contained.

In the end, we both successfully re-clothed. As to whether we were observed in the process remains a mystery.

WHAT LINE-UP?

Expo 86 took place in Vancouver in 1986. The event lasted six months.

By a stroke of luck, I was hired as the manager for the gift and souvenir boutique in the USSR Pavilion. Fortunately, my business background and connection to the Ukrainian/Russian community generated the opportunity.

Although I spent the better part of ten hours per day on-site for the duration of Expo 86, daily errands were run off-site. These errands included banking and most frequently stock replenishing.

All inventory was being warehoused a short distance away. Travelling between the two locations required driving past a food distribution warehouse. During the summer, a strike arose with the street gate being picketed.

While driving past this location over several weeks I noticed one lone striker. There was no other substitute.

Having a labour background, I empathized with his situation. I stopped one day to talk with him. We discussed the nature of the strike and I left giving him a fifty-dollar cheque made out to his union.

No more than a few months later it was reported that he had been stabbed to death. A tragic outcome as far as I was concerned. A passer-by had stopped and murdered him while he was picketing. For no apparent reason.

Months later I became aware of a belated funeral for this individual.

I felt obligated to attend having had a brief association with the gentleman. It was advertised for noon on a Friday at an east-end church.

I arrived early and parked across the street. It was 11:20 a.m. A large line-up had already formed outside the church. I joined the line. It was impressive. I concluded that the murdered victim had a large union and social network support.

The line-up was noticeably solemn. Almost no one spoke. If anyone did it was done in hushed tones. In addition, the line moved ever so slowly. Time also passed at a snail's pace. Looking at my watch I couldn't understand why at 11:40 a.m. we had only moved a metre or two.

Time continued to drag. Why was so little progress being made? Was the church filled already?

I listened intently for any clues but failed to ask any questions. The atmosphere continued to be sombre.

Finally, at noon reality hit. The line-up that I had patiently joined was meant for the food bank located at the side entrance of the church.

Realizing my idiotic mistake, I rushed to the main entrance of the building.

I was met by an overflowing crowd. Not only was the church interior filled but the entrance lobby was as well. Attendees were also milling about outside.

It became evident that I had failed to fulfil my original intention. There was no possibility of paying my respect.

I exited humbled and disappointed.

PIGMENT OF YOUR IMAGINATION

Painting has been a therapeutic occupation for me. I am referring to residential and commercial painting. My satisfaction derives from the ability to make aesthetic changes and witness the effect immediately.

A twenty-eight-year career is a testimonial to the satisfaction that I derived from this field of work. Or should I say pleasure?

Both interior and exterior painting had their rewards. But working outdoors on building exteriors proved to be more gratifying. The reason—more coverage in a shorter amount of time meant it was more rewarding, especially with a sprayer.

Spraying, which was almost exclusive to exterior surfaces in the repainting business, was a favourite of mine. Brush and roll applications were enjoyable but not as much in comparison.

Mid-spring to mid-fall was the prime spraying period. There were times when I would work right up to the last remaining light in the evening.

Paint spraying did have its share of negative aspects. The main one being overspray. After a lengthy session, I could be covered in paint. If the weather conditions were hot, I would wear less clothing. At the end of the day, my face, hair, exposed arms, and clothing could be covered significantly.

This was the case when I painted a house in "forest green." I wound up spraying until 10:15 p.m. one evening. Upon completion, I headed for a neighbourhood grocery store. I needed to purchase food for a late dinner.

While passing through a checkout a young male cashier took interest in my appearance. He commented, "Looks like you've been painting."

Sensing an opportunity to tease him I replied, "What do you mean?"

"Well look at you, you're covered in paint," he retorted.

Again, I feigned any existence of paint. I repeated my earlier statement. "What do you mean?"

This seemed to get his ire up. "Look at you. You look like you've come from the moon. You're covered in green," he uttered in an exasperated tone.

I then countered, "It must be a pigment of your imagination!"

The conversation concluded on that note. I can't even remember if any laughter ensued on his part or with any of the customers that were nearby.

SUICIDAL CYCLING

Delivering newspapers was an extracurricular activity that I engaged in from the age of eleven to thirteen years old. I had a total of three different paper routes. Two existed at the end of each school day and one in the early morning preceding school. The routes were not done simultaneously. As I quit one, another one was taken on.

Each route provided interesting experiences both positive and negative.

Making money was a great motivational factor at that age. The majority of customers were a pleasure to work with. One experience that stands out in my mind deals with an early morning delivery on a Sudbury late-autumn day. I used my bicycle on this route.

As I was peddling down a street from one house to another, I realized that I had forgotten a delivery to one of my customers. I immediately slammed on my brakes.

Unbeknownst to me, the road was covered in black ice. The rear end of my bike instantly swerved, spilling me to the hard pavement. There was a loud thwack. This sudden, unsuspecting event terrified me momentarily.

As I picked myself up a passing worker approached me asking if I was all right. To my surprise, I had no broken bones. Just pain that subsided quickly.

Once I recovered, I reversed my direction to make the delivery that I had previously missed.

Then I returned along the same road on which I had had my earlier accident. As I approached the same spot I decided to experiment. What if I tried my brakes ever so slightly? Would I cause the bike to veer again?

No sooner than applying the brakes did the bike flip on its side causing me to slam onto the road once again. It was identical to the first occasion. Fortunately, there were no broken body parts and no head injuries, just a repetition of the pain.

I questioned the logic of my decision to try the brakes again. "How stupid could I be?" ran through my brain. It was a lesson learned. One that I never repeated.

EMPTY GAS TANK X 3

The late spring of 1968 is somewhat jumbled in my mind. Events that occurred may have been in 1969. However, for some reason, I'm sure the account that I am about to relate must have taken place in 1968.

The primary fact that supports this belief is that I owned a 1956 Volkswagen Beetle at this time and not a year later. On the other hand, my finances were far more destitute in 1969 which tends to support the story being based in 1968.

Anyways, here goes.

Gas gauges did not exist for Volkswagen Beetles in those days, including in my 1956 model. If I needed to check the gas level, I had to follow a rudimentary process. First, the hood had to be lifted. The gas tank was there. Second, the gas tank cap needed to be removed so a wooden ruler could be inserted into the tank, then dipped and removed. The level of fuel left a mark on the wood surface.

This procedure was both time-consuming and bothersome. As a result, often I put off the fuel check. Procrastination was my operative mode.

But I paid an unfortunate price. I ran out of gas several times.

Because of my financial misfortune at the time, I was only able to purchase fifty cents worth of fuel at a time. My worst-case scenario took place in a one-week period. My '56 "bug" ran out of gas three times. The third time occurred on a Sunday evening when all gas stations were closed.

I remember the frustration, the stupidity of the whole affair. How could I be so idiotic? Why couldn't I have been more sensible?

I was forced to walk home, which was a fair distance. And I had to abandon the vehicle until the next morning.

CAT SITTING

Paula was a close friend in the mid-seventies. In fact, she introduced me to my first wife. Peter, another friend at the time, was a mutual friend to Paula and me. We travelled in the same political and social circles.

It was no surprise to hear from Peter that he would be cat-sitting for Paula. She was leaving town for the weekend.

Having spent the Friday night at her apartment, Peter gave me a call Saturday morning. I detected that the company of a cat was not meeting his need for adequate social interaction. He invited me over for a visit. I obliged.

After arriving mid-morning, we sat in the rather small kitchen. He offered me a coffee. As political activists, we carried on a lively discussion about contemporary events.

From time to time, Peter appeared agitated about the house cat. It wasn't to be seen—not when I entered and not while we were talking. To me, calling the cat seemed a futile strategy. However, Peter did try. He checked all the rooms. No luck.

He opened the kitchen door to the outdoors. Again, no success.

Despite being perplexed about the whereabouts of the cat, Peter carried on with our conversation. It was interrupted intermittently with a cursory check inside and outside the apartment. Obviously, Peter was concerned.

It was only when Peter decided to open the fridge door that the mystery was solved. Out came the cat.

In the process, Peter displayed a combination of utter surprise and total relief. I couldn't avoid bursting out with laughter. Peter quickly joined in.

How ironic.

BAND-AID SOLUTION

After moving away from Sudbury in 1976, I lost touch with my friend Peter. It was only in the eighties that I returned to the city for visits. My parents and three siblings still lived there. By that time, I was married and had children.

On one of these trips, my two daughters accompanied me. I decided to take them down to Lake Ramsey for a swim. This was a boyhood haunt. I wanted to share some of my childhood memories with Katie and Emma.

After a swim, they asked to visit the playground. It was located a short distance from the beach.

As we approached, I noticed Peter standing with his back to me. He was supervising a young boy about five years of age. I presumed that he was Peter's son.

As I got closer, I was still undetected by my old friend. In the process, I noticed that his son, wearing shorts, had five band-aids scattered across one leg and three across the other leg. I counted them for accuracy purposes. It was quite comical to see.

Peter still wasn't aware of my presence let alone who I was. He was too engaged with his son.

Having previously had a very convivial relationship with him I decided to surprise him with a risky approach.

Within a few metres of father and son, I offered the following comment loudly: "Anyone with a child having that many band-aids could be charged with child abuse."

Peter instantaneously turned around bristling with anger. It was a picture to behold. Fortunately, and just as quickly he realized who I was. The intent in my accusation was dispelled equally as fast.

With the ice broken we renewed our acquaintance, introduced our offspring, and caught up on news.

In retrospect, I wouldn't recommend what I had done that day to anyone unless there is a rock-solid friendship between the parties.

AN ANGEL VS. A DEVIL

In 1960 I became a teenager. It was also the year in which my religious convictions were at their peak.

As a member of the Ukrainian Catholic Church, I was totally immersed. I attended Mass as often as possible, not only Sundays but weekdays. I was an altar boy.

Following an early morning Mass, I can remember Sister Josephine telling me, "You're an angel." So, it became even more of a self-fulfilling prophecy. I tried to be more dedicated to my religious beliefs.

The contrast came later in the year. It was the lead-up to the Christmas season. The Ukrainian Catholic nuns were responsible for preparing a seasonal concert. I was asked to participate in a skit which was to be presented in the Ukrainian language. It required several rehearsals.

After having been deemed "an angel" earlier in the year it was ironic that I was asked to play the role of a "devil." The actual performance was hilarious.

The nuns had sewn a custom-made devil's outfit for me. Its most prominent feature was its tail. It was long, curved, and pointed. With a blackened face and a high-energy performance, the audience roared at some of my antics and spoken words.

It was quite a year.

BEEN THERE, DUNG THAT

The year following the tragic tsunami in Southeast Asia, Sue and I made a trip to Thailand. Koh Samui was our destination for a winter getaway.

We enjoyed the Thai experience tremendously. Everything ranging from food, hospitality, weather, beaches, Thai customs, and seasonal celebrations was exemplary.

We had a ball. Witnessing a traditional Buddhist wedding on the beach next to our resort was one of the highlights. The bride and groom arrived on the back of an elephant—not exactly a guaranteed mode of transportation to "get you to the church on time."

Our need to venture from our vacation spot was almost non-existent. The resort was idyllic.

Notwithstanding this sentiment, we did take advantage of a brief four-hour tour of the island. The minivan with only eight tourists conveniently stopped at a handful of attractions. Temples, monkeys, and natural geological sights were included.

One of the highlights for Sue and me was a roadside stop at a waterfall. Upon exiting our vehicle, we were introduced to a group of three or four elephants. These were domesticated and smaller in size. An opportunity to ride the elephants to the waterfall was available to us at a cost of course.

We chose to hike one kilometre instead. The excursion was delightful.

The falls themselves were uneventful. After spending a brief amount of time there we began our return. Shortly into the walk, we realized something was amiss. Not only did it feel unfamiliar, but the trail was covered in elephant dung.

This wasn't the path we had taken up to the falls. Recognizing an opportunity, I asked Sue to remain on the path for a photo shoot. She complied, and I took several photos.

My ulterior motive was to eventually frame one of these photos and inscribe it with the words, "Been there, dung that!"

If you haven't already detected my addiction to puns, then be forewarned.

PROMISED RESURRECTION

During an extensive fifty-one-day campervan trip through much of Northern British Columbia, the Yukon, Alaska, Northwest Territories, and Alberta, Sue and I enjoyed a cornucopia of sights.

Abundant wildlife and spectacular scenery kept us captivated for the most part. Museum artefacts and uniquely built Northern structures such as log cabins proved equally interesting. One item that caught my eye was on the streets of Revelstoke, British Columbia. As we were sightseeing in the downtown area, I spotted signage on a building that read "Brandon Funeral Home." Ironically and immediately to the right, a second business advertised "Second Chance."

I thought to myself that if indeed the funeral home was proposing a second chance, I just might want to walk in and investigate the grand offer.

OUR HILARIOUS WEDDING

The year 2002 was eventful for Sue and me, primarily due to our marriage. It was the culmination of six years of courtship.

The wedding was planned for an August date at our home.

The ceremony took place on a spacious rear deck overlooking a sizeable garden. Seating was available for the one-hundred-plus guests on the grass.

All six of our adult children were participants in our wedding party. A professional pianist friend provided accompaniment for two of our offspring musicians—a classical violinist and an accomplished vocalist with a beautiful voice. With a gorgeous weather day, we couldn't ask for anything better.

Once most of our guests had arrived and were seated, the male entourage strode onto the rear deck. Dressed in tuxedos, Sue's two sons and I looked as if we had stepped out of a wedding magazine.

In the glaring sun, we waited patiently for Sue and our four daughters to join us. I decided they were probably still preening themselves inside the house. An inordinate amount of time seemed to pass. Still no sign of the ladies.

We began to look back in anticipation of their arrival. The guests were visibly becoming impatient.

Finally, the ice was broken by Sue's brother John.

In a loud voice he volunteered, "If my sister doesn't come out soon, I'll have to marry Fred myself!" His comment was met with a roar of laughter.

In short order, the female entourage arrived and joined the men on deck. With Sue now by my side, the marriage commissioner approached us. The ceremony began. It was an exceptionally touching affair until the grand finale.

When the moment came to pronounce us man and wife with our newly acquired married name, Mr. and Mrs. Pawluk, the commissioner committed a major faux pas.

As she stood directly in front of Sue and me, we were introduced as Mr. and Mrs. Halsey-Brandt. This was Sue's surname from her previous marriage.

The reaction was instantaneous. My head fell back, and I let out a tremendous guffaw. Sue's response was identical. The guests followed suit. I can't remember ever cracking up to such an intensity.

The outcome was in direct contrast to the commissioner's embarrassment. She cringed before us.

Once the laughter subsided, she attempted an apology. Sue and I tried to deflect her embarrassment. Not wanting to prolong the situation, the commissioner directed us to a table a short distance to our left to sign the marriage certificate.

As Sue took her first few steps leading the way, I heard the tear of fabric.

I had been standing on her train. Once I removed my foot, I reached down to grab her train. The intent was to avoid further damage.

With her train freed, Sue continued moving. Bent over, I tried moving with her, grasping for her train. To all observers, it was a futile situation.

One guest took note and commented to the entire gathering, "Fred must think it's a drop sheet." Again, an uproar ensued. Those knowing my painting background understood the humorous connection.

In my opinion, the experiences of that day demonstrated that reality can be funnier than fiction.

$18.45 AUTO REPAIR

Automobile accidents are notorious for a variety of reasons: injuries, deaths, vehicle damage, confrontations, and eventual disputes.

None of the above applied to a 1969 accident for which I was responsible, except for the damage costs. These amounted to eighteen dollars and change.

How could this be you might ask? Impossible! It's not plausible. Well, here is my explanation.

As I travelled along a busier Sudbury road, I came upon a taxi pulled over in my lane. It had stopped alongside the curb to deposit a customer. Not being in a particular rush, I slowed my Volkswagen Beetle to a complete stop, directly behind the cab. Patiently, I waited for the taxi to resume its journey. Seconds turned into a half minute and time progressed even more slowly.

In turn, my frustration grew incrementally. What was taking him so long? What was the problem? This was ridiculous. "It's a typical taxi driver that doesn't care about anyone else," I thought.

Finally, I made my desperate move. Quickly looking over my shoulder and checking the left-hand mirror, I saw the coast was clear. I turned my wheels to the left and lurched forward.

Bang! My right bumper just barely caught the corner of the cab. I stopped immediately, pulled back to my original parked position, and got out with the taxi driver to survey the damage—the red tail-light reflector. Once I provided my information we departed. The arrangement was to have the taxi repaired and I would be then contacted to reimburse the costs.

Within a week I was presented with the invoice for $18.45. I gladly paid.

NICE JUGS!

Sue and I couldn't have been more pleased with our wedding day. Even the blunders added character to the affair.

There was another interesting element to that day. Claire, a long-time and close friend of Sue, had offered to act as a greeter. Her offer was much appreciated.

She welcomed all guests as they arrived at the front door. They were either ushered or directed to the rear of the house and into the seating area.

As a last-minute suggestion, Claire recommended that water be made available for the guests. The temperature was unseasonably high. In addition, she volunteered two jugs to serve water. "I have just the right jugs for the job," she exclaimed.

There was adequate time for her to return home and retrieve them.

Claire's people skills worked wonders. She made everyone quite comfortable in advance of the ceremony.

At the conclusion of the evening, with most guests departed, Claire began to bid her adieu. Sue and I thanked her profusely. As she gathered her jugs, I suggested that we take a photo of her with them.

She kindly agreed, holding the jugs proudly in front of her, about shoulder high. Again, I sensed a perfect opportunity. Once the photo was developed, I suggested to Sue that it should be framed and a metal plate attached with the inscription, "Nice Jugs, Claire!" Sue agreed.

Once it was completed, we made the delivery. Luckily, Claire was not offended by the double entendre. She accepted our gift with a hearty laugh and a thank you.

FIDDLING GONE AWRY

Richard Mendez was a fellow Sudburian whom I met in 1974. Although an English college instructor by day, he was most passionate about his avocation: country fiddling.

As the artistic director and coordinator for the local folk festival, I booked him to perform. He proved to be an asset in the fiddle workshops. His repertoire acted as a counterpoint to the other fiddle styles.

Once the three-day July event was completed, all musicians and organizers parted ways.

In late fall I was pleasantly surprised to receive a phone call from Richard. He described an upcoming situation that might be of some interest to me. A country band had asked him to join them for a Saturday afternoon matinee performance. The hotel was in an isolated community twelve miles outside Sudbury.

The one proviso according to Richard: "It's redneck country. With your long hair, there could be trouble. If you decide to come, make it for three o'clock Saturday."

I took his warning under advisement and made no promises to come.

When Saturday rolled around, I decided to make the journey. I wasn't going to be intimidated.

Arriving around three thirty in the afternoon, I found Richard in the lounge. He was sitting at a table surrounded by the locals. They welcomed me to join them. Not only was Richard treated with free beer, but I was as well.

Yet the band hadn't called Richard to join them on stage. While they played, couples danced. One of the male participants was impossible to ignore.

This gentleman was wearing bedroom slippers. In his early sixties, he was constantly pulling up his trousers. His belt was missing. The loose-fitting pants kept falling down from his waist as he gyrated to the music.

It wasn't long before someone took advantage of his dilemma. Just as the trousers were plunging again another dancer, from behind, pulled them to the floor. All those that were watching burst into laughter. While the slacks were crumpled on the floor the owner casually looked around for the culprit. The perpetrator played innocent and continued dancing.

The amusement maintained itself for two reasons. One, his underwear was an offensive yellow colour. Two, he was in no hurry to pull up his fallen trousers. When he finally did, dancing resumed.

Shortly after this hilarious episode, Richard was beckoned to the stage. Together they performed three or four songs before Richard was approached by the same character with the loose-fitting pants.

He explained that he too was a fiddler. Could Richard lend him his fiddle?

Richard resisted his request and carried on with the next song. Despite the earlier rejection, the wannabe fiddler persisted.

Finally, Richard relented. He passed on his fiddle. This gentleman climbed onto the stage. A discussion arose with the band members to determine what song was common to both parties. When this was resolved they began to play together.

Not long into the song the infamous pants began to droop. Before reaching mid-song, they fell to the floor. All eyes were on the owner. The patrons were howling. It intensified as he ignored the situation and carried on with his fiddling. At the completion of his one and only contribution, he surveyed the room looking for Richard. All the while his pants remained crumpled at his feet on the stage floor. His yellow underwear was highlighted by stage lights.

Only when Richard arrived to retrieve his fiddle did the gentleman reach down to gather up his trousers. The room was in hysterics the entire time.

At the time it occurred to me, "What if a liquor inspector entered the premises?" The joint would have been closed.

Never, never will I experience a scene as uproarious as I witnessed that day.

CUT HER UP

As we baby boomers were threading our way through the educational system in the sixties extraordinary demands were being made on the system. More teaching resources were required to service the bulging school population. This was especially the case at the high school level: younger teacher trainees were allowed to pre-empt the completion of their education and teachers that should have retired were kept on.

Our Latin, French and math teachers fit this latter category. From a teenager's perspective, they appeared quite elderly.

Miss Russell, our Grade 12 French teacher, was a prime example. Her age wasn't exactly known, but she had excessive wrinkles and we did learn that she had studied French in France slightly after WWI.

A student named Dan sat directly behind me in Miss Russell's French class. He had returned to school after a two-year hiatus.

I had learned that Dan had spent the previous two years apprenticing as a mortician in Timmins, Ontario. With knowledge of this background, it wasn't shocking to hear some of his experiences.

He shared his worst with me. It required picking up the human remains of a person hit by a fast-moving train. Being winter, Dan was required to search in the snowbanks alongside a lengthy section of the tracks.

I also learned of one of Dan's morbid fantasies in Miss Russell's class. With him sitting behind me, I was tapped on the shoulder one day.

I responded by turning around. "Would I ever like to cut her up," he whispered in my ear. I couldn't contain myself as I looked at Miss Russell ever so closely. She was old looking.

I suffered contradictory emotions. I wanted to laugh at the preposterous proposal but didn't want to get caught laughing out loud for no apparent reason . . . and then having to explain the outburst.

Fortunately, Dan's comment didn't go any further than the two of us.

TINGLING LIPS

Sue and I had been invited for dinner by our friends Jean-Jacques and Jacqueline. They hosted us outdoors on their recently completed patio.

The summer weather was exceedingly conducive to an enjoyable evening with wine, food, and conversation. The banter eventually got around to figs. We had recently delivered some fresh figs to JJ and J. Having been citizens of Algeria at one time, they were completely familiar with this tropical fruit. In fact, they were connoisseurs.

Sue and I were surprised to learn that the outer skin should not be eaten. We always ate the outer membrane.

"The skins cause your lips to tingle," JJ pointed out. "Fred, don't they cause your lips to tingle?"

"Only when I kiss Sue," I responded.

Over the outburst of laughter, JJ managed to come back with, "Oh, Fred!"

DUELLING AUNTS

In 1977 my father joined my wife, six-month-old daughter, and me for a trip to Manitoba. We lived in Ontario at the time but still had many family members living in the prairie province, my parents having both been raised there.

Two of my father's older sisters, Nellie and Dora, lived next door to each other. Although both were widows with no dependents, they maintained separate detached houses in Teulon, Manitoba. This small community was located approximately forty-five miles due north of Winnipeg.

We arrived at their homes without advance notification. Both aunts welcomed us with incredible enthusiasm. I suspected two reasons: Firstly, at seventy-one years of age, my dad was the baby in the family. Secondly, they rarely all visited together. This was an unexpected opportunity for them to catch up on news and reminisce.

What became an amusing development was Nellie and Dora's attraction to my daughter Katie. They were extraordinarily competitive when it came to her. It was comical to see them playing tug of war with her. If one aunt held Katie in her arms, the other one would playfully try to pull her away. These were women in their late seventies.

After overnighting at Aunt Nellie's, we moved further north to visit a grandmother, more aunts, uncles, nephews, cousins, and my dad's brother.

But before leaving, Nellie asked a favour of us. Could we pick her up on our return to Winnipeg? We agreed.

The next four or five days proved to be exceedingly rewarding. Situations that arose with family members left me with lifetime memories, most of which would never have materialized if it were not for my father.

Upon returning to Teulon, we found Aunt Nellie packed and ready to go. There was no delay other than bidding adieu to Aunt Dora. We loaded ourselves into the vehicle with my aunt in the back seat and shut the doors. Aunt Dora was waving enthusiastically at her sister's window.

I started the engine and was about to put the vehicle into reverse, but before we had a chance to move, Aunt Nellie, looking directly at her sister, said, "I don't like my sister."

My dad, wife and I were floored. We were flabbergasted at her candidness.

I tried to detect if Aunt Dora had heard or understood the nature of what was said. She hadn't.

Obviously, this was not a case of sisterly love.

POLITICAL APPRENTICESHIP

It is difficult to comprehend that as a grade school student my education included hands-on political experience. This situation would be unacceptable in today's politically correct climate.

As a twelve-year-old I was asked to participate in the election campaign for our school principal, Mr. William Edgar. Having been a successful incumbent city councillor for several years, he decided to take a run for the mayoral position.

Mr. Edgar's election campaign team solicited the support of some of his students. As a Grade 6 student, I suspect that this grade may have been the youngest in age. And it wasn't necessarily a case of exploitation. We were offered one and a half cents per household pamphlet we delivered.

The bitter pill was that the election was taking place during the worst of winter weather in Northern Ontario. We were required to distribute leaflets the weekend preceding the January 15, 1960, election day. It was bitterly cold. In addition, we trudged through knee-deep snow in the more isolated settings.

Little did I know that this was an initiation into my future political arena. Over time I ran politically five times, ranging from school board, city council and member of parliament.

POPE'S SON

Over the years, Cuba has been a very desirable travel destination for me. My first trip was in 1982. Three subsequent trips with Sue took place in the early 2000s.

This country remains close to my heart for a great number of reasons: music, climate, tropical fruit, rum, politics, and most importantly Cuban hospitality. I would return at the drop of a hat.

Our 2002 winter trip proved to be a highlight. Jibacoa, our all-inclusive resort, was off the beaten path. Located halfway between Varadero and Havana it offered a more relaxed, isolated environment. In contrast to the densely developed resort of Varadero, the oceanfront reef allowed us an opportunity to snorkel. Sea life was abundant.

In addition, we were able to run through the countryside in either direction from our resort. It was our way of rationalizing our food and alcohol consumption.

To explore Cuban history and culture we signed up for a day tour of Havana. This excursion was to conclude with dinner and entertainment at the famous Tropicana Night Club.

Twelve tourists including Sue and I made the trip. Once we arrived in Havana our first stop was a rum factory. After being ushered onto the ground floor, we were met by a gregarious Cuban tour guide. His English was impeccable.

He first gave us a general introduction to the rum-making process. We learned about the initial production of molasses from sugar cane. The molasses, once fermented, generated rum.

Our guide elaborated: "We produce rum anywhere from one year old, three years old, five years old, seven years old, and older. But our seven-year-old rum is our most popular."

He proudly added, "Our oldest rum is fifty-nine years old. When the pope came to visit us in 1996, we gave him a bottle of the fifty-nine-year-old rum."

At this point, he led us up to the second floor. There, he showed us some of the rum-making equipment on display and went into more detail about the process. We were then given free time to view the displays and ask questions.

Our guide invited us into the hospitality room where coffee was being served. It was complimentary. However, if we chose to include a shot of rum, one US dollar would be charged. There was no hesitation. We each paid the required fee.

Once consumed, Sue's comment, "That's the best coffee I've ever had!" came as a surprise. It was ironic because she rarely consumed alcohol.

Next stop for our group was another display room, one door over from where we had our coffee break. The guide organized us into a horse-shoe-shaped circle. Standing at the open end facing us, he continued with his talk. Tall glass display cabinets lined the perimeter of the room.

In the midst of his speech, our host turned around and pointed to a bottle inside a cabinet. He repeated his earlier statement. "This is a fifty-nine-year-old bottle of rum just like the one we gave the Pope in 1996."

I patiently waited for the conclusion of his presentation.

Seeing and attempting to seize an opportunity, I tapped him on the shoulder. "May I introduce myself to you?" I offered. "I am the Pope's son!"

Without missing a beat, our genial guide retorted, "and I am the Pope's son too!"

"Then you two must be brothers," came an observation from one of our tour members.

This humorous injection to our gathering brought our tour to a most satisfying conclusion.

I still suffer the regret that I was unable to convince the host to part with a fifty-nine-year-old bottle of rum.

OLD MAN MISTAKE

During a trip into lower Manhattan by subway, my daughter Katie and her four-year-old twins managed to find seating together. I, on the other hand, grabbed a single seat directly opposite them.

As the train ride progressed, Freddie and Aretha's behaviour became more and more unruly. They refused to remain seated and flopped all over the floor.

Katie was becoming quite flustered with their antics. When they slid across the aisle, approaching me, Katie admonished them. "Don't go near that old man."

"Don't you recognize your own father?" I offered. She momentarily hadn't realized it was me.

STEALING COPPER

The following story was related to me by my father. It took place in the early sixties.

Hockey was the recreational mainstay of men even then, and probably more so with just the original NHL's six teams.

When it came to hockey two important factors came into play in a town like Sudbury: Firstly, this community had a sizeable French-Canadian population. If you included the surrounding area, they were the majority. This fact created tremendous support for Les Canadiens. Secondly, the workforce involved in the nickel mining industry was male dominated. The mines and refineries were a hotbed for NHL hockey fan rivalry.

Throughout the season, betting, gambling, and hockey pools were ubiquitous. They provided a source of entertainment for the men in an otherwise hostile working environment.

When the playoffs came around, the entire scenario reached a crescendo. Sides were taken and defended devotedly.

One individual in particular, Mr. Martel, a diehard Montreal supporter, was the equivalent of a pit bull terrier. If his team reached the playoffs, he would take on all bettors.

Considering the perennial strength of the Canadiens, he succeeded often. Nevertheless, one of the early years in the sixties produced a quandary for him.

His beloved team did reach the finals. Passions were running high, and a fifty-dollar bet was placed with a fellow worker. If the Canadiens took the Stanley Cup the sum would be his.

Keep in mind that fifty dollars at that time amounted to half a week's wages. Well, Martel's team failed to win the finals. He was devastated.

How was he to save face in the act of acknowledging payment of his debt?

He concocted a nefarious scheme that incorporated the fact copper was the second most produced metal at his workplace.

Martel graciously made good on his bet. He brought fifty dollars in loose pennies to work and handed over the sum at the beginning of the work shift. Well, before the shift's completion he notified security that copper was being stolen. He identified and described the individual. The gate through which his rival was to exit was also pinpointed.

Sure enough, the gentleman was stopped at the gate as he was leaving work.

A quick visual search was made by security with no success. Then he was asked to open his lunch pail. The copper was discovered. But it wasn't the copper anticipated by security. The joke was on them. And the betting winner suffered the embarrassment of being searched.

That culprit Martel had the last laugh. Such clever revenge.

SADISTIC SCHOOL JANITOR

Dwight and I were the best of friends. Not only did we live four houses from each other, but we were also one year apart in age. During the winter of 1957–58, we spent a great deal of time together involved in outdoor activities. On a bitterly cold Saturday morning we made plans to play hockey on an outdoor skating rink. It was located at Prince Charles Public School, a ten-minute walk from home.

Once we arrived, we decided to change into our skates in a sheltered area. The front entrance to the school provided a windbreak from the cold sub-zero wind.

While sitting on the freezing concrete pad, bare fingers numb, we struggled to get our skates on. Well, before we could finish, we were interrupted by Mr. Clark, the school janitor.

"You better get out of here or I'll take your hockey sticks and burn them in the furnace," he threatened. It was totally unprovoked. Why would he want to intimidate us?

We didn't respond verbally, but as a result of his warning, we hastened our task, picked up our winter boots, and quickly proceeded to the rink. It was no more than twenty metres away. Within a minute of stepping onto the ice, Dwight and I realized that in our panic we had forgotten our hockey sticks at the school's front entrance.

Rushing back to where we changed proved fruitless. The hockey sticks were gone. We peered into the school to see any sign of Mr. Clark but to no avail.

It was a moment in which we lost faith in humanity.

ATHENS' CON ARTIST

My 1973 arrival in Athens, Greece, preceded my girlfriend by three days. I had time to kill. After booking myself into a youth hostel, I made it a point to sightsee.

Syntagma (Constitution) Square was the hub of Athenian activity as far as tourists were concerned. Along with foreigners came con artists. These enterprising businessmen were out to exploit. It was no different than anywhere else.

Thinking myself worldly enough, I engaged with a very well-dressed Greek man who was promoting a bar. His offer, "I'll buy you a drink," sounded non-threatening. After all, it was exactly noon in sunny Athens.

I accepted his offer. My thinking was that if there was any hint of trouble, I could run. I also was aware of the Tourist Police, meant to protect travellers from exploitation.

My friend, the businessman, explained, "It is only a few blocks to the bar." Off we went together. A lively conversation ensued. After three or four blocks, I questioned his initial indication of the distance.

"Only two more blocks," came his quick response. We were still in a respectable part of Athens, so I wasn't overly concerned. I was suspicious, yes, but not feeling threatened. More walking and more smooth talking.

I lost count at seven or eight blocks. It was probably ten blocks before we arrived at the entrance to the promised bar. We descended one short flight of stairs into the establishment.

I was immediately led to the bar. "What will you have my friend?" he asked.

"A beer," I replied.

"One beer for my friend," he beckoned to the bartender.

Once the beer was provided, the con artist introduced me to a waitress. As he departed, the assigned friendly hostess suggested that we move to a table not far away. Once seated, she asked, "Can I order some champagne?"

"Yes," I replied, assuming that only a glass would be served.

No sooner said than done, a full bottle of champagne on ice was delivered and served to my genial hostess. My alarm bell was beginning to ring. The conversation continued only to be interrupted by my need for a beer refill. My rationale—since the first was free I could afford this one.

Before I had a chance to finish the second beer, the young lady enquired, "Can I have another bottle of champagne?" Up to this moment I hadn't been paying attention to the quantity being consumed.

"No!" I replied emphatically. "Call the waiter. I want the bill," I added.

The waiter was beckoned. A brief conversation arose between him and the hostess. I couldn't understand. It was conducted in Greek. Literally, it was all Greek to me.

The waiter retreated to the bar before returning with the bill. During that brief period, I contemplated my strategy.

When the bill was presented, I digested the details very carefully. It totalled 840 drachmas, slightly more than thirty Canadian dollars. They even had the audacity to charge me for the free beer. This all had taken place in a brief span of fifteen minutes.

I leaned over in the direction of my female companion and whispered, "I'm not paying the bill!"

Shocked, she reiterated my comment. "You're not going to pay the bill?"

"That's right, I'm not going to pay for it!"

Before I could complete that last statement, she screamed to the waiter in Greek. Whatever was said prompted the waiter to rush to our table. When I confirmed my intention not to pay, he raised his arm, fist clenched in a threatening way.

I countered with "Call the Tourist Police!"

His reaction was amazing. He immediately became compliant. "How much are you willing to pay?"

I proposed 330 drachmas, roughly twelve Canadian dollars.

My offer was accepted. I paid the bill and left thinking that this was a valuable lesson. And thankfully a relatively inexpensive one.

BEING AND NOTHINGNESS

I met a fellow traveller in Athens who had suffered the same experience as I had of being lured to a bar. His situation proved to be more financially draining.

We were both residents at the same youth hostel. In a conversation over lunch, he began to confide his recent experience. It was identical to mine. He was lured to a bar and taken for fifty dollars. He was almost in tears. His emotional display was almost laughable. "Why would they do that to me?" he exclaimed.

I chalked up his apparent exploitation to naivety. In contrast, my exploitive session was the result of a calculated gamble. Despite the difference, we were both losers financially.

Knowing that I had three days to kill at the hostel, I prepared an action plan. Before leaving Canada, I had purchased a paperback copy of *Being and Nothingness* by Jean-Paul Sartre. Existentialism was a mystery to me. I wanted to learn. At over a thousand pages it was an ambitious plan.

Once making my way through the introduction, I dove into the body. By page three I had comprehended very little. I decided to start over. I reread pages one through three, this time more slowly and carefully, but without much greater success.

I put the book aside for another day. I needed to clear my head. A fresh start was needed. Then on my third attempt, I conceded before page three.

The remainder of my three-day stay was spent offering *Being and Nothingness* to the first taker. I was successful.

The book title was an appropriate description of the whole process that unfolded in my futile attempt to master a topic.

ÑUTTY IDEA #1

It was my first and only trip to the Hawaiian Islands. The arrangement was to meet Sue in Maui following her singing competition in Honolulu.

We had booked accommodation through a close friend at Kihei. The November weather was splendid. With an eleven-day span, we were able to take in a lot of activities: snorkelling, sightseeing, grocery shopping, dining out, and running. The last activity took place every other morning before breakfast.

Our running itinerary was primarily on the beach and grass and along a boardwalk path. Eventually, we were forced to travel along the roadside, sometimes on sidewalks. We usually ran forty minutes out and back.

Towards the end of our stay, I began to extend my segment further down the road, leaving Sue behind. On the third last day, I discovered a cache of nuts on my run. They were lying on the ground beneath tall nut-covered trees. Out of curiosity, I gathered one to take back to our condo. I wondered if it was a Macadamia nut.

Sure enough, after cracking the shell I could see the nut was identical to a Macadamia.

We had previously purchased plenty to enable us to make the comparison. I shared the excitement with my wife. "I know exactly where there is a free source," I explained. "We can drive to the location later in the day to gather more." Sue was a Macadamia aficionado as well. She was on board.

When we eventually harvested a small amount, we took them back to our condo and shelled them.

It was remarkable how we lucked out. Free nuts. We left the shelled nuts to dry for the next twenty-four hours.

Roasting, of course, was required. A quick search on the web provided the needed procedure: ten to fifteen minutes at 325 degrees Fahrenheit. I placed the nuts on a cookie sheet and popped them into the oven. At the allotted time I checked the nuts, but they were sweating a considerable amount of oil. I retrieved one and compared it to our purchased version. Not satisfactory. Our nuts were far from being roasted adequately in comparison.

I continued the process in dribs and drabs. More oil oozed out as time progressed. They were beginning to turn yellow, unlike the commercial variety. I began to sample our version with a bite now and then. Sue sampled one and found it to be bitter. It was not for her.

I wasn't about to give up. My expertise in wild mushroom hunting, I thought, would serve me well.

Fifty minutes in total passed before I gave up the roasting process. I had consumed the equivalent of three nuts in the interim. By this stage, the nuts had yellowed even more so due to the excessive oil sweating. I was off to bed.

We were one day away from returning home to Canada. The worst was to come. I awoke at four thirty in the morning with severe abdominal pains accompanied by diarrhoea.

The discomfort continued unabated for the next four hours. It was severe. Repeated visits to the toilet were required to deal with the diarrhoea.

Finally, when Sue awakened at eight thirty, I related my agonizing story to her. "I have to get medical attention."

Within the next hour, we were able to locate a hospital emergency room. It was US Independence Day, so all other medical facilities were closed.

After being triaged, I was seen first by a nurse and then a doctor. I related my symptoms plus their suspected cause—the roadside nuts.

While I was hooked up to an intravenous to rehydrate, the doctor researched the nut possibilities on the web. He returned with the verdict. I had eaten kukui nuts, better known as candlenuts. They were highly toxic unless well cooked. The Hawaiian natives considered them laxatives.

The pain dissipated within the next hour, and I was released.

It was a valuable lesson learned. Do not eat nuts from the roadside. They're too expensive. The medical bill was $2,700.00 US for one hour of treatment. Fortunately, travel insurance covered the expense.

THREE DOLLAR BILL

Shopping is a ritual practised by many at the beginning of each school year. This is more prevalent in Western society. School books, school supplies, and clothing are the primary purchases.

For elementary school students, parents are the ones that normally determine what is bought. When it comes to high schoolers, young adults usually make clothing choices for themselves.

This was the case for me as I entered Grade 10. My mother allowed me the liberty to make my own choices.

It was early September, and I headed downtown to Eaton's. A new shirt happened to be my goal. After a period of concentrated browsing, I found an appealing one. I immediately headed for the cash counter situated in the middle of the clothing department. Once there I was served by a young lady. She appeared to be my age, around sixteen, probably a student working part-time.

The sale was rung up. The total came to eleven dollars and change. I presented her with fifteen-dollars in the form of a ten-dollar and five-dollar bill. With her till open, she began to determine the change required to reimburse me.

I was floored when she said, "I'm sorry, I don't have a three-dollar bill to give you. Will a one and a two do?" I couldn't believe what I had heard. Was she simply confused or was she deliberately pulling my leg?

I looked at her closely, trying to determine the answer. My conclusion leaned towards the former theory. She was bewildered.

"Yes, one-dollar and two-dollar bills would be fine," came my response.

I walked out of Eaton's amused at what had happened. So much so that it remains both a mystery and an entertaining memory to this day.

FORGETTING TOOTHPASTE

While travelling in Costa Rica, one of our first excursions took place in the cloud forests. The experience was fantastic. It was the first time Sue and I had experienced jungle treetop walks, tarantulas, and tropical bird life, including unlimited hummingbird sightings.

At the end of a two-day stay, we departed by van in a small tour group. Our destination was the Manuel Antonio National Park in the southwestern part of the country.

Once we checked into our accommodation in Quepos, we realized that our toothpaste was missing. It must have been left behind.

Our first errand the next day was to purchase toothpaste at a local pharmacy. We were able to communicate our needs in our limited Spanish. Upon our eventual return to our lodgings, we quickly realized that we had forgotten our toothpaste purchase at the pharmacy. For the second night in a row, we were without the key ingredient to brush our teeth.

However, an accidental discovery was made. The original toothpaste was found deep inside our luggage. What a relief. But the mysterious unearthing posed questions as to our competence.

The next day we trudged the thirty minutes to the Quepos pharmacy in hopes that we would find our previous day's purchase. Sure enough, as soon as we entered, a staff person recognized us and immediately handed over a bag with our toothpaste. A sincere *muchas gracias* was offered.

YOU LOOK AWFUL

The annual Ambleside Mile, a race available only to master runners, took place in West Vancouver, British Columbia. The age category at the time was forty years and older. Both male and female entries were welcome.

This event had two very appealing qualities. The first advantage was that it preceded the annual West Vancouver Days parade along the same route. With the spectators lining both sides of the street, the race was exhilarating for the participants—a rare audience opportunity.

The second advantage was the nature of the course. There was a net drop in elevation from start to finish. In other words, it was downhill.

My running coach encouraged me to enter this event in the first year of my return to running. My racing experience was quite inadequate as far as I was concerned. Although apprehensive, I decided to participate.

On the day of the race, I prepared myself with the other competitors near the start line. Sue, my wife, who accompanied me, decided to position herself at the finish line. She wanted to see me cross at the end.

Once the gun signalled the start of the race, I quickly realized how physically demanding the event was. It was a mad sprint from start to finish. I was caught up in the push and pull of the other competitors.

My level of discomfort seemed to increase exponentially along the route. When I crossed the finish line, I immediately doubled over in an attempt to catch my breath. Completing the race provided me with both mental and physical relief, intensely so.

Sue quickly approached. As she witnessed the state of my physical condition she asked, "How do you feel?"

"Great!" I replied. As far as I was concerned, the worst was over.

"You look awful!" she observed. It was impossible for her to comprehend the sense of relief that I was experiencing. But I still laughed, realizing the irony of the situation.

FOREVER TANGO

Forever Tango was the name of a professional Argentinean touring group. It comprised a magnificent troupe of dancers as well as an equally inspiring orchestra.

I first fell in love with tango music during Expo 86. A serendipitous attendance to a Montreal-based group Fantango made me a fan forever.

Years later when I became aware of an impending Forever Tango performance, I didn't hesitate in purchasing tickets. Without any previous exposure to this group, their Argentine bloodline impressed me. I had no doubt they would be incredible.

And so, my prediction proved true.

The musicianship was incredible with the bandoneons and violins; the music was emotionally tingling. But most impressive of all were the erotic visuals of the tango dancers. The combination of sexy costumes and sensuous dance moves created a surreal evening of entertainment.

The complexity of the dance movements seemed to intensify as the evening progressed. The performance concluded in a crescendo of stupefying tango acrobatics. The female dancer was twirled about, ending up suspended above the head of her male partner.

This brought the house to a standing ovation. We were left with a feeling that what we had seen would be humanly impossible for others to replicate.

As the intensity of the ovation died down, I noticed friends who were sitting five or six rows in front of us. They were seated quite close to the stage.

I managed to call out their names and gain their attention. With the applause having died down, I deliberately shouted, "Sue and I are going straight home to practise." All those within hearing range burst into laughter.

They realized how preposterous my intentions were.

ASLEEP AT THE ACROPOLIS

In my three-day layover in Athens, Greece, awaiting the arrival of my girlfriend from Canada, sightseeing became an avenue to kill time. Walking was my primary means of transportation, and naturally, the Acropolis was high on my list.

Arriving at the base of the Acropolis, I met a young American fellow traveller. He impressed me with his knowledge of the local geography. He suggested we buy food for lunch and trek up the Acropolis to a taverna. I was on board.

When we reached the Acropolis summit my newfound friend directed us to a very makeshift-looking structure. Its exterior cladding consisted of corrugated metal. This was the taverna—not very impressive to my eyes.

Our arrival time was slightly past noon.

We entered to discover a vast number of large oak wine casks. They were tiered two high. The only people present were an elderly proprietor and three or four equally elderly patrons sitting at a single table.

Having no ability to communicate in Greek, we attempted to gain the owner's attention using sign language. We managed to succeed. After sampling two or three wines in their traditional way we settled on a glass each.

Combining our cheese, olives and bread with the wine couldn't get any better. This was as pleasurable and laid back as could be.

We bided our time in conversation, food, and wine. From time to time, we would survey the room. The proprietor had dozed off and the other customers were busy in a lively discussion.

After nearly an hour, our wine had run out. More was required. We resisted the temptation to wake the owner. Looking over at the other table the men appeared to be suffering the same dilemma—empty wine glasses.

Finally, one of the gentlemen approached the sleeping landlord and awakened him. He immediately checked his watch to discover that the siesta period had already commenced. Instead of meeting our request for more wine, he aggressively chased us out the door and slammed it shut.

To our North American experience, this was mind-boggling. Why would anyone turn down business at midday? All we could do was reflect on how unusual and amusing a situation we had just experienced.

CHEAPER OUZO

As part of my 1973 European backpacking trip, the island of Rhodes played a significant part. My girlfriend and I spent two and a half months there.

Initially, the town of Rhodes was our base. While staying at a pensione, we spent time sightseeing and purchasing groceries and alcohol.

The town centre housed a fruit and vegetable market surrounded by shops.

Many of these retail stores catered to tourists. It was in one of these that I purchased a bottle of ouzo. The cost seemed reasonable at 90 drachmas or 3.60 Canadian dollars. Besides, I was craving the national Greek liqueur.

With my bottle in hand, my girlfriend and I headed to the outdoor market. We needed fruit and vegetables. It wasn't long before we were confronted by an elderly vendor. Seeing my bottle, he motioned to see it. Not being able to speak each other's language, our conversation materialized in the form of sign and body language.

When he recognized the bottle's contents, he quizzed me as to the cost. I indicated the price. He immediately demonstrated the symbol for "crazy" with his finger circulating rapidly around his temple. This gesture was followed with his arm outstretched and a forefinger pointing straight ahead and then around the corner to the right. At the same time, he voiced a figure of fourteen drachmas or fifty Canadian cents.

Somehow, he communicated that bringing an empty bottle was required. Sure enough, we did visit this winemaking or u-brew shop. The price for a bottle of ouzo was exactly as promised. It turned out to be a mecca for inexpensive alcohol. Samples could be tasted from the large wine casks. Wine was available for as little as four drachmas per litre. But we always splurged for a wine bottle refill at eight drachmas.

We visited this location repeatedly over the duration of our two-and-a-half-month stay. It was paradise as far we were concerned. And we had to thank the good-natured vegetable vendor. His generous concern for our financial welfare was a trait that all Greeks demonstrated to us. They were the most hospitable people I had ever met.

In fact, on two occasions when I attempted to reciprocate, the Greeks were offended and refused to accept my offer. Their behaviour was defended with, "You are our guests. We buy for you!"

TWENTY-FIVE CENTS OR ELSE

Twice a week I attended Ukrainian language school. These sessions took place in the evening during my eleventh and twelfth years.

To get there and back I needed to take public bus transportation.

One evening as I was waiting at the bus stop, an older man approached me. His advance startled me. "Give me twenty-five cents or I'll call the sheriff," he demanded.

Although this increased the degree to which I felt threatened, I took solace in the fact that there were other people in proximity. Nothing untoward ever happened to me that evening.

One amazing recollection is that the gentleman that confronted me was Indigenous. I made a mental note there and then not to consider him as being representative of all Aboriginals. In my heart, I didn't want the incident to cause me to discriminate against other members of Canadian society.

In retrospect, I feel that I've succeeded.

IRRESISTIBLE ICE CREAM

As part of my 1971 European trip that included my experience at the Munich Hofbräuhaus, Venice was one of the stops.

My girlfriend and I arrived by rented car quite early in the morning. We parked our vehicle and waited for the next ferry to arrive. The ferry was required to reach the islands in the lagoon that comprised Venice.

We passed the time by walking up the street towards a row of buildings.

One intrigued us. It was an Italian gelato shop. A refrigerated window display contained an assortment of scrumptious-looking items.

One item appealed to us, and the listed price indicated about six hundred liras or one Canadian dollar.

This was completely out of line as far as we were concerned. This was in 1971 when ice cream cones in Canada could be purchased for under twenty-five cents. We continued our walk for a short time before turning back. Of course, we passed the same shop again—the one with its appetizing ice cream delights. We stopped to ogle at the window display.

After discussing the pros and cons of purchasing our preferred ice cream, we gave in to temptation. Walking into the store, our six hundred liras were exchanged for our cool treat.

We exited the building and jointly devoured our purchase. Our reaction was identical—what a fantastic treat. The cost was well worth it.

Without hesitation, we re-entered the ice cream parlour. We each bought a second cone and away we went completely satisfied with our decision. So much for prudence.

What a wonderful introduction to Italian gelato!

GORGEOUS LEGS

Sue and I were married in 2002. It was a second marriage for both of us.

Several months after establishing what appeared to be a promising relationship in 1996, I asked Sue for a photograph. This would keep her in my thoughts when we weren't together physically.

She would only provide me with a photo when she was able to locate a suitable one. The photo she settled on not only included her but her best friend at the time, Madalon. They were seated side by side on a sofa.

The photo was much appreciated. However, a slightly disturbing aspect of the snapshot began to grow on me. It dealt with Madalon's attire. Whereas Sue wore slacks to cover her legs, Madalon didn't. She was wearing pantyhose. As it turns out her exposed legs were a distraction. Every time I tried to focus on Sue, my eyes diverted to Madalon's legs.

It was so disconcerting that I knew a solution was required. Asking for another photo might have been an insult to Sue. Instead, I decided to remove Madalon and her legs from the snapshot. A pair of scissors provided the means.

When I shared this development with Sue, she was quite amused. When it was shared with Madalon, she feigned embarrassment and then amusement. When it was shared with Madalon's elderly mother, she considered it hilarious.

As an aside, I discovered that Sue's legs were equally gorgeous when exposed. This just wasn't the case in the photo provided to me at the time.

SHOW ME

When I was a child, Wasyl and his older sister, Nadia, were our neighbours across the street. For a brief period, Nadia and I were playmates. She was seven and I was five years old. We were playing in front of her house one day, and without any previous indication, Nadia spontaneously asked me, "Do you want to show me your peepee? I'll show you mine." Without hesitation, we both dropped our pants to reveal our genitals.

I can still distinctly remember her profile. It was my first exposure to the female anatomy.

To this day I have never had a similar offer from a female.

DOM PERIGNON

When we relocated to Richmond, British Columbia, friends and family were naturally left behind in Ontario. Although we continued regular communication, it wasn't an adequate substitute for being physically together.

News of one of my wife's closest friends, Marcelle, travelled our way within a year or two after leaving Ontario. We learned that she had been diagnosed with breast cancer. She also decided to decline any medical intervention such as chemotherapy and radiation.

In addition, Marcelle quit her teaching job. News came that she began changing her lifestyle in a way that could be best described as completely "throwing caution to the wind." Being charged with shoplifting was one example—specifically a bottle of Dom Perignon. At sixty-five dollars a bottle, it was one of the most expensive items in the liquor store inventory.

We also learned that an old friend, Don Kuyek, defended her in court. It proved to be successful. Marcelle was found not guilty. However, Don read the riot act to her: "Don't ever try shoplifting again."

It was not too long afterward that we received word that Marcelle and her husband would be visiting us on the West Coast. My wife especially was excited about the news.

The day after their arrival Marcelle confirmed the events that had transpired in her recent past, most notably the "Dom Perignon" incident.

As she completed the account of her lawyer's warning not to shoplift, Marcelle nonchalantly offered, "Would you like some Dom Perignon?"

Our jaws dropped. We couldn't believe what we were hearing. Had she stolen one successfully? Without being told outright, we assumed this to be the case.

Sure enough, out came the promised bottle. Were we accessories to the crime?

BEEF AND GREENS

One of my favourite friends during the early seventies was a character named Lesiak.

What endeared him to me was his ability to make me laugh. He had this uniquely uncanny talent. Storytelling was one of his strengths. Quite often his tales would unravel like a ball of wool in the paws of a cat. They became never ending.

This process was even more exaggerated when liquor or drugs were consumed.

Another wonderful quality belonging to Lesiak was his generosity. A helping hand was a common contribution on his part.

Shortly after taking possession of my first house in 1972, Lesiak offered to prepare a dinner for a group of mutual friends. It was to take place on a Saturday. Because of my work commitment, I was only able to join the dinner party at the end of the day, so the gathering was already in progress when I arrived. I found Lesiak in the kitchen resolutely tending to his dinner creation: beef and greens. Every so often he would open the oven door to check his tray of delight.

Finally, Lesiak announced that dinner was ready. Gingerly, out came his offering. But misfortune struck. Lesiak lost his grasp and the entire contents fell upside down on the floor.

I can remember him collapsing onto his knees bellowing, "My beef and greens, my beef and greens!" It was a tragic comedy. Despite this misfortune, I couldn't avoid laughing. Lesiak was almost in tears. His noble efforts had almost come to naught.

The beef and greens were still salvageable. Lesiak scraped them off the linoleum floor onto the tray. I can't recall if there was any attempt to clean the food before reheating it in the oven.

It wouldn't have mattered anyhow considering we were all under the influence of beer and marijuana.

PERMEATING POT SMOKE

Marijuana first became prevalent with the baby boomers of the sixties and seventies. It was ubiquitous. Prices then were unbelievably low—as low as fifteen dollars for an ounce.

I have no clue as to its street value today.

So, with its easy accessibility, the opportunity was there. So many of us took advantage. For me, it was a combined case of experimentation and peer pressure. I personally didn't sense any serious negative impact. During this time, I was able to acquire a full-time job, save money, and buy a house by the age of twenty-four.

Most social gatherings included the use of marijuana. One of these gatherings took place in the basement rec room of a friend's parents. Nothing untoward took place other than smoking pot, listening to music, conversing, and laughing a lot.

As the evening progressed, our host Lesiak became progressively paranoid.

He was concerned about his parents upstairs being able to detect our illicit activity. To determine whether there was any concern, Lesiak would go upstairs from time to time.

Upon each return to the basement, he became increasingly agitated. "The smell is getting stronger and stronger. My parents are going to find out!" he would claim.

The other members of the group were unconcerned in comparison. We were having too good a time. In fact, Lesiak's paranoia was quite comical to observe. It seemed to be exaggerated and unwarranted. And the situation didn't deter Lesiak from sharing the joints that were being passed around.

It became evident to me that as Lesiak accumulated more pot smoke in his nostrils and lungs he mistakenly interpreted that more pot smoke was permeating upstairs.

On his final visit upstairs and subsequent return, our host was in a state of panic. "There's more smell than ever. It's everywhere," he reported. "My parents are going to find out. We've got to leave!"

Without a moment's hesitation, we were ushered out unceremoniously.

We never did hear any negative repercussions from Lesiak regarding that infamous evening of smoking pot.

FLYING CHICKEN

A considerable number of years before I met Virginia, a very dear friend, she had the following experience I thought was well worth sharing.

Virginia was leaving a supermarket with a bag of groceries in one hand and a hot rotisserie chicken in a heavy plastic bag with handles in the other. While walking between closely spaced vehicles to get to her car, she passed by an SUV with the front passenger window partially open. Without warning, a smallish dog lunged viciously out the window, its fangs missing her face by no more than six inches.

Instinctively, she tried to fend it off by swinging the bag of chicken. Before she could get away the nasty beast came at her again, this time lunging even farther out the window. Again, Virginia flailed the bag in self-defence.

Suddenly, the bag had no weight and the dog had disappeared. She backed up and looked to see what had happened to her chicken. She discovered the bag had burst, hurling the chicken accurately but unintentionally through the window of the SUV, and splattering the greasy contents all over the front seats and console. The dog was happily gorging on its free meal.

Virginia drove to the other side of the building, hoping to evade witnesses to the event and went back into the store to buy another chicken.

ELEVATOR TRAUMA

Shyness was a chronic debilitating malady for me during my early years. I can remember literally hiding outdoors when friends came to visit my parents.

I would not respond to calls well after dark until the last guest left the house.

This continued well into my mid-teens. Girls especially did me in. I was extremely uncomfortable in their presence. Having two slightly younger sisters did not alleviate my anxiety.

One notable example took place at the age of twelve. My mother was hospitalized.

During a visit to her seventh-floor room, she asked me to purchase a bottle of pop for her. She explained that the beverage machine was in the basement.

I entered the elevator on floor seven expecting to travel directly to the bottom. But it came to a halt shortly after on the sixth floor. The doors opened to reveal seven, yes seven, nurses waiting to come onboard. I sank into despair instantly. This confrontation amounted to a death sentence as far as I was concerned.

I can recall blood rising into my scalp. I must have turned every embarrassing shade of red. The nurses entered, turned their backs to me and carried on with their conversation.

As we travelled downward my only thought was, "When will they get off?" I was so traumatized that I can't recall which floor they exited. Only when they departed, and the elevator door closed behind them did I feel a sense of relief.

The remainder of the trip down and back to the seventh floor proved to be gloriously uneventful.

PLAYING SANTA CLAUS

Christmas 1972 was something else. It was a time of total bliss. A satisfying job, money, a house, a new girlfriend, and a compatible house partner made it so.

As Christmas Eve approached, my girlfriend suggested that we make the rounds on that night. Visiting friends and family would be a wonderful way to spend the evening. In fact, her employer could supply a Santa outfit for the occasion.

I thought it would be a great idea to dress up as Santa Claus.

Prior to setting off that night, we indulged in a considerable amount of alcohol and pot-smoking. Once I donned the Santa outfit, Suzanne and I jumped into a vehicle with our friend Paul.

Our first stop was a family friend of Suzanne's. She was a stranger to me. As we entered her home, she quickly recognized the existence of Santa Claus. "Oh, Santa, give me a kiss," she exclaimed.

As she approached me with her arms outstretched, I noticed her obesity. I started to cower. This was the last place I wanted to be. I was trapped. But I was obligated as Santa to fulfil the compassionate role. We kissed. Pleasantries were exchanged and we were on our way.

As we travelled the roadways of Sudbury, I recognized a Polish Catholic Church. It was 11:45 p.m. Parishioners were streaming towards and up a long staircase into the church. I yelled to Paul, our chauffeur, "Stop." I wanted to get out and visit. I didn't feel intimidated for two reasons: I had occasionally attended this church in the past and the alcohol and pot provided a loss of inhibition.

I crossed the street and began to walk up the stairs. As I approached the church entrance animosity towards me became increasingly apparent. Men, mostly, whispered, "Get out, get out. We don't want you here." Despite the antagonism, I continued until entering the vestibule.

It was there the resentment turned to bitterness. I was convinced that if I proceeded any farther, I would endanger myself. With Suzanne and Paul close by, we retreated to our vehicle.

The next stop was Suzanne's brother's home. A niece and two nephews were expecting Santa Claus. When we pulled into the drive close to one o'clock in the morning, I observed three sets of hands and three noses smattered against a frosted picture window.

As Santa approached, the breadth of their innocent smiles was unmistakable. The glow on their faces was worth all the joys in life combined. It compensated for the two previous episodes.

A PANNED PERFORMANCE

Upon entering Grade 11, I already had two years of French studies under my belt. Mrs. Penas, our French teacher, was preceded by a reputation that was not at all flattering. It turned out to be one that boys especially exploited.

However, to be fair to her Mrs. Penas proved to be quite tolerant with regards to our antics. A lack of control is another way of describing her classroom capability.

Part way through the year she issued a challenge: "Would anyone like to write a short play in French and present it in front of the class?"

Carleton, Herb, and I consented. We were willing to take up the challenge.

I must point out that my two playwrights were the class brains, and I was the class clown.

We spent one evening constructing our masterpiece. Then came the performance. It took place during class time.

I simply can't remember one iota of the content. It did draw laughter considering it was our attempt at humour. However, the satirical content proved not to be as pleasing to Mrs. Penas.

Upon completing our performance, Carleton, Herb, and I descended from the raised platform.

We were met with her mildly critical comment, "Remind me never to ask you to do a play again."

It generated a great deal of mirth, and we took so much delight in our effort.

THOUGHT YOU WERE DEAD

Aunt Dora lived to 102 years of age. She was the last survivor in a Ukrainian–Manitoban family of six. My father was the youngest and managed to live close to 83.

Having spent most of my teenage summers in Manitoba, I came to know her. She was exceedingly cheerful with lots of energy.

It was in the 1970s that she settled in Teulon, located approximately forty-five miles north-northwest of Winnipeg. At first, Aunt Dora lived in a detached house with her husband.

She stayed there after his death until her nineties. A seniors' home became her home for the remainder of her life.

My mother would try to call on Dora every other year when visiting from Ontario. One of these stopovers occurred when Aunt Dora was in her late nineties.

It is important to mention that my mother was twenty-five years her junior.

At this get-together, Aunt Dora could not recognize my mother. It was obvious that her memory had deteriorated. To spark a recollection my mom spoke to her in Ukrainian.

Fifteen minutes into the conversation the light bulb went on, and Dora exclaimed, "Anne, I thought you were dead a long time ago!"

FORBIDDEN MOONSHINE

On the trip we took to Manitoba with my father in 1977, one of our stops was a visit to my dad's nephew, Johnny Timchishen. Seeing him was a high priority for my father as they had bonded at some time in the distant past. Johnny considered Dad his favourite uncle. The admiration was mutual.

We found Johnny's farm northeast of Arborg and arrived unannounced. He was extremely surprised and happy to see my father. We were welcomed with open arms.

Once seated in his kitchen, Johnny proceeded to tell us about the latest development in his life. He had been busted by the RCMP for making moonshine. Johnny was lamenting the fact that he had purchased a brand-new copper still in Winnipeg.

After setting it up in the loft of his barn, he put the still into production.

The resultant "white lightning" was made available for sale to friends and neighbours.

Not long afterward, Johnny noticed an RCMP vehicle parked on the road abutting his farm. Over the next week, the vehicle maintained regular surveillance.

It was when Johnny and his family returned from a Saturday outing that the worst was realized.

The RCMP had entered his barn and discovered the still. The still was destroyed and Johnny was charged with his illegal activity.

As we sat around the kitchen table, Johnny related the terms of his eventual conviction. "I was given a one-year probation. I'm not to have any connection with moonshine."

As he concluded this statement, Johnny turned to my father and offered, "Would you like to try a little?" We were flabbergasted that he would even consider the risk.

Sure enough, he announced, "I'll be right back," as he disappeared into the basement.

My cousin returned with a jar of clear-looking liquid. A small amount was poured for each of us. We toasted and sipped a tiny sample. Firewater would have been the best description for Johnny's offering.

It was torturous to swallow even the minutest quantity. But we were obligated not to offend our host.

Our stay ended shortly after with us giving Johnny our heartfelt appreciation, more so for the delightful story than for the actual moonshine we consumed.

MISMEASURING

When I came into Sue's life, she already owned several properties. I often refer to this period as my BS days, that is, before Sue.

One of her assets was a beautiful half-acre waterfront location on the Sunshine Coast. She had purchased it with an existing ninety-year-old rustic cabin situated on the shore of the Georgia Strait. Sometime after, a rental house was built on the bluff above.

For many years, the cabin was used by her family as a full-time summer retreat, but as an isolated structure it fell to vandalism during the quiet winter months.

Windows were broken to gain access. The cabin contents were of minimal value and therefore very little was ever taken.

When we discovered another window broken, I assumed the responsibility to remove the broken glass and clean it up. In addition, I measured the opening to eventually purchase a replacement pane of glass. In the meantime, I boarded it up.

An order was placed with a glass company upon our return to Richmond. On our next visit to the cabin, I began the process of installing the plate glass. I soon discovered a blunder. The new piece was too small. The height and width were incorrect. They were both one inch too short. I couldn't believe my incompetence. How could I have made such a simple error?

I took out the measuring tape again and remeasured it, this time with greater care. In fact, I double-checked.

We returned to the same glass shop with the mismeasured sheet of glass for recycling purposes. We placed a second order, this time with the correct measurements.

We paid for the second pane of glass and returned to the cabin. Once the temporary boards were removed, I proceeded to fit the sheet of glass into the frame.

The resulting fit was even more disastrous to my psyche than the first.

I now questioned my intelligence. It was beyond incompetence. The dimensions of this new piece were identical to the first go around. How could this happen?

Sue commiserated with me. But the problem had to be solved. Where was I going wrong?

Out came the measuring tape for the third time. I checked it for a possible defect. Sure enough, this made-in-Asia product was at fault. Instead of the tape beginning at zero, it began at the one-inch mark. As a result, any measurement with this tape was short-changed by one inch.

Being now completely cognizant of the source of the problem, I remeasured the opening accurately.

When we reappeared a third time at the same glass outlet, we were met with incredulous looks. With large smiles, two staff members jumped to our assistance.

The entire dilemma was explained, and we placed a third order. The staff took pity on us. No further payment was requested.

I'm happy to report we successfully installed this pane of glass without it causing us any more grief or pain.

LOVE AND MARRIAGE

My first visit to the home of a retired couple was to quote on an interior painting job as per their request.

I rang their doorbell, located beside their street-level front door. The lady of the house answered. After initial introductions and pleasantries, her husband joined us.

The conversation continued for a brief time until we were suddenly interrupted by water cascading onto the woman's head.

Looking up to the entrance ceiling, we observed a small steady flow of water coming through a light fixture socket.

"Oh, I forgot! I left the water running in the kitchen sink," explained the wife.

Both husband and wife quickly ran upstairs with me in pursuit. Sure enough, the kitchen sink was overflowing. Water was streaming onto the floor and finding its path of least resistance through the electrical light fixture below.

"How stupid can I be?" she uttered. The lady had been interrupted by me ringing the doorbell.

The most remarkable aspect of the event was the fact that both husband and wife laughed at the mishap. No harsh words were shared. No condemnation occurred. To me, this was quite an education. As it turned out they did hire me to do their painting. In the process, they taught me a valuable lesson. This couple demonstrated that a successful relationship incorporated a great sense of humour and good communication skills.

I have tried to emulate these two principles ever since in my life.

THE GRASS IS NOT ALWAYS GREENER

A farm is the perfect setting to literally learn about greenery. Greenery is necessary to maintain life. Green pastures feed millions if not billions of livestock worldwide.

Springtime is the optimal time to witness the rebirth of plant life. Infinite shades of green are generated by Mother Nature. All that is required to appreciate this wondrous transitional period is your senses, specifically sight and smell.

For domestic animals such as cows, taste also plays an important role.

When dairy cattle are put out to pasture in early spring, their food needs to be rationed. After a long winter indoors, too much fresh alfalfa—the cow equivalent to chocolate for humans—can be hazardous to their health.

Cows can produce dangerous levels of gases from excessive alfalfa consumption. Bloating and death can occur.

In one situation, I was rounding up dairy cattle from a field of alfalfa. They were given a short two hours to feed. It was early spring, and they had not had sufficient time to adapt to this legume.

Sure enough, I discovered one cow lying on its side, severely bloated and dead. It illustrated to me that although the "grass may be greener" it's not necessarily desirable.

This lesson was reinforced on another occasion involving the corralling of the milking cows. They were to be brought into the barn for afternoon milking. Again, they were feeding on alfalfa pasture.

As I approached the herd, I noticed one cow nudging at a section of the fence. The cow quickly broke through it and ran at full speed to the middle of the adjoining field, then stopped. The rest of the herd followed in succession.

I watched the lead cow lower its head, open its mouth, and snatch a clump of grass. This was not alfalfa. As soon as she discovered this fact she scrambled back. The remaining herd mimicked the exact process modelled by the first cow.

Observing the entire scenario was living proof that the "grass is not always greener on the other side."

FRED HACKETT'S CLASS

Fred Hackett was my Grade 11 homeroom teacher. He also taught history to our class.

Mr. Hackett loved to inject theatrics frequently in classroom situations. Dramatic effect became his signature characteristic. Politics would bring out the greatest emotional response from him. However, student disturbances could also instigate a strong response from him.

Here are a few situations that arose in his class during that school year.

I happened to sit right behind Irene, who sat at the front of the room directly facing Mr. Hackett. Being the era of the Beatles, Irene turned around asking, "Can I comb your hair down?"

"Sure," I replied. After reaching in her purse for a comb, she proceeded to comb my bangs down over my eyes.

It didn't take long for Mr. Hackett to notice. He stopped teaching and issued the edict, "If you don't comb your hair back up, this class will not continue!"

Irene retrieved her comb and returned my rearranged hair to its usual place.

It is hard to believe that an innocuous incident like that would cause such a furore.

On another occasion, Mr. Hackett confided to our class that he was finally getting rid of his pet guinea pig. There were two apparent reasons for his decision. The pig was constantly tearing up the paper used on the cage floor and his patience in having the animal had run out.

At that point, I raised my hand. "Yes, Fred?" he questioned.

I volunteered, "I guess you could say the situation was a 'bore.'"

This was my feeble attempt at a pun with a triple meaning. I can recall that the response was rather muted by both Mr. Hackett and my fellow classmates.

On yet another occasion, a male student, one and only once, simulated the sound of an overhead bomb being dropped. We had somehow learned that Mr. Hackett had suffered shellshock during WWII. A few supporting students ducked for cover.

In the process, Mr. Hackett momentarily thought he was under wartime fire. His terrified reaction brought an uproarious response from the class. It should go without saying that he was not amused with the episode.

ONE + ONE DOES NOT EQUAL TWO

One plus one does not always equal two. My daughters taught me that.

Daughters, Katie, age fourteen and Emma, age eleven were visiting. I had been divorced from their mother for several years.

They arrived on a Sunday morning at my residence. I had planned to make them breakfast, but a shortage of milk prevented me from completing my preparations. Fortunately, a convenience store existed next door.

I asked my daughters to go over and purchase the necessary milk. Specifically, I told them, "I need two litres of two percent milk." I gave them some money and off they went.

Returning a short time later they proudly presented me with their acquisition: two one-litre containers of milk, each being one percent. My reaction was one of stern disappointment. "How could they manage to get it so wrong?" I thought.

I reproached them with, "I told you I wanted two litres of two percent milk."

"But Dad," they replied, "we did get you two litres of two percent milk. One litre plus one litre equals two litres and one percent plus one percent equals two percent."

Katie and Emma beamed with pride. They couldn't have been any more pleased with themselves. They had pulled a fast one on me using pure arithmetic logic.

MYSTERIOUS MISSING MONEY

As I was the eldest child, my mother often sent me on errands. The corner store was a frequent destination for me to purchase food items.

I may have been ten years old when I returned from one of these chores. I handed the purchase to my mother whereupon she asked me for the change. I reached into my coat pocket where I had placed the coins. Nothing. I dug my hand a little further and swished it around. Absolutely no luck.

"Mom," I exclaimed, "I don't have any change."

"What do you mean, you don't have any change?" she countered.

"Mom, I put the change in this pocket, and it's gone," came my frustrated reply.

"What did you do, spend it?" she accused.

"No, Mom, I didn't spend it. Maybe the change fell out of my pocket," came my defence.

"Then go back to the store and retrace your steps to see if the change fell out of your pocket," commanded my mother.

I made my way back, scrutinizing the ground at every step for lost coins. At the same time, I continued to search my coat pockets desperately. I had no success after completing the full trip to the corner store. I was becoming very neurotic about the disappearance despite knowing that I did not intentionally misuse the funds.

On the return home, I paid attention again to every minute detail of the ground along the route I travelled. I still had absolutely no luck by the time I arrived home for the second time.

"Well, did you find it?" my mother demanded.

"No," I said with trepidation. I was anticipating punishment for my misdemeanour.

Out of desperation, I tried to search my right-hand pocket once again. For some reason, I felt the bottom of the coat below the pocket. To my surprise, something seemed to be inside the lining. As I searched more deliberately, sure enough, my disappearing coins mysteriously reappeared. I turned my pocket inside out to discover a hole at the bottom. The coins had fallen through.

I dug out the coins and handed them over to my immense relief and my mother's forgiveness.

I COUNT MONEY

During my twenty-eight-year painting career, I crossed paths with a great number of client personalities. These ranged from clients who created substantial difficulties for me to clients who made relationships with them enormously rewarding. Fortunately, the latter comprised most of my clientele.

One wonderful couple was James and Katie Ko. They had emigrated from Taiwan and settled in the Vancouver area. In my estimation, what made them exceptionally pleasant to work with was their Buddhist beliefs.

They displayed warmth, understanding and patience amongst many other wonderful characteristics, all of which fostered a beneficial relationship with someone like me.

Over time I also discovered that they were very wealthy. Notwithstanding this fact, they were immensely modest. James usually coordinated the painting details and Katie the financial transactions. Payment was always in cash.

I first painted for James and Katie for their Vancouver house. It was a minimal exterior project. Not too long afterward I received a request to repaint the complete interior of a newly purchased house in North Delta. They had sold their Vancouver location. Their undemanding nature made my job uniquely rewarding.

Within a year, to my surprise, James and Katie called me to repaint the exterior of a third house. They had sold and bought again.

When the job was near completion, Katie asked if she could make me lunch. I happened to be working by myself on this day. I accepted and entered the home at noon.

I found Katie preparing a vegetarian stir fry. In the midst of her cooking, she turned to me announcing, "I don't do this in Taiwan."

I immediately questioned, "Who does it for you?"

"My servants do this," she replied.

As a Canadian, I was quite astonished by her admission. I questioned her further. "Then what do you do?"

"I count money!" came her reply.

I was dumbfounded. Her account was totally out of context for someone like me. How could someone of such wealth be so down to earth, so generous in nature?

It certainly appeared to be a significant contradiction.

GIGGLING DAUGHTER

Farm life not only produced a cornucopia of food products but an abundance of unique experiences. One experience involved my daughter Katie at the age of fourteen months. It took place in the dairy barn after an early morning milking.

Our regular daily morning routine started with a five o'clock feeding of the cows and then the actual milking. Our breakfast then followed. After this, we returned to the barn to clean out the manure and clean the equipment in the milk house.

The milk house was separated from the main part of the barn by a simple wooden swing door. A box stall was located on the barn side directly opposite the swing door.

One-month- to two-month-old calves were kept in the box stall. They were intentionally isolated from their mother in order to wean them, but the calves still needed to be fed milk. This was done by placing a calf's mouth into a partially filled pail of fresh milk. At the same time, two fingers were inserted into the calf's mouth to simulate the mother's teat. The intention was to train the calf to suck the fingers and at the same time draw milk into its mouth. This was required at each feeding until the calf learned to manage the process independently.

I had taught Katie the art of feeding a calf using this method.

On one of the occasions when I was in the milk house cleaning equipment, I had left my daughter feeding a calf. While performing my duties I was alerted to a continuous sound emitted from the other side of the swing door. I knew it came from Katie but running water interfered with my ability to comprehend the nature of her vocalizations. In a state of panic, I rushed through the door anticipating some crisis.

Instead, I found Katie giggling uncontrollably. Her hand was suctioned in the calf's mouth, and she was suffering an extreme case of being tickled. The suction created by the calf was overpowering for a fourteen-month-old. She couldn't pull her hand away.

CORN FED FRED

Being a typical impoverished university student, I discovered an inexpensive food source, corn. In the immediate vicinity of the University of Waterloo campus, vast quantities of corn grew on farmers' fields.

As I drove by on numerous occasions, I realized that the corn fields offered an opportunity for a free food source. I thought, "No farmer would miss a few ears considering the vast amount growing."

So, I helped myself one day. I pulled over on an isolated country road out of sight from any farmhouse. A dozen heads of corn were a perfect amount for me.

Over the next three days, dinner included corn on the cob. On day one, I found the corn to be rather bland and not sweet at all. But it was free. In addition, the water in which the corn was boiled, mysteriously turned yellow.

Dinner on day two produced identical results. Tasteless corn and yellow water. But I devoured the corn, nonetheless.

It was only on day three after completing the same dinner ritual that I realized the truth. I had been eating cow corn. No wonder I had such unimpressive results. It wasn't sweet corn that I had been eating.

The remaining inventory of corn was quickly ushered into the garbage bin. I chalked it up to a university education.

SHOOT ME

One of the most difficult issues I had to deal with in the painting business was dealing with stratas. More specifically, dealing with people in those stratas.

Success in achieving a contract to paint didn't stop there. Having to negotiate with the strata council and owners proved to be of epic proportions on several occasions.

The most difficult dealt with two warring factions in a sixty-five-unit townhouse complex. We were contracted to repaint the complete building exteriors plus all the property fencing. It was a sizeable project.

Prior to the start of the project, all negotiations were arranged with the existing strata council. This included their colour-choice decisions. Once this was determined we were ready to begin.

We power washed the exterior surfaces in advance of the painting, and we leased a boom lift to reach the three-storey height. We began painting on the day that the lift was delivered.

Within two and a half hours of commencing, everything came to a halt. Two strata factions, the current council and the previous one, were at odds over the colour choices. We were ordered to cease. Their differences seemed insurmountable.

I waited until the next day for direction, but one was not forthcoming. Consequently, I decided to contact a litigation lawyer. The delay was costing me money.

A letter was drafted and sent to the strata council. It stipulated the daily costs that were being incurred by my business and that would require compensation.

An emergency meeting was conducted by the property manager with the two warring groups. I received a phone call from the property manager the following day. He reported, "We had a two-and-a-half-hour meeting. Those people don't know how to get along! I told them that the delay will cost them money, so settle your differences!"

We received the go-ahead the following day. The painting progressed for three weeks with ongoing conflicts. Just prior to the third payment draw the property management requested that we guarantee the completion of the project in writing.

After consulting with our lawyer, we were advised that it was no different than the original contract agreement. The guarantee was signed. We continued painting. Payment was made for the third draw. The strata environment became progressively caustic.

It became so unbearable that after consulting with our counsel, we pulled out permanently and sacrificed the final payment.

No negative consequences arose out of our decision to terminate.

In my final consultation with my lawyer, he shared the following comment: "Earlier this year I dealt with a strata problem for my mother. She owns a townhouse in a strata. It amounted to people who were on a power trip." He added the warning, "If you ever hear that I've become involved in a strata purchase, shoot me!"

"What an admittance and condemnation of stratas," I thought.

BOILING POPCORN

When I was invited to spend an evening with fellow university chemistry students, little did I know it would turn out to be a unique lesson in science.

We were attending Laurentian University in Sudbury, Ontario, at the time. Our second-year chemistry class developed into a friendly group.

The invitation came from a classmate. She included me and two others. In addition, her own roommate was present. The gathering took place in their basement rental suite.

It was early evening and we entertained ourselves with card games. I can't recall if alcohol was present. It probably wasn't since the atmosphere was very low-key.

When the roommate offered to make popcorn, we indicated approval. We continued playing cards while the popcorn was being made. The chef was easily visible from our dining room table.

With competition in the card game intensifying, we became oblivious to the time. Finally, we realized that an inordinate amount of time had passed. And still no popcorn. We looked over to the popcorn maker. Collectively we asked, "When is the popcorn going to be ready? What's taking so long?"

Our jaws dropped when she explained, "The water hasn't boiled yet!" We couldn't believe our ears. Sure enough, we spotted a full pot of water on the stovetop.

Our volunteer cook was under the assumption that popcorn was made by inserting the kernels into boiling water. We had to explain the correct procedure to her. Her embarrassment was unparalleled.

Later, we learned that the roommate had led a sheltered life. Due to a physical handicap, she had been raised without any expectation to learn cooking essentials.

UNCLE JOE'S FARM

Despite the demands of working on a farm for summers as a teenager, I was treated wonderfully on my Aunt Pauline's cattle farm. Her husband Joe, Uncle Joe to me, and my nearest cousin in age, Jimmy, were my close allies.

One midday under a hot sun Uncle Joe decided to butcher a rather large pig. It was probably about three hundred pounds. He had enlisted a friend to help. Once slaughtered, the hog was placed on its back on a makeshift wooden table set up in the farmyard driveway.

From a short distance, I could observe the two men cutting open the full length of the pig's belly. Copious flies were swarming about. With his bare hands, Uncle Joe lifted out as many entrails as he could manage high into the air.

"Freddie, can you hold this for me while I cut around?" he asked matter-of-factly.

"Absolutely not," I replied in disgust. I quickly disappeared.

As far as I was concerned there couldn't have been anything more offensive I could have been asked to do.

In a separate incident, Jimmy and I were stacking bales of hay outdoors in the form of a pyramid. As we reached a height of twenty bales, about thirty feet, we became aware of an unusual roaring sound some distance away. From our viewpoint, we could distinguish a car travelling towards us along the dusty country road. It was approximately half a mile away.

Jimmy and I were perplexed as to why it was making such a bizarre noise and moving so slowly. As the car drew closer, the racket intensified. It seemed like an eternity before the vehicle finally pulled into the farmyard.

We quickly realized the absurdity of the situation. The car had been driven in first gear the entire distance with the gas pedal pushed to the floor.

The driver turned out to be Jimmy's alcoholic uncle. As he staggered out of his vehicle, the severity of his drunkenness became apparent. He could only mutter a few indistinguishable words, jump into the car, and turn back.

As fifteen-year-olds, Jimmy and I could only express amusement at the situation we had witnessed.

This third episode came as a challenge from Uncle Joe.

He challenged Jimmy and me to a foot race. We accepted. The setting was the country dirt road in front of the farmyard. A set distance of about fifty metres was determined.

There was adequate time for me to strategize. Three facts were evident to me. Uncle Joe, being the oldest by twenty-seven years, would be at a disadvantage. Jimmy, who was bulky, wasn't exactly fleet-footed. Unless I collapsed en route, the race was mine to win.

But that was not the scenario that I intended. All I wanted was for Uncle Joe to win and for me to outpace my rival cousin Jimmy.

And this was exactly the outcome: first, Uncle Joe, second, me, and third, Jimmy.

It was wonderful to see the sincere delight in the winner's facial expression and the disappointment in my cousin's.

TRIPLE TREAT

While taking a road trip through the Gaspé area of Quebec, we discovered a plethora of soft ice cream businesses. Previously unbeknownst to Sue and me, la crème glacée was an important part of Quebec culture. It was almost as ubiquitous as maple syrup. In fact, la crème glacée à l'érable became our favourite dessert/reward during our stay.

At one of our ice cream pit stops, we placed an order for two regular-flavoured soft cones, chocolate dipped. The server, a young teenager, prepared the first one for Sue successfully. But when the second one was being dipped upside down into the chocolate cauldron, the server lost her grip. The cone fell into the chocolate syrup and was quickly swallowed up.

The young woman panicked, initially not knowing what to do. In the space of five seconds or so she managed to locate a pair of tongs.

The cone was extracted, and she was about to discard it into a garbage receptacle. This time I panicked. *"Non, non, je desire ca,"* I blurted out.

I saw it as a unique opportunity. I wanted it. The cone had been coated with at least triple the regular chocolate quantity.

Fortunately, the server agreed to make the sale at the regular price. I licked that cone to my heart's delight.

I don't anticipate this scenario will ever happen again.

SLAPPING OF HANDS

Young children can be such a delight.

One example of this took place during a Christmas concert at the Vancouver Ukrainian Hall. My daughters participated as dancers, and I participated as a choir member in the organization of United Ukrainian Canadians.

In this concert, the focus was on the younger performers with the youngest being three to five years in age. Their experience was extremely limited. In most cases, they had only four months of dance training.

With a full house consisting of siblings, parents, and grandparents, the youngest group proved to be the most entertaining. Their naivety and inexperience provided amusement. Two older dancers led the group on stage.

On the first occasion, when they were to form a circle by joining hands, all teamwork broke down. Girls and boys alternated. However, one of the boys refused to accept the outstretched hand of a girl. In fact, he slapped constantly at her offer.

This caused the audience to break into hysterics. There was no way that this young man was going to hold hands with a girl.

The circle routine quickly ended with the dancers separating themselves. They danced solo for a brief amount of time until the dancers were required join hands again. As the circle reformed, hands were again extended. Again, the same delinquent boy refused to hold the girl's hand. The slapping process was repeated to the hilarious approval of the audience. It took an extended time for the laughter to subside.

It had to be one of the most amusing performances I have ever witnessed.

BEE KEEPING ADVICE

A newspaper advertisement caught my eye. It was early 1971.

The ad promoted a talk being given by an out-of-town beekeeper. I was intrigued. It was to take place on a Saturday morning.

Despite my good intentions, I arrived late. The formal part of the talk had been completed. When I entered the room, a question-and-answer session was ending.

Fortunately, the beekeeper was generous enough to give me the time to answer my questions. He shared his expertise with me even after everyone left. But he concluded with a warning: "If you ever decide to bee keep, remember it is a dangerous occupation, especially for men."

My curiosity was aroused. "What do you mean?" I asked.

"If you get stung on the penis," he replied, "it can be excruciatingly painful. When you go to get medical attention, make sure you get medication for the pain but not the swelling."

The beekeeper took great delight in relating this anecdote. And I took great pleasure in his sense of humour.

DRIVING UPSIDE DOWN

During the winter of 1968–69, Bob and I frequented an out-of-town hotel lounge five to six nights a week. It was wasteful in retrospect, but it was what we did at the time.

To make the round trip of twenty-four miles I depended on the use of Bob's vehicle.

On one of these evenings, we met up with two young ladies. We arranged to share the same table for the night. At closing time, Bob and I split up. I was to travel with the woman who owned a vehicle. Bob offered to drive the other woman who was without a car.

It was a perfect setup, or so we thought. Our intentions were not necessarily noble.

Upon exiting the cocktail lounge, we realized the weather had turned for the worse. While we were inside drinking, freezing rain had fallen. The roads had become treacherous.

This fact didn't prevent my female companion from taking to the highway.

We were both drunk. Her inhibition to speed was non-existent. I remember looking at the speedometer and seventy-five miles per hour registered in my mind. The roads were covered in a coat of ice.

Shortly after making this observation, all consciousness of what transpired next escaped me. I blame my drunken state.

When reality hit, we were lying on our backs on the interior roof of the car.

The vehicle had flipped and was lying upside down. My partner was in shock and screaming. My attempts to calm her down proved successful after several tries.

"Are you injured?" I asked.

"Just my hands. They're cut," she replied. I assessed myself as well. Nothing serious that I could determine.

It was totally disorienting. We were drunk in an overturned vehicle. "How do we get out?" I wondered. "How do we open the doors to get out?"

As I tried to move around, my bare hands couldn't differentiate between broken glass and snow and ice. I was afraid to place too much pressure on anything with my hands.

Most importantly, we still needed to vacate the vehicle. It was still a mental quandary to comprehend how to turn the door handle and how to push out. When I finally figured it out, I exited first and then helped my friend.

Shortly after, an Ontario Provincial Police car arrived. The officer asked about our injuries. Minor lacerations to our hands and one to my scalp were all that were evident. We were very fortunate. The police officer was unconcerned with any drunkenness. He indicated that the freezing rain had caused a rash of accidents.

However, he radioed for transportation to take us to a hospital for treatment.

When we arrived at the emergency ward, we were met by my family doctor. He recognized me and looked at my female companion. I can remember the expression on his face. It was the greatest smirk you could imagine. I surmised that his grin was prompted by the nature of my apparent date. For lack of a better expression, "She was quite homely."

After being treated for our minor lacerations, we were sent home. As a postscript, two related events occurred: I did meet my accident companion the following week. We briefly discussed the event, and no further contact took place. She impressed me as a very articulate and intelligent individual despite her lack of physical beauty.

At the time I still lived with my parents. I intentionally kept the accident from them. However, it was only a matter of days before my mother confronted me with, "Why didn't you tell me about the accident?"

There and then I realized that the truth is always revealed.

WHY DID?

The road traffic I was in came to a standstill. The light had turned red preventing advancement in all three lanes heading north. It was bumper to bumper except for a small opening generated to allow a truck to enter from a side lane.

The truck was attempting to cross over three lanes. This commercial vehicle wasn't just a regular run-around variety. It was gigantic in proportion to most of the automobiles in the vicinity.

I happened to notice the signage on the truck's side: Sunrise Poultry.

Instantaneously the question arose in my mind, "Why did the Sunrise Poultry truck cross the road?"

BROKEN AXE HANDLE

This must be one of the funniest episodes that I have witnessed. It transpired in a mere second. It was totally unpredictable and totally ironic.

Tofino, British Columbia, had become our favourite getaway after having moved to the West Coast. The vistas in Pacific Rim National Park took our breath away. And we established Green Point Campground as our home away from home.

Our first trek down to Long Beach nearly resulted in the drowning of our daughter Katie. She was two and a half. The incoming waves were so alluring that she rushed out ahead of us to meet them. The resulting impact swept her off her feet. She disappeared. With the waves receding and the undertow, we had no knowledge as to where Katie was.

I had already begun a desperate sprint to where we had last seen her. Fortunately, with the water rushing out to sea her body became exposed. She was lying face down in the sand still breathing and alive. Just about every orifice in her body was saturated with sand.

It was quite amazing that she suffered no trauma. She displayed no fear of water the next day. Despite this fact, we did not take our eyes off her for the remainder of the vacation.

The second year we were joined by my wife's twenty-year-old cousin Johnny. Two years before his visit to Tofino, we had worked on his father's dairy farm in Milton, Ontario.

On the second day of camping, we decided to build a fire in our campsite pit.

We had already picked up the free firewood and were set to go. But we quickly realized a missing ingredient—an axe. We had forgotten it at home.

Johnny offered to go and scout for one around the other campsites. He returned in short order. The occupants of the adjacent campsite lent Johnny a brand new long-handled axe.

He offered to do the chopping. We were in good hands. Johnny had been born and raised on a farm. With a wood-burning kitchen stove, wood chopping was almost an everyday event.

Johnny placed a piece of firewood on the chopping block. As we watched, he wound up for his swing. The axe came hurtling down. On impact, there was a loud "thwack." Instead of the firewood splitting, the axe handle snapped in half.

Johnny's aim was not true.

Our reaction was instantaneous. Johnny, a friend, my wife, and I broke into uncontrollable laughter. How could someone with so much expertise screw up so easily?

It took us a considerable amount of time to recover from this hilarious occurrence. We must have replayed it two or three times following the actual event.

Johnny did return next door to apologize for breaking the axe handle. The owner showed remarkable tolerance in not wanting to accept financial compensation for the damaged axe.

The broken axe handle story has remained a treasured memory for those of us who witnessed the incident.

FIRST FARM MEMORIES

My earliest memories of being on the farm are numerous. There are three accounts I recall that took place on my grandparents' Manitoba farm when I was five years old. Baba and Gido were my mother's parents.

Shortly after arriving, I became aware of where the milk came from. I had seen it with my own eyes. It grossed me out. I refused to drink this version of cow's milk.

But it only took one day of deception to change my mind. I awoke in the morning and was told that the milkman had delivered earlier. I was easily convinced as my mother pulled out a familiar-looking milk bottle filled with cold milk. This is what I drank contentedly for the remainder of my farm stay.

My father was responsible for the next ruse. While he was hand-milking a cow in the barn, I kept my distance up in the loft. I simply found being near cows and manure obnoxious.

My father called me from below. I was able to stick my head through a cut-out in the loft floor in response. At that instant, my dad filled a cow's teat with milk, bent it upwards in my direction and squeezed it with great force.

The milk squirted upwards of fifteen feet, hitting me directly in the face. I can remember being furious with my father. I spit whatever had entered my mouth and madly thrashed at my face to remove all remnants of milk.

The third memory involved me bathing. No indoor plumbing existed on Baba and Gido's farm. So, in my case, they devised a simple plan. After the morning milking, the cows were led to the water trough and then put out to pasture. A fifty-gallon metal barrel cut in half lengthways provided the trough. It was filled with water from an adjacent hand pump.

With the cows away the trough was drained, scrubbed, and refilled. Once the water was heated sufficiently by the sun, it was ready for bathing. My sister and I enjoyed the rustic experience.

I can't recall having a more unique cleansing than that.

EASY DRUNK X 2

My first wife and I stayed on a dairy farm from 1976 to 1978. While there we became teetotallers, not necessarily by choice. It was a simple case of being so isolated that the opportunity for socializing was rare. Liquor was not kept in our household.

When the occasional off-farm visit offered the chance to drink alcohol, two important factors came into play for me. First, there was the effect of having abstained for an extended time. And second, the daily farm labour had made my metabolism exceedingly efficient. Food and drink were processed remarkably fast.

On our first outing to a Toronto nightclub, I consumed two beers. The return trip to the farm took one hour. I fell asleep shortly after. But the effect of the beer caused me to wake up in short order. My stomach was churning, and I felt dizzy.

I rose from the bed very carefully with the intention to head straight to the bathroom. Not disturbing my wife was a high priority. But it failed. I fainted and collapsed to the bedroom floor with a loud thud.

My wife awakened in a state of shock. "What's wrong?" she shouted.

"Nothing," I replied in the faintest of voices.

It didn't take long for her to discover the nature of my problem.

On a second occasion, we were invited to celebrate my birthday on a Sunday afternoon. My uncle hosted the event at his apartment in Hamilton, Ontario.

Prior to the dinner, alcohol was made available. I chose a beer. I remember sitting on the living room sofa feeling noxious and suffering vertigo before completing that first beer.

I carefully stood up, planning to make my way to the bathroom. My intention was to not alert others to my dilemma. But it failed again. As I negotiated myself into the hallway, I collapsed and hit the floor with a familiar thud.

My uncle's wife, who happened to be closest, screamed, "Fred, what's wrong?" Everyone rushed to my aid. I managed to revive quickly and carry on into the bathroom.

The experience was most embarrassing. I feared others would assume that I had a drinking problem. In fact, I did. It was a case of not drinking excessively but my body metabolized alcohol super efficiently.

CHOP SUE-Y

Ever since Sue built her cottage, I've been responsible for the provision of firewood. The wood fireplace was something we treasured primarily during the cold weather months. It was designed to adequately heat a one-thousand-square-foot home.

Fortunately, there was a sufficient source of trees on the half-acre property to supply ample firewood.

However, this required me to have a process for felling the trees, bucking up the trunks, rough splitting the wood, and storing it. Once the wood was sufficiently cured, it needed to be further split or chopped.

For the longest time, Sue left the chopping to me. She was too intimidated by the process mainly due to safety concerns.

But in recent times, Sue was making the trip to the cottage more frequently on her own. This situation necessitated that she split the wood to provide cottage heat.

So, the occasion arose when she remarked to me, "I'm getting good at chopping firewood!"

Her statement offered me the opportunity to remark, "We'll have to call you

Chop Sue-y from now on."

HELLO DOLLY

I had pulled up to our neighbourhood liquor store to return a number of empties. As I was about to enter, I met an acquaintance who was returning bottles as well. He was loading them onto a sizeable four-wheel dolly.

Ted kindly spoke up, "This is my last load. You can use my dolly if you wish."

"Yes. That would be great," I replied. I waited for him outside.

It was a few minutes before Ted returned. "Here, it's all yours," he offered.

"I just have one load to bring in. It won't take me long," was my reply.

When I returned with the dolly, Ted and his vehicle were no longer at the front entrance. "He must have forgotten I had his dolly," I thought. "I'll return it."

I knew where Ted lived. His house was easily identifiable. As the retired Richmond fire chief, he had placed an antique fire truck on his property.

It was only a ten-minute drive away. Well, it became a nightmare. I circled a four-block area looking specifically for that property with a fire truck. I had no luck. I couldn't even recognize his house, which I knew had an unusually high turret.

Round and round I went until I gave up in futility. Then a brainstorm hit me. "Go and check a phone book to determine his address. He probably moved," I thought.

It took several retail stops to find the required information. But I lucked out. Ted's new address was within a five-minute distance.

I pulled up in front of his house, sensing relief that I had finally found him. Checking my watch, I realized that a full hour had passed since I had started my quest.

Ringing the doorbell brought Ted's wife to the entrance.

"Is Ted home?" I asked.

"Yes," she replied. "I'll get him."

"Ted!" she shouted as she disappeared into the house.

When Ted appeared I quickly stated, "I have your dolly. You left before I had a chance to return it to you."

"But that's not my dolly. It belongs to the liquor store!" came his reply.

I was dumbfounded. What an idiotic situation to be caught in. Ted laughed and I laughed at this misunderstanding.

Off I went, returning to the liquor store. I unloaded the dolly from my van and surreptitiously pushed it through the store to the return area. Not a word was spoken, nor was a question asked between me and the staff.

OPERA PANIC

I first became aware of my wife's episodic impatience when we were attempting to find a parking space in Vancouver.

We had driven into the city to attend an opera. The performance was to start at 8:00 p.m. At 7:50 p.m. we were desperately circling several blocks for a vacant parking stall. It was bumper to bumper. Others were in the same dire situation.

At that point, Sue opened her passenger door, informing me, "I'm getting out. I don't want to be late!"

"What about me?" I questioned. "You can't desert me like that! We're in this together!"

"I don't care! I don't want to be late!" she continued.

I countered emphatically with, "Don't you dare leave me or I'll just drive home!"

There was a moment of reconsideration on Sue's part as she closed her door. Fortunately, we found a parking space within two minutes.

We ran to the Queen Elizabeth Theatre, arriving just one minute before show time. As we approached the entrance, an usher was advising everyone, "There's no need to rush. There's a medical emergency. The opera is being delayed."

During the process of being seated, we learned that an audience member had suffered a heart attack. He was lying on the floor of an aisle receiving medical attention. We also learned that his pulse could not be found. The individual could not be moved until a pulse was detected.

The theatre remained in a hushed state until 8:40 p.m. when the individual had reached the desired condition to be taken away.

When the performance finally began, the first scene involved a lone bass singer acting out a death scene. This caused the audience to gasp in horror at the remarkable ironic coincidence taking place.

HARRY'S VISIT

My connection with Harry was rather tenuous.

He was somehow associated with the somewhat clandestine performing group called "Perth County Conspiracy Does Not Exist." They were based in the Stratford, Ontario, area.

As the coordinator of the Northern Lights Folk Festival, I invited some of the members from Harry's group to perform in 1974. After arriving for this event, the group informed me that Harry was unable to attend. He had been sentenced to a six-month jail term. The crime: possession of nine hundred pounds of marijuana he had grown.

He pleaded that the entire quantity was for personal use. Of course, there was no intent to traffic. Unfortunately, his defence failed.

Now fast forward to late fall, November to be exact.

I received a phone call from Harry. He had just arrived by bus in Sudbury.

"Can you put me up for the night? he asked. "I'm passing through on my way to Sault Ste. Marie tomorrow."

"No problem," I replied. "Where are you?"

"The Nickel Range Hotel," he answered.

"It will take me about twenty minutes to get there," I instructed.

"Great!" he responded. "I'll be waiting on the front steps."

Sure enough, when I pulled up in front of the Nickel Range, Harry was standing there.

"Harry?" I enquired. He immediately approached and entered my vehicle. We introduced ourselves and headed back to my home, the same twenty-minute duration.

Shortly after arriving, Harry announced, "I forgot my shopping bag. I left it on the front steps. I'll phone the hotel and ask them to check to see if it's still there."

Harry made the call. "I just left your hotel a short while ago. I forgot a shopping bag on your front steps. Could you please check to see if it is still there?"

The staff person at the front desk stepped outside, found the item, and brought it inside. "I have it," the clerk informed him.

"Could you hold it for me? Harry asked. "I'll be there as quickly as possible!"

Obviously, Harry was taking things for granted. His expectation to have me drive there and back a second time in addition to housing him for the night was quite extraordinary. And we were essentially strangers.

I relented. We jumped into my vehicle for round two. As we drove into town, Harry was demonstrably concerned about his forgotten paper container.

"It's full of pot—eight pounds," he informed me.

As soon as I heard those words, paranoia overtook me. A nonstop series of questions ran through my mind. "What if someone looks inside the bag? What if the marijuana is discovered? What if they call the police? What if we arrive and the police are waiting for us? What will happen? Should we turn around and not take the chance?"

As we continued towards our destination, I rationalized the situation as follows: The pot belonged to Harry. I had nothing to do with it. If he was apprehended inside the hotel I would simply drive away.

As we approached the front of the Nickel Range, I was extremely watchful of any suspicious activity. No one was stationed outside. I stopped my van and Harry exited. He disappeared inside, moments later reappearing with a shopping bag in hand.

We made it home.

DON, DON, AND DON

While driving, our radio is always operational. It is our source for all things: news, information, and music.

When mention was made of an upcoming Don Juan Opera broadcast, I immediately identified with it. Sue and I had seen it performed at the Sydney Opera House.

Then just as quickly I realized that I was mistaken. It dawned on me; it wasn't Don Juan it was Don Quixote. We'd seen Don Quixote the ballet, and not Don Juan the opera.

So much for my feeble attempt at punning.

POLITICAL ADVICE AT THE URINAL

The Law Society of British Columbia decided to host an important conference in 1996. It dealt with the aftermath of the previous year's Quebec referendum on separatism.

The minute loss on the part of the "Yes" side drew great concerns on the part of Canadians who were opposed to Quebec seceding.

"How do we prevent that eventuality?" was the thrust of the conference.

The panel consisted of a cross-section of fifteen high-powered Canadians. They ranged from a former prime minister, a Liberal cabinet minister, a British Columbia cabinet minister, a judge, constitutional lawyers, and academics.

At the time, I was still heavily involved in the political arena. Having run as a candidate in the 1993 federal election, politics and the Quebec issue resonated with me. As a result, I attended the conference at the University of British Columbia (UBC).

Many aspects of the one-day event were exceedingly stimulating—the opinions, the debates, the personalities, and the keynote speaker.

I felt quite comfortable in this environment. I had gained considerable insight over the previous four years. During the 1992 Charlottetown Accord debate, I had the opportunity to challenge Joe Clark at a public meeting. As a candidate in 1993, I became well educated as to the nature of Quebec aspirations. In 1995, I spoke with a Parti Québécois member of parliament.

One of the facts that I researched dealt with the federal government's constitutional authority to nullify any provincial attempt to separate.

I put this piece of evidence to a very distinguished judge when we met in the men's room. Side by side, each at our own urinal, relieving ourselves, it was a once-in-a-lifetime opportunity to talk to him.

His reply to my query proved to be disappointing. He felt invoking federal supremacy over a Quebec sovereignty decision would be foolhardy.

So much for seeking a legal opinion at the urinal. Fortunately, it was one of the rare occurrences where a legal fee was difficult to levy.

MANUFACTURING GUILT

At times auto accidents can bring out the worst in people. This is something I experienced with a two-vehicle collision in 1991.

While driving along a major artery in Richmond, British Columbia, a smaller vehicle bounded out of a side street, crashing into the front end of my painting van. His view had been obscured by a large five-ton truck. Witnesses corroborated the fact that he had erred.

Immediately following the collision, I managed to vacate my vehicle, but the other driver didn't. It appeared he was suffering a neck injury. I called 911 requesting an ambulance. Then I made a second cell phone call to the job site explaining my situation.

The other driver then requested the use of my cell phone. One call was made by him and then another. I retrieved my phone when he demanded it for a third call.

Shortly after, ambulance and RCMP vehicles arrived. Once a medical clearance was given to the other individual, the RCMP officer interviewed him. By the time I was been interviewed, the wife of the other driver arrived.

She was obviously distraught, as she interrupted the RCMP constable. "It's his fault," she claimed, pointing in my direction. I was taken aback. How could someone not present at the scene of the accident possibly accuse blame with certainty.

"Please don't interfere.," the police officer responded. "Could you stand back!"

The interview process continued. Once again, the woman interrupted. "It's his fault!" she exclaimed.

This time the RCMP replied much more emphatically. "Please shut up. If you interfere once more, I will arrest you!"

It was a remarkable experience to witness someone so desperate that they would destroy their own credibility in such a blatant manner.

BEAR SPRAY

"Bear Spray Available" read the sign. I pulled my vehicle over to investigate.

The advertisement was featured on the exterior of an outdoor outfitter business. As avid ocean kayakers and hikers, my wife and I have crossed paths with bears on two occasions.

Consequently, I was intrigued by the opportunity to learn about bear spray. I planned to purchase some.

Once inside, I proceeded to a counter where a staff person was available. The first question I posed was, "Is this stuff guaranteed?"

"Absolutely not!" came the response. I was dumbfounded. How could a product be sold without any form of guarantee?

"What do you mean no guarantee?" I asked.

The clerk explained, "Well there are many reasons why bear spray doesn't work. For one, people will panic and drop the can. People will panic and spray it in the wrong direction. People will panic and release the spray too soon—before the bear arrives. A strong wind may blow the spray in the wrong direction. That's why there's no guarantee for bear spray."

With all those provisos I left the store empty-handed.

DECEPTIVE SMOKER

As an employer in the painting business, I learned that cigarette smokers were inherently less productive than those who didn't smoke.

Therefore, I made extraordinary efforts to screen potential employees. I did not want to hire smokers.

In consultation with labour standards, I learned that I could not discriminate in the hiring practice. The accepted requirement was to advertise with the stipulation, "Non-smoking is preferable." When it came to hiring David, I implemented this condition. He indicated that he was a smoker but only "at the end of the day." Not being completely satisfied with this answer, I still hired David as he claimed he had experience as a sprayer. This skill was an asset as far as I was concerned.

And so, it happened on his first day of work. After fifteen minutes into the job

I asked David if he could do some spraying.

"I need to get my respirator from my car." he replied.

He disappeared down to street level. My curiosity was aroused when it seemed that David was taking an inordinate amount of time.

From the second-floor window, I glanced at his vehicle, and to my astonishment, David was crouched in the driver's seat obviously dragging on a cigarette.

I couldn't comprehend how someone could be so dishonest. It took this individual only fifteen minutes on the job to destroy my trust in him.

HAIDA GWAII TOILET

Haida Gwaii, formerly the Queen Charlotte Islands, is one of the most fascinating places on Earth. Its remoteness and beauty make it so.

With that kind of attractiveness, I and several family members have made three trips to the southern half, Moresby Island.

In all cases, we flew into Sandspit. From there we arranged an inflatable boat passage south to Juan Perez Sound. There we were outfitted with ocean-going kayaks.

Our plans always consisted of touring for seven days.

On one of these occasions, we arranged to be picked up on day four. We intended to visit Ninstints on Anthony Island. This World Heritage Site is located at the southernmost point of Haida Gwaii.

What makes it a historical gem is the fact that the location represents the advanced civilization of a First Nations people. The site today consists of a deteriorated village and its famous mortuary poles.

Haida Watchmen are assigned to oversee and protect various historical assets.

When Sue and I visited Ninstints, the Haida provided an informative tour. In addition, we were welcomed into their place of residence. As we surveyed artefacts and Haida art, the question of bathroom facilities came up. "Where do we go?" None could be seen to exist in their building.

We were kindly pointed in the direction of a path. This one-hundred-metre trail meandered through untypical West Coast foliage. Trees were considerably shorter on this rocky outcrop.

When we reached the designated toilet, we were both amused and shocked.

It could be best described as a partially completed open-air outhouse with a seat suspended over a crevice in a rock formation. Looking down, the drop to the ocean floor was a death-defying seventy feet.

This was the extent of their sewage system. It's the most memorable one I've experienced.

PICKLED PEPPERS

John Niechoda, a friend, was a man of many interests and talents.

Amongst his many interests were his love of food and food preparation. During one of the summers that I was employed with John, he grew hot peppers. These weren't ordinary hot peppers. They were derived from seeds of Polish origin.

In addition, John pickled them. This increased their potency exponentially. On the two or three occasions that I tried his pickled peppers, I suffered an instantaneous reaction.

Just one bite and swallow would cause my scalp to rise from my skeleton—all within one second from ingestion.

I am not exaggerating the situation. Nothing compared to its intense effect then and now.

With this in mind, I allowed some of these peppers to dry for a few months. I decided to use them in a pasta sauce.

My daughters, ages nine and six, were my dinner guests. In the preparation, I was chopping the peppers into very thin slices. It was at this point that Katie and Emma curiously asked, "What's that, Dad?"

"Hot peppers," I replied.

"Can we taste one?" they enquired.

Knowing that they were exceedingly potent, I decided to let them just lick the residue on my fingers. When both were given the opportunity, they immediately exclaimed, "Dad, you're trying to murder us!"

Sadly, after a two-year production, John misplaced the seeds. We were never to have the opportunity to savour the delight of that most intense sensory experience again.

POWER OF PRAISE

It's amazing what a compliment can achieve. In one case it led to my marriage. In fact, it was my second marriage.

I was shopping for produce, and so was an acquaintance from the past. We engaged in a conversation.

I had previously known that she had divorced, but it did not enter our discussion. My situation was identical. That did surface in our talk either.

The conversation ended abruptly, shortly after she paid me the following compliment: "You're looking very good."

Sensing this was a sincere reflection of her opinion I countered with, "We'll have to get together for a coffee."

She seemed to recoil in response. "I think I've got to go," she replied.

At the same time, she rejoined her friend and disappeared.

I did follow through and arrange a coffee date. Our discussion dealt with each other's children and catching up on past events in our lives. But no sparks evolved. And no further plans were made.

Having learned that Sue was in the process of moving and planning a house renovation, I decided to delay any further contact. When I did contact her three months later, she was surprised. She had thought that I was disinterested in her.

The call materialized into a date, which eventually snowballed into further dates.

Six years later we were married. All six of our children participated in the wedding party. We were praised as "soul mates."

And it most likely would have never materialized if not for Sue's initial compliment.

WHERE'S BRITAIN?

Climbing aboard a flight from Amsterdam to London, I expected the event to be of short duration. After all, it is a relatively short distance. At least that was my impression.

The mid-afternoon journey proved to be pleasant and unremarkable. It was unremarkable because the view was obliterated by giant lofty, billowy clouds. Visibility below the clouds was non-existent. I yearned to see the topography of the English Channel. But to no avail. After what seemed like an unreasonable amount of time, I turned to my seatmate. As a native Brit, I expected he would relieve my curiosity. "Where exactly are the British Isles?" I asked.

"Just look for the biggest cloud. Britain is right below," came his reply.

HASH BROWNIES

Fez, Morocco, offered an unbelievably intriguing culture for me in 1973. I experienced so much in my short nine-day stay, even if it was curtailed by a severe case of dysentery.

Events ranged from butchered meat dripping with blood being loaded onto our bus while entering Morocco to beggars desperately grasping at our bags of food in the streets. Offers were made on two occasions to purchase my girlfriend by "well-meaning businessmen." After all, a Caucasian woman was worth ten camels by the desert Berbers tribes compared to three camels for a Moroccan female.

We were treated to tea and lunch sessions by rug merchants in order to garner our patronage. Befriended by a young Moroccan male, we learned the Islamic custom of multiple marriages. We visited kief dens. We witnessed child exploitation.

A secured campground with a swimming pool cost the equivalent of twenty-five cents per person per day. It was at this campground that we met two young American hippies. They gave us the impression they were travelling together and had been friends for just a brief amount of time.

They inadvertently entertained us with a contentious issue. One had in his possession hash brownies. The other pleaded desperately that the treat should be shared with him. But to no avail. No matter what arguments he used, he couldn't convince the other to divide the brownies.

"But I'm your friend! How could you be so selfish?" he argued.

That was countered with, "They're my brownies. I made them. I'm not going to share them!"

As observers, we were splitting a gut. The scene was reminiscent of two toddlers fighting over a toy. It could easily have been fodder for a Cheech and Chong skit.

Finally, the aggressor changed tactics. "If you won't share the hash brownies with me then why don't you share them with our new friends?" referring to my girlfriend and me.

This provoked serious contemplation on the part of the owner. The argument intensified until the brownie possessor ultimately relented.

"All right, I'll give a brownie to each of you," he remarked.

At the very moment the brownies were handed to us, the pleading individual pounced on the generous friend. "How could you share your brownies with strangers?" he quarrelled. "You have only known them for a few minutes. We've known each other for days, and you won't give me one brownie!"

This ironic dilemma kept us in stitches. It was uncontrollable laughter.

I can't honestly say if any sharing eventually took place between the two. But I think it was due to the mere fact that I can't recall any further dispute.

HIPPIE BANK ROBBERY

In the early seventies in Sudbury, Ontario, a group of hippie pot dealers decided to supplement their finances by holding up a Bank of Montreal branch at a prominent shopping centre. Four Corners was located across the street from a lake on the southwestern outskirts of town.

The well-planned robbery included positioning a motorboat at the lake to use as their getaway vehicle. The daytime raid succeeded. The thieves acquired their desired cash at gunpoint, and they managed to escape using their novel strategy. But somehow, they were eventually apprehended.

It was later that I met one of the conspirators. In an attempt to finance his legal defence, he was selling pot.

The second connection was a lot less obvious. It took a considerable amount of time to decipher.

This same Bank of Montreal branch was the financial institution that I dealt with as well. It was conveniently close to my home.

For at least a year to a year and a half, I sensed an unusual coldness in the service they provided me at that branch. I couldn't understand why I was receiving such unsmiling and perfunctory treatment.

Then the light went on. I was a hippie with long hair. They probably associated me with the hippie bank robbers who had traumatized them. I had been unofficially declared persona non grata by the bank employees

CHRISTMAS GIFTS ON FIRE

Christmas 1958 was quickly approaching. As an eleven-year-old, it was an exciting time in my life.

Two of my friends, Zenon and Joe, lived in separate suites in a four-unit multiplex just four properties from my parents' place. It was commonplace to entertain ourselves at their homes.

It was a Saturday morning, a few weeks in advance of Christmas that Zenon decided to take advantage of his parents' disappearance. We learned that they had left for a shopping trip into downtown Sudbury.

The moment they were out of sight, Zenon notified us that he needed to inspect the Christmas gifts that had already been purchased. They were stored in a closet in their attic suite.

While Zenon vanished upstairs, a small group of friends played in the yard below. It may have been twenty to thirty minutes later that we were alerted to smoke billowing from a roof area of the house. This coincided with Zenon's parents' unit.

The sound of a siren was quickly followed by the arrival of a fire truck.

While the fire was being extinguished, Zenon appeared and explained what had happened.

Because electrical lighting was non-existent in the closet, Zenon decided to make use of matches and a candle to view the presents. In the process, some clothes caught on fire.

Happily, no serious damage occurred. I made my way home before Zenon's mother and father returned. Anticipating what might happen to Zenon, we had no wish to stay.

During the following week, we learned first-hand from Zenon the consequence of his investigative technique. "I'm not getting anything for Christmas this year," he reported.

ATTEMPTED SEXUAL ASSAULT

Traumatic experiences in childhood are deplorable. Those involving sexual assault are especially despicable. In my case, it was an attempted sexual assault.

As a paperboy, it was my duty to not only go door to door to deliver newspapers but to also collect money from those households once a week.

One of my clients lived in an attic suite. Climbing a narrow interior staircase was required to access his apartment.

On no previous occasion did I have a negative incident with this individual. However, the exception came on one occasion when I neared the top of the staircase. I was there to make my weekly collection.

I was met by the occupant, dressed only in his long-john underwear. After asking him for payment, he methodically approached me. Almost within arm's reach, he abruptly lunged for my genitals. Fortunately, being fleet-footed I was able to easily escape.

I honestly can't remember if I received any payments that day. I'm sure the trauma of the event has fogged my memory.

Notwithstanding this fact, I recall continuing to deliver papers to this household, including climbing that interior stairwell. I exercised extreme caution each time, placing confidence in my ability to escape quickly.

Amazingly I never shared this experience with anyone until last year. Exactly fifty-seven years transpired in the interim.

ÑUTTY IDEA

Preceding a typical marriage, a customary engagement usually occurs. As part of this process, an engagement ring becomes a focus.

This was no different for Sue and me. We had the exceptional benefit of a professional jeweller who happened to be a client of mine. Arena was able to provide very competitive pricing by keeping her overhead down. She worked out of her condo suite.

We arranged to meet her so Sue could personally choose a design for her ring. Once done, Arena indicated a two-week production period.

When I was contacted for the pickup, I decided to surprise Sue rather than just notify her of its completion. I brought it home prior to her return from work.

I decided to make her hunt for the engagement ring. It was hidden in our second-floor walk-in closet. I created a path of in-the-shell hazelnuts. It began at the bottom of our curved staircase, climbed the staircase, across the upper hallway, into our master bedroom, through the bedroom, into the master ensuite, through the ensuite, reversing back into the bedroom, through the bedroom, and ending at the hidden location in the walk-in closet. The filberts were spaced about a foot apart.

When Sue arrived home, she quickly noticed the unusual layout of the nuts. "What's going on?" she asked.

"Just follow the nuts," I insisted. So, she did.

I followed her as she crawled along the carpet, seemingly amused by the extraordinary situation. When Sue finally arrived at the end of the hazelnut line, she had difficulty finding the treasure. I intervened to help her. Her discovery very much pleased her although she was certainly aware of its anticipated delivery.

It was a matter of a week or two that the full account of this story was related to a gathering of her four adult children. When one of them, Jennifer, asked, "What made you think of doing that?"

I replied, "It was only a nutty idea."

So much for a witty attempt.

YOU WOULDN'T BELIEVE

Hiring university students every summer was a regular part of my painting contracting business.

Over the years my own daughters and two of my stepsons became employed in this capacity.

During one of those summers, my daughter Emma and stepson Chris worked together as part of my painting crew. This occurred during my formative years of establishing a relationship with Chris's mother, Sue.

We lived together in Sue's family home with all four of her children ranging from fourteen to twenty-three in age. It just happened that Chris and his brother Michael shared a bunk bed in a ground-floor bedroom, directly below their mother's.

On occasion, this made them privy to whatever sounds were generated from above.

This was alluded to by Chris on one job site. He and Emma were painting together in a section of a house within hearing distance of me.

I was pleased to listen to their convivial conversation. It reflected a compatible relationship within a blended family.

However, I was taken aback when I heard Chris mention, "I sleep directly below my mother and your father, and you wouldn't believe the sounds I hear."

I heard Emma at first gasp in astonishment and then burst out laughing.

She countered with, "That's too much information. I don't want to hear more."

I assumed that they did not know of my proximity. It was a revealing moment for my daughter as well as me. I discreetly muffled my laughter.

Knowing that Chris was comfortable enough to tolerate me in the circumstance described was a satisfying realization of my acceptance into the family.

BIZARRE FELLOW TRAVELLER

At one point in June 1973, my girlfriend and I were in front of the American Express office in Barcelona. We were searching for a ride north to Amsterdam.

After a brief time, we were successful. We made a connection with people travelling north in a van. They were willing to make space for us for a reasonable amount of money. At four o'clock, we were to meet back at the American Express office for our departure.

While milling about at this location, I noticed a most unusual character. He too was walking back and forth. His appearance was somewhat gaudy—yellow and green hand-painted shoes for one. He was also considerably older than the rest of us.

When we returned at the appointed time and began to load into the van, this same individual climbed in as well with his dog in tow. With a total of seven or eight passengers, my girlfriend and I ended up at the rear of the van directly across from the strange man.

The trip to Amsterdam took approximately fourteen hours. It was nonstop. During that time, we discovered many disconcerting facts about this Australian travelling companion.

He laughed repeatedly in the manner of a laughing hyena. He alternated between eating food and picking ticks out of his dog's fur. He would crush the ticks between his fingers and then go back to eating with the same hand.

My girlfriend was revolted by his behaviour. She moved as far away as possible. Our proximity to this man and his dog tested our tolerance to the limit. It was a situation that we wished never to repeat.

MANAGER OF MY UNIVERSE

After establishing a relationship with my second wife, Sue, over several years, I became aware of many of her wonderful qualities. Not all were apparent at the outset of our courtship. It takes time to develop knowledge of one's partner.

One of these qualities was her organizational skill: specifically, her ability to manage many aspects of my life. She often made recommendations that became an asset to my personal and business decisions. In fact, Sue had a particular talent in financial matters that proved beneficial.

Consequently, I began to compliment her as the "manager of my universe." From time to time, I would share this opinion with others. In many cases, my intent was to amuse but the fact remained true.

While working one day for a friend mutual to Sue and me, this fact was shared with her. Besides being amused, she offered the following advice: "When you return home tonight and Sue does as well tell her that you are the centre of the universe."

I took this under good advice.

I arrived home first. When Sue walked through the door, I immediately related the conversation I had had with Myra. Then I shared her suggestion, alluding to the fact that I should be considered the "centre of the universe."

My intent in sharing the opinion was twofold: one, to test Sue's reaction and two, to see if it would create any preferential treatment for me.

Not to my surprise, the latter proved to be erroneous, and the former drew a hearty laugh.

So much for the experiment.

SMOKING AT AGE FOUR

It may be difficult to believe that a child of four could become addicted to smoking. But it is true.

To the discredit of my father, he encouraged my younger sister Margaret to begin smoking at that age. I and my other three siblings were spared his ill-intentioned influence.

Margaret was allowed to share cigarettes with my father. He encouraged her. And we still have actual proof in the form of photographs taken at the time. In these captured moments, Margaret is riding her tricycle with either a lit cigarette in her mouth or a cigarette butt.

I can vividly remember her on many occasions dismounting her tricycle, picking up a butt, placing it between her lips, jumping back on her bike, and pedalling away. Everyone found Margaret's habit quite amusing. Her reputation preceded her.

Friends and family became quite aware of this endearing little girl.

When a visiting family friend discovered this fact, he promised to cure her there and then. As a cigar smoker, he lit one up and shared it with her. After finishing the first one. a second cigar was started. During this session, Margaret became violently ill. She was nine at the time.

It worked. Margaret was cured until the age of twelve when she took up the habit again. It continued into her early fifties after many futile attempts at quitting.

It is to her credit that Margaret was finally able to rid herself of her nicotine addiction. Unfortunately, what we know today about the ill effects of cigarette smoking had little bearing on the novelty of enticing a young girl to take up the habit.

DESIRABLE ÑANNY

This story originates with my stepson Chris, his wife Jodi, and one son.

Over a family Easter dinner, our daughter-in-law Jodi related a recent development in their nanny situation.

After a successful two to three years with Chris and Jodi's children, their nanny decided she needed a change, so she was moving on. My stepson and his wife made an intense effort to find a replacement that would be satisfactory to all concerned—the two sons, mother, father and of course the nanny. Everyone's work or school schedules needed to be accommodated.

Their recruiting endeavour paid off when they found a university student with great qualifications who came highly recommended.

At the conclusion of the nanny's first day, Jodi returned home first. After relieving the nanny from her duties, she questioned her two sons as to how the day went with their new nanny. Everything was positive. However, Oliver, age five, added his commentary. "I think Daddy should marry her." Jodi was taken aback.

"But what will happen to me?" she asked.

Oliver quickly responded, "You can move somewhere else." Again, Jodi was shocked to hear these words emanating from a five-year-old. Just what motivated his thinking process?

Fortunately, Jodi had a good sense of humour about it.

To the best of my knowledge, no untoward developments have occurred since.

FARMING AT ITS LAZIEST

In the summer of 1975, I volunteered a week of my summer vacation to work on a farm belonging to my fiancée's uncle on Manitoulin Island in Ontario.

I thought it would be an excellent refresher course, an opportunity to help, and a chance to get to know my future in-laws. Little did I know the circumstances related to the operation of this farm.

As it was a dairy farm, I expected I would be given a wealth of milking-related responsibilities, starting my day before sunrise and ending at dinner time. This proved to be untrue.

For a start, this farm had only a cream quota. The milk portion could not be shipped nor sold. This substantially reduced the workload.

My first day was somewhat typical: early morning milking with chores after breakfast. This was followed by a round of checking the fencing with my soon-to-be cousin. The remainder of my day and week proved to be extremely idle.

My typical day began around eight o'clock with the morning milking, then an extended breakfast. After a brief barn visit, everyone retired to the house for extended TV viewing.

A prerequisite vegetable garden was non-existent. There was a complete lack of motivation to cultivate one despite the fertile soil on which they lived.

And the pièce de résistance was when a sudden rainstorm occurred. The cousin announced that water was leaking through the ceiling in his bedroom. He quickly rounded up a pail to collect the drips.

"How long has there been a hole in the roof?" I asked.

"Seven years," he replied.

I was flabbergasted by his answer and the situation on this farm. I chalked up that week as a complete waste of time.

FISHING WITH TWINKIES

In the summer of 1985, Harry, a friend and commercial fisherman, asked if I would be interested in joining him on a salmon fishing outing. He needed a deckhand on his gillnetter. As I was between jobs, I gladly accepted. The anticipated experience thrilled me.

The destination was the Strait of Juan de Fuca. We would go during the brief sockeye opening allowed by the Department of Fisheries and Oceans.

In addition to preparing the boat and fishing gear, Harry purchased groceries. I was to be the cook. The expected outing was to be three days.

Once all was ready, off we sailed for the Strait.

During the expedition, I quickly learned and realized the extent of Harry's consumption habits. He was a smoker, bordering on chain smoking. This was accompanied by a constant need for coffee. Both routines convinced me that Harry should be counteracting his intake with wholesome food.

I was willing to prepare sandwiches, pasta, vegetables, and anything that may be nutritionally beneficial. On the first occasion, Harry replied, "I'll have a Twinkie."

Not having previous knowledge of what a Twinkie was, I searched for one in the hold. Sure enough, I found a package of them.

I passed the offending junk food to Harry. I couldn't believe this was his first choice over the other food items he had purchased.

This scenario was repeated throughout the remainder of the trip. Cigarettes, coffee, and Twinkies were Harry's mainstay.

Although I prepared hot meals for myself, I can't remember him ever partaking.

The whole experience amazed me. I couldn't believe someone would abuse himself to the extent that Harry did on that fishing outing.

THE CAT CAME BACK

As former Manitobans, my parents frequently returned there from their adopted home of Sudbury, Ontario. As children, my siblings and I would make the trek with them.

For one such trip, our family cat was left in the care of our neighbours.

Upon our return two weeks later, we discovered that our cat had disappeared. It was nowhere to be found. As kids, we were devastated. We were attached to it as any child would be. Our parents explained that the cat must have gotten lost and possibly been adopted by someone else.

Out of sight and out of mind described the situation as time passed until that September when the cat suddenly arrived. Our "cat came back" and we were elated. But how could this happen? It had been two months. As far as we were concerned it was a miracle.

As children, we had many questions. Finally, the truth was revealed.

Our parents admitted they had no longer wanted to have the cat, so it had been given to our neighbours to be disposed of. They placed the cat in the trunk of their car on a trip to Espanola, a town forty-five miles due west of Sudbury. There it was released.

Our cat managed to make its way back over a period of two months. It was an amazing feat as far as we were concerned.

I can't remember if we forgave our parents, but more importantly, did the cat forgive them?

TOPPLING RCMP HORSES

I was visiting my good friend Dave Tolonen, aka Bucky. At the time, he was living in Cranbrook, British Columbia. On his suggestion, we decided to take a short drive up the highway to Invermere. Bucky painted a picture of Invermere as an interesting, quaint town to visit as it catered to tourists.

After viewing some of the sights, we stepped into one of the gift shops. The typical Canadiana souvenirs, those appealing to out-of-country clientele, were ubiquitous.

As I was passing through the aisles, I came across a display of plastic horses, each mounted by an RCMP officer. It was a replica of the famous RCMP Musical Ride. Each figurine was about ten inches tall by twelve inches long. I was intrigued. Picking up one, I analysed it before setting it down on its glass display.

It immediately toppled into the adjacent one, triggering a domino effect. I felt compelled to place them upright again. In my first attempt, I may have stood two or three of them up before they all tumbled like dominoes again.

The problem quickly became apparent. These cheaply made horses were incredibly unstable. Each horse stood on three legs only—one was raised. It took a great deal of my concentration to get each figurine to balance.

By the time I began my second attempt to stand them up, Bucky, observing from a safe distance, was completely in stitches. I begged him to come over to help, but he absolutely refused. His laughter became contagious. I began to laugh uncontrollably. This deteriorated my ability to concentrate on the task at hand. No matter how much effort was expended on my part, I was unable to get the complete set to stand.

Bucky must have laughed hysterically for at least five minutes. I abandoned the display as we both exited the premises unable to contain ourselves.

ALCOHOLIC TRICKSTER

As senior high school students in early spring 1967, my friend Myron and I decided to skip school one day to raise some spending money. Our plan was to spend spring break in Toronto.

We set out early on a cold March morning to the local "Temporary Employment Office." There we discovered a whole new world.

The office was filled with homeless men who had been sent out of the nearby Salvation Army shelter until evening. These men fit into two categories: those who were unemployable but needed a place to keep warm and those who needed employment to fund their addictions.

The office operated on a first-come-first-served basis. When you entered you would register and be put on a waiting list. As calls came in, usually for mere hours of employment, men would be sent out as required.

As we patiently waited for our turn for a work call, Myron and I overheard several overwhelming stories. In one case, ink and aftershave lotion were being consumed by some of these desperate men as a substitute for alcohol.

But the most amazing account was provided by a man who was obviously bright but had fallen on hard times. He indicated that he had previously been in a similar employment office in Toronto. When he entered the second-floor establishment, he became aware of the fact there were around fifty men ahead of him. His chances of getting employment that day seemed remote. It was first-come-first-served.

But he had a trick up his sleeve. He exited the office onto the street and went around the corner to a phone booth. He made a call to the same office impersonating a hiring officer for the Dominion Glass Company, which happened to be on the other side of town.

"How many men do you have available?" he asked.

"Fifty," came the reply.

"Good," he said. "Can you send them out as soon as possible?"

This scammer said he waited patiently as fifty men streamed downstairs and out onto the street. As soon as they disappeared, he quickly returned to the hiring office to register as first in line.

Although Myron and I did succeed in being hired, the experience paled in comparison to the mind-boggling events overheard by us that day.

LAUNDRY TO PETRO-CANADA

Having a cabin to go to on the Sunshine Coast was a treasured experience. Sue had been doing it for decades in her previous marriage. Now that I was in the picture, I was introduced to the same rewarding practice.

The ritual was to travel to the cabin on Friday after work or early Saturday morning. Typically, we would catch the ferry and return on Sunday evening.

On one of these return trips, we stopped at a Petro-Canada station in West Vancouver. After fuelling up, Sue suggested we throw out the small amount of garbage we had. I promptly deposited the white plastic bag into the nearby waste receptacle.

We continued on our way, arriving home less than an hour later. Once there we unloaded our vehicle of food and clothing. In the process, we opened the other white plastic bag that contained our soiled clothing. To our shock, this bag contained our garbage. We had mistakenly dropped off our laundry at Petro-Canada instead of the garbage.

We immediately phoned the gas station attendant and explained our folly. We asked if he would check the garbage receptacle for us. Fortunately, he found and retrieved it. We arranged to pick up our laundry the following Wednesday.

To this day we continue to travel to and from the cabin on the Sunshine Coast, and in the process, we pass through West Vancouver. From time to time when the same Petro-Canada station comes into view, I will turn to Sue and ask, "Do we have any laundry to deposit today?"

SIX FOOT SEVEN IN A NIGHTIE

First told by Claire, this story was later corroborated by her brother, the protagonist.

The event took place in late November. Ross and his wife Vickie, who resided in a bungalow, were sleeping at the time. Their bedroom was located on the main floor, closest to the front door entrance.

Unbeknownst to them, the front door had blown open sometime in the early hours of the morning. Their shut bedroom door prevented their awareness of the situation.

When the paper boy arrived to deliver the morning newspaper, he discovered the open front entrance. He called out to see if anyone was home but got no response. Being highly concerned about this unusual situation, he managed to locate a phone and dial 911.

Two police officers were dispatched to the address. Upon their arrival, they proceeded cautiously to the open front entrance.

Anything was possible. There could have been a break-in. There could have been an assault on the occupants. The residents might be hostages in a botched robbery attempt.

Before entering, the police tried to determine if anyone was present. Their loud voices finally awakened Ross and his wife.

Ross, who had slept naked, quickly grabbed Vickie's nightie and wrapped it around his waist.

What made this scene completely preposterous was the fact that Ross stood six foot seven inches tall. Not only could his size be intimidating, but Ross was an exceptionally fit human specimen. As an avid outdoorsman, he hunted by bow and arrow. By day he worked physically as a BC Hydro linesman.

So, there was Ross covered only in a nightie, opening his bedroom door to determine what was the matter. There he met the two police officers who in turn were confronted by this giant of a man dressed ridiculously in next to nothing.

When Ross did recount this tale to me, he explained that he had recently installed new weather stripping in the front door jamb. As a consequence, the door had not been closed properly that eventful night. In conjunction with a strong wind, it precipitated an unforgettably hilarious affair.

HEAD TO TOE IN LILAC

Although I didn't live on campus, occasionally I would take "advantage" of the university cafeteria food. Its reasonable price was countered by the questionable nutritional composition of the prepared food.

In one of my weaker moments, I decided to have Sunday dinner at the cafeteria.

I remember being in the assembly lineup with a hundred or so other students. We made our decisions based on the menu choices for that day. With trays filled, we proceeded to the dining area.

Shortly after sitting down to eat, our collective attention was drawn to one student. He entered the room walking quite deliberately, but his appearance and behaviour were what captivated us.

He was dressed head to toe in one colour. His t-shirt, jeans, socks and running shoes were all lilac. It was as if his entire wardrobe had been washed together with a purple colour bleeding throughout.

But what really boggled our minds was his colour-matching German WWII helmet.

He continued to mesmerize us as he sat down with his tray of food. Once seated, he removed his helmet and placed it upside down on the table. He then scraped his plate of food into his headgear, completing the process by pouring a glass of milk over the top.

Those present including myself were completely flabbergasted. We were all in stitches.

His behaviour was bizarre. At the time I assumed he was drunk. But this may not have been the case. A typical display of drunken rowdiness was not evident. Everything he did was done in a very quiet and subdued manner. He kept to himself and didn't converse with anyone else present.

It certainly was a most amusing mealtime.

FLYING PORRIDGE

Porridge has been my breakfast mainstay for literally decades. For many of those years, I consumed it 350 days a year.

In more recent years, I would soak my special concoction overnight in enough water to help reduce the cooking time. This porridge consisted of slow-cooking oats, a mixture of nine cracked grains, ground flax seeds, and whole chia and sunflower seeds.

And so, this breakfast tradition continued when Sue and I were touring New Zealand and Australia by campervan in 2013.

The porridge mixture on one day was soaking in a cooking pot, stored in an overhead compartment at the rear of the van. I felt secure with it there as we drove along the highway before breakfast. A manual lock prevented the compartment door from opening. Or so I thought.

Before we reached a suitable location to cook breakfast, a highway incident caused me to slam the brakes. Instantaneously, the overhead cubicle door cracked open.

The saucepan with its contents shot across the length of the van. Spillage was everywhere: seat cushions, floor carpet and furnishings.

Our hearts sank immediately realizing the work that would be required to clean it up. It was one of those moments when you just want to throw up your arms in surrender and shout, "I give up!"

LACTOSE INTOLERANCE

While spending fifty-one days on the road in Canada's far North, Sue and I encountered our fair share of mosquito-infested areas.

Our itinerary included Central and Northern British Columbia, the Yukon, Alaska, the Northwest Territories, and Alberta. In some of these locations, we were terrorized by mosquitos.

Despite applying insect repellent and eventually donning netted head coverings, the pesky critters seemed to defy our defences. This was more so the case at night inside our campervan. As we attempted to fall asleep the constant buzzing of these infiltrators drove us crazy. No matter how many we eliminated with our constant swatting, there would always remain one or two to exacerbate the situation.

We were on guard, night and day.

At one point we were eating lunch inside the van. As I looked over towards Sue, I noticed a mosquito on her left wrist. Without hesitating, I slapped at the insect. In the process, the cup of milk in that same hand flew across her body splattering her and the door window on the opposite side.

Milk was everywhere. Sue was not a "happy camper" with me. And what made the situation even worse was her discovery that the milk stains on her pedal pushers could not be removed.

Obviously, this was a case of her clothing demonstrating "lactose intolerance."

FIND SOMEONE BETTER

An interesting development took place within two years of my marital separation from my first wife, Margaret.

As part of my new career, I was sent to London, Ontario. A two-week training session was a prerequisite prior to being immersed in the work program.

London also happened to be the home of my wife's favourite aunt, also named Margaret.

I was contacted by Aunt Margaret and invited out to a Sunday lunch. I was quite surprised since my marriage had ended quite acrimoniously.

Why would I be offered this invitation? Despite my apprehension, I was pleasantly reassured of her noble intentions.

Besides the usual pleasantries, Aunt Margaret did ask some prying personal questions. The one that I recall the most was, "Are you seeing anyone?"

"No," I replied. "I'm really not interested in a relationship at the moment."

I was taken aback when she countered with, "I hope you find someone better than Margaret."

"Would you care to elaborate?" was my response.

"No," came her reply. The topic was pursued no further.

It was an interesting revelation to hear someone who was considered the "favourite aunt" of my former wife indicate a smidgeon of contempt for her niece.

As an afterthought, if my ex ever got wind of this story, I'm sure she would fly into a rage denying that this could ever have possibly been true.

HOLY MACARONI

During a family Christmas Eve gathering, our grandson Matthew perked our interest with his latest high-school experience.

Matthew, as it turned out, was involved in a cooking course. He shared his most recent experience in preparing a creative version of cooking macaroni.

His creation involved baking a potato, then scooping out the contents and inserting a scoop of cooked macaroni and cheese. It was obvious to us that Matthew took great pride in his accomplishment.

At this point, my curiosity was aroused as to how well he scored with his endeavour. "Matthew," I asked, "did you 'pas ta' test?"

WE LISTEN

A close friend of Sue's hosts an annual post-New Year's open house for a great number of friends and neighbours. As a rule, we attend if we are in the vicinity.

I am much more of a stranger at the gathering compared to Sue. She once lived in the neighbourhood.

On one occasion I was introduced to a gentleman who happened to be an architect. We engaged in a very revealing conversation about the field of architecture.

During the previous year, he had been hired to problem-solve for the Architectural Institute of British Columbia (AIBC). It seemed that the reputation of architects had fallen into disrepute. The reason: "They didn't listen."

Architects were becoming notorious for ignoring their clients' wishes. Despite the obligatory consultations between the two parties, eventual decisions favoured the professional advisor. Clients were becoming disenchanted.

This is where my newfound friend came in. He was contracted to analyse the predicament and advise as to how to reverse the negative impression.

I can't recall if he shared the actual recommendations that he provided to the association. But I remember the gist of what he said: "Listen and incorporate the wishes of the client. Don't ignore them."

When an eventual decision was implemented by the Architects Association, my friend threw up his arms in disgust; AIBC hadn't even listened to the advice provided by one of their own.

ULTIMATE WATER FIGHT

On a beautiful fall afternoon, we organized a co-ed football game on the University of Waterloo campus.

We played the match on a grassy flat area alongside a stream. Rising immediately above us was an extensive series of grassy knolls. And beyond this several student dormitories spread over a distance of a few hundred metres.

The distance from the dorms to our makeshift football field was about a hundred metres with an elevation drop of approximately ten metres.

This Sunday setting was rather peaceful, or so we thought.

During our touch football game, our attention was captured by an episode of water warfare. We witnessed a large contingent of students from one dorm attacking a group from another dorm. The attackers were armed with plastic dorm waste bins filled with water. They ran from their home base over to the defenders' building. But the defenders were equipped with identical containers full of water.

Once the attackers emptied their containers, they retreated to their residences. They were immediately followed in hot pursuit by their combatants. Once they released their weaponry, they too returned to their defences.

Below we were mesmerized by the goings-on. Our game was pleasantly interrupted as we erupted in laughter.

With a lull in the proceedings, we resumed our football competition. But it wasn't long before our game was disrupted by a second attack being mounted by the original perpetrators.

Once again, they came running across the grassy knoll with water bins in hand. However, the defenders were better prepared this time. Fire hoses had been unravelled and dragged outside to counter. It was a hilarious scene. High-pressure water versus hand-thrown water. The defenders had the advantage.

It was spontaneous entertainment at its best. Once the standoff extinguished itself and rumours of campus police circulated, we resumed play.

It wasn't long before we witnessed an army of students descending on us. They were running towards us with water-filled waste bins. We were completely taken by surprise. There was no time to evade them. We were outnumbered and defenceless. I tried. But it was fruitless.

We ended up in the stream. I spotted a smaller male attacker and grabbed him by the collar. The only satisfaction I gained was dragging him into the stream. I was successful.

Our football game had disintegrated into chaos with every member completely soaked. We were never to meet again.

SPARE TIRE IN DETROIT

My friend Grant MacKinnon and I made an extensive two-week trip to Southern Ontario and parts of the Northern US in the summer of 1969.

The opportunity arose due to a strike with our employer at the time. So, we jumped in my Volkswagen bug and headed south from Sudbury.

Our first stop was Toronto, then Hamilton, Windsor, Detroit, Rochester, and eventually home.

Detroit became a destination because Grant had an uncle living in nearby Dearborn, Michigan. We spent the first night with them before venturing into Detroit. Attending a Detroit Tigers afternoon baseball game was our goal.

At that time, Detroit had a notorious reputation as the "murder capital of the USA." Grant's uncle and aunt were so fearful that they hadn't been in Detroit for the previous three years.

When we did drive into town for the baseball game, outdoor parking was available near the stadium. Our first major league game proved to be memorable. The winning Detroit pitcher happened to be Denny McLain. For that season he became the winningest pitcher with thirty-one wins.

When we returned to my vehicle after the game, I remarked to Grant that I was concerned that we didn't have a spare tire. Considering the additional distance that we planned to travel, I felt we needed a spare.

Looking around in the parking lot, I could see the potential of stealing one from another Volkswagen Beetle. It would make me feel more secure having that spare. All that was required was a quick jacking up of the rear end, removing the nuts, and loading up the tire.

When I put this brain scheme to Grant, he was absolutely horrified. He would have nothing to do with it. After all, we were in the heart of the "US murder capital."

It was his trepidation that convinced me to reconsider my plot. We exited that parking lot without attempting the unthinkable.

It may have saved our very own lives.

UPHILL SKIING DISASTER

Suddenly at the age of twelve, I decided I wanted to ski.

Somehow, I convinced my parents to provide the skis and boots through the auspices of Santa Claus. It was Christmas 1961. Despite my request for a set of downhill skis, I was surprised to find them under the tree. Money for my family was always a dilemma.

Although I was extremely pleased, I could not utilize them immediately. The harness came unattached. It needed to be installed and fitted to my ski-boot size.

Fortunately, my good friend Paul Quenneville had older siblings who had the ability to perform the task.

When the mission was accomplished, I took my virgin skis to the closest downhill location: Ramsey Lake Park. The ski run could be best described as a bunny hill. A rope tow no more than thirty metres in length acted as our means to ascend the gentle slope.

This would be my first actual attempt at the sport. I had no previous experience.

Everything was new to me including rope tow etiquette. I lined up for the lift, waiting my turn. The process was to grab the rope when no one was ahead of you.

If I recall correctly, my first one or two ascents were quite successful. The downhill segments were more of a challenge. I know that I fell but the gentleness of the slope negated any serious consequences.

It was on my third attempt at the rope tow that I failed miserably. As I was waiting for my turn to grab the rope, the two people in front of me were in limbo. They simply were not in a hurry to take their go round.

As I waited, I became increasingly impatient. Finally, without due consideration, I seized the rope. It immediately lurched me forward. I crashed through the two offending skiers. As our bodies collided, my skis ripped across and under the other skis.

When I finally released my grip on the rope, the scene was a disaster. All my bindings were completely ripped from their foundation. Screws had popped out, leaving gaping holes.

But more devastating was my pride. I was embarrassed to the nth degree. I gathered all my belongings to vacate as quickly as possible.

Now I had to deal with the quandary of hiding the damage from my parents. I surreptitiously brought them into the basement of the house and placed them out of sight.

At my first opportunity, I contacted my friend Paul who in turn had his older brother reattach my bindings to the skis. Only then did I breathe a sigh of relief.

SYDNEY OPERA HOUSE

After touring the Southeast Coast of Australia for ten days, Sue and I arrived in Sydney. Travelling by campervan, we set our GPS for the famous opera house.

Being a Saturday, we decided to pull right up to the scenic building. We intended to see what performances were taking place that evening. In addition, viewing the sight was a high priority for us.

With our high-top vehicle, access to the actual structure was prohibited by security. However, Sue pleaded that we had just arrived from Canada and needed to check the entertainment. The guard kindly radioed ahead and authorized us to proceed to a parking spot just outside the magnificent staircase leading up to the entrance.

When we reached the box office, we learned that the ballet Don Quixote was being performed that evening. Tickets for two were available at CAD 330.00. The price came as a shock since we had been travelling on a cost-conscious budget.

Sue looked at me with a quizzical look. "What do you think?" she asked.

Completely cognisant of this once-in-a-lifetime opportunity, I responded, "Let's do it."

Once the fee was processed, we drove up the street four blocks away and began our dinner preparation. Here we were camping and eating on the street a mere six hundred metres from an iconic edifice.

Once our meal was completed, we sponge-bathed, changed into our best casual clothes and walked to the opera house. With time on our hands, we toured the exterior perimeter of the building under the darkened sky. We clicked our cameras incessantly to record the extraordinary beauty. We continued the process upon entering the building.

Although the ballet performance was the highlight of the evening, a coincidental meeting with a transplanted Canadian proved to be quite amusing.

As a gentleman excused himself as he threaded his way past us in our seated positions in advance of the show, we learned of each other's Winnipeg roots. This common bond precipitated a lively discussion prior to the opening act.

It continued during the intermission. Hockey, weather, and Winnipeg were the subjects bantered about. We hit it off. A great deal of laughter ensued.

I used my usual commentary when dealing with a fellow Winnipegger: "If you know the book titled *Men are from Mars, Women are from Venus*, I'm planning to write a sequel titled *Men are from Mars, Women are from Venus, and I'm from Winnipeg.*

My brief encounter with this individual proved to be mutually entertaining.

It ended with us meeting him on the street following the ballet. We passed him as he sat on a sidewalk bench. Strangely, a hockey stick was dangling from his hands. Why there and why then were questions left unanswered.

IT VOICE ACTIVATION

While vacationing on the Big Island, Hawaii, Sue and I satisfied our craving for Canadian news updates by going on the web. We specifically sourced the CBC site.

Sue became exceptionally excited by one news item she read within a few days of our arrival. The feature dealt with the latest developments in IT voice activation.

In the process of witnessing her enthusiasm, I remarked, "Why are you getting so excited? You've been voice-activating me ever since we met."

STALKING GEORGE

George, a neighbour of ours, became a source of increasing conflict over the years. His habit of walking his dog off-leash in defiance of the existing by-law proved to be the irritant.

As runners on the Richmond West Dyke, our paths were often impeded by George's free-running dog. The straw that finally broke the camel's back came in January 2011.

On that occasion, one of his two off-leash dogs ventured onto our property. When I investigated the situation, the mutt mounted an aggressive barking challenge towards me. George continued his walk oblivious to his dog's action.

This incident was the first of a handful of formal complaints I lodged with the Supervisor of Animal Control up to 2014. On each occasion, George was visited by a bylaw officer. For each subsequent period, George would comply for a brief period. His dog would be leashed and then allowed to run free again. Not only did this create a conflict when we met on the dyke, but George would also impart bullying language in our direction.

With consistent defiance by George to obey the on-leash regulation, the Animal Control Supervisor recommended that I take photos. The request was easily achieved.

Shortly after the photos were provided, we learned that George had been fined for the first time. This brought out the worst in him. As a result, he contacted the RCMP and claimed that I was "stalking him." If it were not so serious it would be completely laughable—a desperate attempt on his part.

Upon investigation, an officer interviewed me about the allegation. I had the supervisor's email recommending I take photos. It corroborated my actions.

The police officer's conclusion was to notify George to obey the bylaw. I was advised to avoid him as much as possible. But living within six houses of each other makes the recommendation difficult.

Consequently, George scowls and offers his middle finger at every opportunity as I drive by his property.

DARING DWAYNE

I don't know exactly why Dwayne Brown and I didn't get along, but it was a fact. As twelve- or thirteen-year-olds, we didn't see eye to eye.

The first and possibly only confrontation that remains in my memory took place on Morris St., Sudbury, Ontario.

I happened to be across the road from our house playing directly in front of Uncle Paul's house. It was there that Dwayne confronted me as he was walking in the direction of his home.

For some inexplicable reason, he stopped. An argument ensued. Dwayne picked up a rock and threatened to throw it at me. As he wound up, I decided to mount a strategy. With Uncle Paul's car parked in the front yard, I would use it as a decoy. I placed myself at the rear of the car alongside the bumper. My plan was to taunt Dwayne. If he dared to heave the rock at me, I would duck. The rock would then hit Uncle Paul's vehicle. I would then run into my uncle's house and report the damage and exactly who the culprit was. I knew exactly where Dwayne lived.

The give and take continued. Dwayne was positioned on the street no more than two to three metres away from me. I would goad him to throw the rock and he would wind up as if flinging it. Sure enough, after three or four feigned attempts Dwayne let go of his missile.

I ducked successfully and the rock sailed over my body, directly impacting the rear window. The sound of broken glass sent Dwayne and me in opposite directions.

Dwayne ran home and I ran to tell Uncle Paul.

"Uncle Paul," I reported, "someone threw a rock and broke the rear window of your car."

"Do you know who did it?" he asked.

"Yes! It was Dwayne Brown and I know where he lives."

I then led Uncle Paul down the street three blocks and pointed out the house. I disappeared as he proceeded to knock on the door.

It was the next day that I learned that Dwayne had admitted his guilt. His father offered to pay the cost of the repair. And I managed to survive unscathed.

That wasn't the only run-in I had with Dwayne.

On a few occasions, Dwayne had bragged that he had a colour TV. In the era of 1959–60, this was unheard of. We considered him to be a liar.

An opportunity arose one day to challenge his bravado. A group of two or three friends and I happened to be passing by his house. Coincidently, Dwayne appeared on his front porch.

"Dwayne," we asked, "can we see your colour television?"

"No, you can't. Besides, there isn't anything in colour right now," he excused.

After a brief period of challenging Dwayne for proof, we walked away convinced that he was a blatant liar.

CANOEING CAPSIZE

It began as an innocent paddle with Sue. Albeit it took two attempts to convince her to join me.

We set off in our canoe from our cabin on the shore of Georgia Straight. We had no destination in mind until ten minutes into the expedition.

"Why don't we paddle to Roberts Creek?" I suggested.

"That's too far," came Sue's reply. It just happened that two of her offspring and their families were vacationing in cabins along the same shoreline. Although we often drove to visit them, travel by water would be much more laborious.

The conditions were ideal. The water was calm and flat, and the early evening summer temperature was ideal. So, Sue gave in to my proposal.

The paddle was physically demanding, more so for her, but we persisted with occasional breaks. As we approached the cabins from two hundred to three hundred metres offshore it was difficult to identify them.

"There they are," commented Sue.

I disagreed. "I don't think that's them." After all, I had better vision when it came to distance. So, we continued our effort for another four hundred metres until we realized we had gone too far.

As we reversed our direction, Sue reprimanded me for my visual impairment.

Our eventual arrival came as a complete surprise to everyone. We hadn't notified them in advance. Besides, it didn't seem credible that two seniors, approaching seventy, would attempt such a journey.

After the canoe was pulled into shore, we spent a few hours socializing. When it came to the return paddle, Sue begged off. Her son Christopher agreed to replace her. I insisted on one condition. He must wear a PFD. Chris was notorious for not wearing a lifejacket when on the water. He agreed to my request.

So, it was just the two of us. "This will be an opportunity to bond together," I observed.

Less than thirty seconds into our departure I realized just how unstable the canoe had become. Two reasons for this were apparent: First, we were in a sitting position rather than a kneeling one. Our centre of gravity was too high. Second, Chris had a hundred-pound advantage over his mother. With the combined disadvantages, each dip of our paddles resulted in a precarious side-to-side rocking motion.

Chris astutely offered his observation. "I think there is a sixty percent chance that we won't make it." However, we persevered all the while experiencing numerous near rollovers.

When we reached the halfway mark, it happened. The canoe spilled over. As we tumbled into the drink, our laughter spontaneously ensued. "There goes the sixty percent," commented Chris.

With the canoe upside down, the two of us in the water, and dusk beginning to overtake us, you would think our survival would be of greatest concern. But it was not.

"Where are my flip-flops and my fishing rod?" was Chris's refrain. Our laughter was incessant. It was only when his missing items were accounted for that we attempted to attend to our predicament. We struggled to right the canoe. Once achieved, bailing out the water came next. Without any container, it proved to be futile.

So, with a waterlogged canoe, we began pulling and hand-paddling to shore. Reality quickly became apparent. Although only fifty metres from shore it would take us forever to get there.

As we struggled in the water, the sight and sound of a motorboat approached. Once it pulled up, we realized how fortunate we were. John, the rescuer, had observed us struggling from his cottage viewpoint. He quickly attached the canoe by rope to the stern. Then Chris and I hauled ourselves into the bowel of the boat.

After a quick trip to shore, the canoe was untied and released to the safety of our rescuer's wife. The vessel was then secured to a buoy offshore. The three of us jumped into a very small rowboat with the owner at the helm. It only took a few strokes before one oar snapped in half. We limped the remaining short distance to shore whereupon John offered his phone to call for assistance in returning to our bases.

Meanwhile, Sue had returned to our cottage awaiting our arrival by water. She was initially shocked to hear my voice on the phone. "Chris and I capsized," I explained. "We've been rescued and are safe. Can you pick us up on the lower road, first driveway on your left past Camp Byng? We'll walk up to the road and wait for you."

The conversation was punctuated with rounds of laughter at our dilemma.

Chris and I must have looked quite foolish on the road for ten to fifteen minutes awaiting Sue's arrival. There we were dressed in our life vests and swimsuits with Chris attached to his fishing rod.

Laughter resonated on several occasions subsequently when the entire episode was shared with family and friends.

OFFER TO COMMIT SUICIDE

In 1985 I was hired as a sales representative for London Life. The next six months were increasingly stressful.

After an initial two-week training period, I was put on a six-month trial period. Productivity in the form of life insurance sales was the measure of success.

My immediate manager, Tom, oversaw my weekly progress. Regular contact with him was a prerequisite.

As the term progressed, it became evident to me that meeting the company's sales targets was extremely difficult. Over time the strain became cumulative. The strain was less evident in Tom. I simply didn't notice his situation relative to mine as much.

However, there was one tell-tale sign. At an open house for Tom and his wife, the evening concluded with me finding Tom lying on his back at the front entrance. He was totally inebriated, unable to get up. It was a bad omen.

Scroll ahead to the end of my six-month trial. Tom called a meeting to review my situation. As far as I was concerned the writing was on the wall.

The early morning get-together began with Tom pacing around his fourth-floor office. I can't remember the bulk of his conversation except for two essential ingredients: one, that it was evident that my employment would be terminated and two, his comment, "If we could only open these windows, we could both jump out." I almost burst into laughter. But the seriousness of the situation prevented me.

"No thanks, Tom," I replied. "It may be a solution for you, but I'm not interested."

There was a silver lining to this apparent dilemma. I awoke the next morning totally and unexpectedly unstressed. It was only then that I realized the excessive anxiety I had been living with.

HELPFUL DUTCH POLICE INSPECTORS

My girlfriend and I planned a one-year trip to Europe to commence at the beginning of 1973. We departed in January. Taking advantage of age-related price differences, we arranged separate flights.

I set out in advance. We were to meet two weeks later in Athens.

Amsterdam was my arrival city. Once there my intention was to visit my friend Jim Laing in a central Dutch city. He had preceded me in his travels by six months.

Prior to departing, I had become aware of an international incident involving a mutual friend, Barry Ainsworth. As a heavy pot and hashish user/trafficker, he had made a trip to Holland. While spending a brief amount of time with Jim, Barry managed to purchase a quantity of hashish. In turn, he subdivided it into smaller quantities. These were packaged and mailed to friends and business associates in Canada.

Authorities in Canada intercepted some of the mailings. Of course, this led back to the source, Barry in the Netherlands. Somehow, he managed to return to Canada and elude the police for some time.

When I arrived to stay with Jim, the Dutch police were still investigating. On the second morning after my arrival, we were awakened by a knock at the door. Two police inspectors discovered me, a new arrival from Canada.

"Can we see your identification, please?" they queried. I politely supplied my passport. They examined it suspiciously. They were hoping to find Barry Ainsworth. "Why are you here?" they asked. "What are your plans? How long are you staying?"

I was able to satisfy them with my answers or so it seemed.

The very next morning Jim and I were called upon again. Same time, same cops.

"May we see your passport?" I kindly provided them with my document. Again, they methodically studied it. There was a distinct air of mistrust on their part. "What are your plans?"

"I'm leaving for the train station," I responded. "I'm on my way to Athens." I had already prepared my backpack.

"May we give you a ride?" came their generous offer. I bid Jim adieu and piled into the police vehicle with the two inspectors.

It was obvious to me that they were quite pleased to see me off. However, in recalling this story I can't remember them ever asking to search my belongings.

BROOM BATTLE

My friend Charlie invited me to visit his acquaintances Garth and Charlene. The purpose: to purchase pot.

We drove out to their rental house, parked in the front, and walked along the path past the landlord`s home on the same property.

Charlie knocked on the door, once, twice and a third time without any successful acknowledgement. We were mystified, considering Charlie had contacted the couple fifteen minutes earlier. They had given us the green light to come over.

Giving up we began our retreat. At the halfway mark along the path, a screen door suddenly opened. Charlene shouted, "Charlie, what do you want?" She appeared quite agitated.

Sensing this, Charlie replied, "Oh, it's nothing. We can come back another time."

Charlene persisted. "But what do you want, Charlie?"

Her doggedness prompted Charlie to blurt out, "Pot. We just wanted to buy some pot."

"Then come in," she responded. We reluctantly reversed our direction. We felt something was seriously amiss but proceeded towards the house.

Upon entering we were amazed to discover Garth cowering in a chair in a corner of the room. In addition, a corn broom with its handle snapped in half lay on the floor. A partially broken wooden chair tottered next to the busted broom.

This scene of destruction was quite disturbing to witness, especially for me.

Garth and Charlene were strangers to me. We had never met. It was an embarrassing introductory situation. Ideally, I would have preferred to simply disappear.

But that wasn't realistic.

Charlene took charge and asked us to sit down. We negotiated the purchase of the pot—twenty dollars for a lid. The room was charged with tension. Garth remained voiceless the entire time. Quickly, Charlie and I excused ourselves.

Little was said between Charlie and me as we walked away. All I could do was assume that a serious domestic dispute had occurred. And we had witnessed the aftermath.

GORGEOUS SUPPLY TEACHER

We were not informed in advance. Our regular Grade 13 chemistry class teacher did not arrive. His replacement became the greatest distraction that a normal eighteen-year-old could ever imagine.

Her name was Brenda Porter. She was the epitome of female beauty: vivacious, wholesome, and extremely shapely. She was a woman that boys of that age could easily salivate over.

Brenda was not unknown to me. I had observed her from afar when I was a high school junior. I admired her for her beauty.

Brenda had graduated three years previously. Her high school credentials included cheerleading and being voted School Queen in her final year.

And here we were being supervised by this gorgeous woman. The time of year, early spring, lent to opening windows to let the fresh air into our chemistry lab.

Paul, my chemistry partner, decided to open the closest window on our side of the room. It just happened to face the open sports field on our campus. Once opened not only did the fresh outdoor air waft in but the aroma of decaying dog faeces did as well. It was unmistakable. The fragrance permeated the room.

Within a minute or two of Paul returning to his chair, Brenda abandoned her desk and casually walked over to the open window. She closed it convincingly.

Her body language via her facial expression indicated she wasn't going to put up with a challenge to her authority.

No sooner had Brenda returned to her desk when Paul nonchalantly rose from his stool and repeated his earlier endeavour. The same window was pried open. Paul was deliberately tempting fate.

The class began to reap the rewards of his effort within moments. The heady scent once again filled the room.

Paul and I deliberately studied Brenda to see if she would react to this second episode. She sweetly looked our way as she began her journey in the direction of the open window. It was indeed a delight in having her direct her attention our way.

Upon closing the window this time, Brenda offered a friendly recommendation: "Please don't try it again."

Paul desisted for the remainder of the class. And I took pleasure in having at least a minimal amount of interaction with our gorgeous teaching replacement.

A CLASS ACT

Sue retired in 2012 after a lifetime of teaching. Her area of expertise was music. Her students comprised pre-kindergarten to Grade 5 during the latter part of her career.

With decades of teaching music, Sue had developed an expertise that was recognized and appreciated by children, their parents, and her peers. In conjunction with Mark, the senior grades' music teacher, she had developed a wonderful concert program twice a year. Christmas and year-end student performances were the highlights of the year for the school population.

Consequently, Sue received a tremendous amount of adoration.

When it came to Sue's retirement, she and a handful of fellow educators were honoured at a breakfast ceremony. Each teacher received a tribute in the form of a speech from one of their peers. The acknowledgement for Sue was done expertly by Mark. Someone who knew her well.

With his oversized cue card in hand, Mark took his place on the podium.

Using his prop strategically, he focussed on the theme of "class act." Many references were made to Sue's ability to handle all classroom situations with class. Children were managed in a professional and classy manner. Over the years special assignments were dealt with in a classy style.

No effort was spared by Mark to maximize his emphasis on "class" in addressing Sue.

However, he cleverly presented a twist when his cue card was reversed offering the printed words "no class."

"Despite all my kind words about Sue, as a result of retirement, she no longer has class. Her teaching days are behind her and so is her class."

This concluding comment caused Sue and the listening audience to howl with laughter. It was a fitting tribute.

FOREPLAY

Buying out my house partner in 1974 meant I needed to find a creative way to pay the additional mortgage. Taking on a renter proved to be a practical solution.

When I made this proposal public, an acquaintance, John, was eager to become my housemate. Although we only knew each other casually, living together proved to be an enlightening experience.

The most informative occasion took place on a sunny summer afternoon.

It began with a gathering of friends, male and female. As we socialized indoors, alcohol and pot contributed to a very relaxed environment. Eventually, someone suggested we go for a swim. We jumped in our vehicles for the three-minute trip down to Long Lake.

After a refreshing swim, we returned home to continue our previous activity: more conversation, more stimulants.

In our inebriated state, the banter somehow turned to sex. In an uninhibited fashion, John offered his opinion. "I personally like at least an hour of foreplay before having sex." The comment snapped me out of my stupor. I as well as the others were somewhat shell-shocked by his blatant admission.

Surprisingly, I reacted quite quickly. "John," I asked, "is this preferably with or without a partner?"

The reaction was spontaneous. Everyone erupted in laughter, including John.

It was intense and prolonged. When the hilarity finally subsided John countered, "Fred, I have no defence, you got me."

PENAS VS. PENIS

The surname of my Grade 11 French teacher presented an irresistible opportunity for the boys. It was too tempting for them not to take advantage of the remarkable similarity between her name and the prominent male part of their anatomy. Mrs. Penas became Mrs. Penis on many occasions throughout the year.

When her attention was required, often a male would raise his hand and simultaneously vocalize, "Mrs. Penis, Mrs. Penis?"

Of course, this played to the amusement of their male peers. Never once did our French teacher indicate resentment or threaten retaliation. She was too timid to offer any defence.

In addition, Mrs. Penas's eyesight was severely limited. She was known to supervise class tests and exams from the back of the room—all the better to catch cheaters. This fact motivated the boys to position themselves at the front of her class—all the better to cheat if required.

On the occasions that Mrs. Penas supervised the lunchroom, boys would roll oranges on the floor between her legs as she stood motionless. Again, her limited vision made her oblivious to our misdemeanours.

During each three-minute class change, Mrs. Penas would position herself in the middle of the hallway outside her classroom. She achieved this by counting a predetermined number of steps from her classroom door to the centre of the corridor. This ritual at each class change provided us with an entertaining ingredient to our otherwise stressful academic workload.

In retrospect, I can honestly admit my failings at the time in being completely uncompassionate towards Mrs. Penas. However, I am aware that she did retire at the completion of that school year. No longer did she have to subject herself to the ridicule of students, including me.

PROFESSOR ABUSED

Second-year-university calculus was a tough one for me but not as tough as it was for our course instructor.

Although apparently brilliant, he did generate student respect. The problem was his youthful age and appearance. He didn't seem that much older than us, his students.

His classes took place twice a week in a mid-sized amphitheatre. He stood at the lowest level, utilizing the blackboards behind him while he taught. I sat approximately a third of the way up the inclined seating arrangement with the troublemakers higher up. My back faced them.

As a result, I never knew exactly what transpired with these individuals or why they became so displeased with the instructor. Their displeasure with him began somewhat gradually with small paper airplanes being lofted down towards him as he faced the blackboard. When he turned to face the class, it was obvious that paper planes had been thrown; they were strewn on the floor.

Over the next three to four weeks, classroom etiquette deteriorated abysmally. Paper planes and pennies were lobbed relentlessly towards the professor, always when his back was turned. They bounced off the blackboard with noticeable noise. Occasionally, these objects would even hit him directly.

For the longest time, he simply ignored the projectiles but finally exploded in the sixth week when he angrily spat out, "Whoever is throwing objects down will be expunged from this university!" The class responded with thunderous laughter.

Although I was a non-participant in the antics and empathized with his situation, I couldn't help but laugh. It was a ludicrous situation. And his threat did not correct the behaviour of the offending students.

The following lecture quickly degenerated, culminating in a huge Bristol board, moulded into the shape of an aeroplane, being propelled into the air.

It was unavoidable. The downward flight captured the immediate attention of the entire class. It skidded to a stop on the theatre floor. We erupted into hysterical laughter.

Once the professor turned around, he recognized the situation. It was completely futile for him to enact any form of remedial discipline.

Although I did see him on campus, he never returned to teach our class.

SHAVING THE BEARD

Beginning in the early seventies, I grew a full beard and maintained it for twelve years until the mid-eighties. During this period, many momentous events in my life occurred, with marriage and parenthood being the two most important.

Katie, our first, was born in 1977 with Emma coming in 1980. So, in their formative years, they only knew me, their dad, with a beard.

In late spring 1985, without any premeditation and consultation, I decided to shave off my beard.

As it turned out, my first public venture was to drive to Katie's school to pick her up. Driving Katie to and from school was a duty I shared with her mother on an alternating basis. Following the usual procedure, I parked the car within thirty metres of the main doors where I could easily see the exiting students.

When the bell rang, signalling the end of the school day, I focused on locating Katie as the students poured out. She came bounding out and headed directly to the playground area close by.

I vacated my vehicle and stood alongside it, simultaneously shouting, "Katie, Katie!" At first, there was no response as she didn't hear me. I repeated, "Katie, Katie!" causing her to look in my direction. However, she was visibly hesitating. "Katie, Katie!" I called again. Still no immediate comeback on her part.

It was then I realized the nature of the problem. Katie didn't recognize me without a beard. At first, I found the situation amusing. But I needed to reassure her I was her dad.

I slowly approached her. "Katie, Katie, I'm your dad. Come and get in the car. We must go!"

Very reluctantly, she walked towards me.

"Get in the front seat," I suggested but to no avail. I wanted to hug her to comfort her, but she resisted my attempt. I kept repeating the phrase, "Katie, it's me, your dad." Finally, she entered the back seat of the car demonstrating a great measure of apprehension.

During the entire process, Katie did not utter a word. The situation was quite surreal.

On the fifteen-minute return home, I explained that I had cut off my beard. "There is no need to worry, Katie."

The ironic thing is that when we arrived home, Emma did not demonstrate one iota of strangeness towards me. In fact, she loved the change in my appearance.

In retrospect, Katie may have been taught in school to avoid strangers. And I was a stranger at that moment.

WHAT'S THE TRUTH?

As an eight-year-old, I was a paperboy helper. I assisted my two older neighbours, brothers Brian and Ardy. They were four and three years older than me, respectively.

I can remember the year distinctly: it was 1955. The headlines that summer featured the boxing fight of the century with Rocky Marciano.

One of our delivery locations was a house that was divided into two suites, one upper and one lower. The upper unit was accessible by a staircase at the house front and the second by a side door at ground level.

When it came to delivering a newspaper at this location, I was instructed, "Deliver the paper at the front. Don't deliver it to the side door because a witch lives there."

For a time, I followed the instruction unfailingly. However, for some inexplicable reason, I diverted from the norm and decided to deliver a newspaper to the side door.

As I opened the screen door to throw in the paper, I was met with the vision of an old, old woman in a kitchen setting. To her immediate left stood an old-fashioned stove with an open oven door.

As I was about to drop the paper the woman commanded, "Get out of here or I'll cook you in the oven!" Her statement struck instantaneous fear in me. I slammed the screen door and ran away without delivering the paper.

Now two things remain a complete mystery to this day. Was the whole affair a figment of my imagination or did it happen as I described? Did the warning issued by Brian and Ardy colour my impression of the woman? Did my brain fabricate the meeting as a confrontation?

I doubt if I will ever know the truth. Out of fear I don't even remember if I shared this episode with my paperboy masters.

Conversely, I do remember that I never again delivered to that side door. I always gave that side of the house a wide berth.

WHY A VEGETARIAN?

What do the following have in common: pork hocks, chicken feet, blood sausage, pork fat, and studenetz (jellied pig's feet)?

For one, they are all meat courses. They also smell foul during the cooking process. In addition, the visuals of these dishes during the preparation stage are quite abhorrent.

All in all, they proved to be so offensive to my senses that I became a vegetarian at a very early age.

My parents, of Ukrainian descent, who came from a farming background were raised on meat. No fault of their own. Their exotic taste in meat proved to be unacceptable to me. I just couldn't handle it. Copious amounts of milk became my main substitute food source over the years.

As a result, I drove my mother crazy. She was burdened with the effort to pacify my food tastes. She was always needing to provide me with an alternative to whatever lunch or dinner menu she was preparing.

No amount of pleading would convince me to consume these items. I would belittle pork hocks and chicken feet by insisting dirt existed between their toes. "How could you eat that?" I would exclaim.

I can remember attending a wedding reception at age sixteen. The dinner included chicken. The man who sat next to me noticed that my chicken was left untouched.

"Aren't you eating your chicken?" he enquired.

"No, I don't eat meat," I replied. His facial expression spoke volumes. To him, I must have been a freak.

ZOMBIE AT THE POST OFFICE

As everyone knows, the post office's busiest time of the year for letter and parcel delivery is the Christmas season. This was even more the case in the past as compared to today.

In the 1960s the sizable increase in business required the post office to hire extra seasonal staff.

During my final high school year, I decided that applying for part-time postal work would provide me with much-needed income—I had a girlfriend. I also had a connection.

The father of a school acquaintance was the manager of the local post office.

After I made an informal request, I got a job there working the night shift, 11:00 p.m. to 7:30 a.m. five days during the school week. It lasted about a month, commencing in late November and ending just before Christmas.

Although I accepted the employment enthusiastically, it quickly turned into a nightmare. I managed to live up to the demands of the job. But I failed miserably when it came to my academic workload and basketball commitment.

My sleep deprivation and physical exhaustion progressively grew during the month-long work schedule.

My daily routine required that I take an after-dinner nap. I would wake up each evening at 10:15 p.m. Often it would take fifteen minutes to mentally orient myself: Where was I? What did I have to do? Where did I need to go? It was a nightmare.

After each shift, I would rush home for breakfast, then head to school and fall asleep in classes during the day. Then after-school basketball practice twice a week would drain whatever energy remained in my body.

The workplace itself provided some eye-opening experiences. For one, the monthly postal distribution of *Playboy* magazine created an unrestrained need to crack open the packaging that enclosed it. Breaks and lunchtime saw the male staff completely engrossed in the magazine. It was one of the perks of the job, albeit totally illegal.

On one occasion, I observed a full-timer pick up an intriguing parcel and deliberately smash it onto the concrete floor. His motivation was simply, "What would happen?" It was complete disrespect for another's property, something I did not condone.

In retrospect, I cannot remember exactly what work I did there. Absolutely no clue. I must have been a zombie.

CINDERELLA'S SLIPPERS

Friends were invited to join us for an evening out. Ukrainian New Year's was the event. It required our guests to commute forty-five minutes from White Rock to meet us in Richmond before continuing another forty-five minutes into Vancouver.

Sue and I suggested that Virginia and Doug consider spending the night at our place. Partying late into the evening would make it difficult for them to travel home. So, they arrived with slippers and pyjamas in hand just in case.

The evening proved to be very worthwhile for our friends. It was their first experience with this celebration of Ukrainian food, cultural entertainment, and dancing.

Upon our return home, Virginia and Doug declined our overnight invitation. They gathered up their slippers, wished us goodnight, and away they went.

Sue and I quickly fell asleep but were awakened within an hour and a half by a voice being recorded on my answering machine. We were both so exhausted that the event seemed like a dream. We did not respond.

Shortly after awakening the next morning another phone call came in. I answered it. It was Virginia. "Can you please check outside to see if you can find my slipper? I threw my slippers into the car last night, but I can only find one. I'm also missing the orthotic insert. It cost me five hundred dollars." Virginia seemed quite agitated.

"Let me go and check," I assured her. "I will get back to you as soon as possible." I headed outside in my housecoat and slippers. I crossed the lawn out onto the street all the

357

while scouting for a slipper. No luck. I repeated the procedure a second time before re-entering the house.

I called Virginia back. "Virginia, no luck. I couldn't see anything."

"I can't understand what happened to it. I thought I threw both slippers into the car," came her response. The desperate tone in her voice convinced me to try again.

"I'll go out once more," I said.

I followed the same path as before, but this time I looked farther down the street in one direction. Something lying on the street caught my eye. It appeared as an indistinguishable dark lump. It was in front of the third property from our house.

As I approached it, I still couldn't make it out. Finally, when I reached down to retrieve it, I recognized it as a waterlogged slipper. The orthotic was still inside. The mystery was solved. I was elated for Virginia's sake.

I phoned her immediately with the good news. "I found it!"

"Where?" she asked.

After my brief explanation, Virginia offered to drive from White Rock to pick it up. However, I insisted that Sue and I would deliver it to her. After a brief amount of back-and-forth, Virginia accepted our offer. I had an ulterior motive. It required a prop, a pillow.

Upon ringing her doorbell Virginia appeared at the door. She was met with her slipper and orthotic on a decorative pillow.

I greeted her with, "Cinderella, I think you forgot your slipper last night at the ball. Not only did you leave your slipper behind but your orthotic as well!"

Needless to say, Virginia burst into laughter and so did we. Doug arrived shortly after to join in the mirth.

FAKE PRO-WRESTLING

For two years in my early teens, I worked part-time at the local arena. Concession sales were where I plied my time. Popcorn, peanuts, ice cream, pop and chips were some of the junk food items we sold.

The events that we catered varied tremendously from bingos to professional hockey with upwards of seven thousand in attendance. Cowboy shows, rodeos, fiddle competitions, ice dance shows, concerts by big-name acts and many other forms of entertainment kept us busy.

But the most entertaining event was wrestling. In fact, the best in the professional wrestling world performed at the Sudbury Arena. We had Gorgeous George, Whipper Billy Watson, Bouncing Bambino, Hard Boiled Hagarty, the Masked Men, Little Beaver, other midget wrestlers and many more.

The wrestling ring was always located in the middle of the ice rink floor without the ice. Fans were seated surrounding the ring as well as in the stands. Wrestling typically drew large and excitable crowds.

The antics of these wrestlers were outrageous at times. Gorgeous George always entered the ring in a full-length fur gown. He was preceded by his female assistant who made two laps of the ring spraying a strongly scented perfume.

One memorable event sticks in my mind due to its farcical nature. It transpired as I rounded the wrestling stage in very close proximity. A timeout had been called and both wrestlers had retreated to their respective corners. Each was being attended by their manager. I happened to be standing alongside one of these corners just below the raised stage. Just as the bell rang to recommence the duel, I noticed the manager above me surreptitiously slap a small plastic pouch, red in colour, into the right palm of his wrestler. In turn, the wrestler immediately rushed out to meet his challenger in the centre of the ring. There was an instantaneous clash. The wrestler with the pouch slammed his open palm onto the forehead of his competitor. Blood, more accurately a red-dyed liquid, immediately appeared, pouring from the point of impact. The receiving wrestler feigned serious injury and at that point, I burst into uncontrollable laughter. How preposterous could this be? Did no one else notice amongst the thousands who attended?

I walked away from this scene to carry on my sales duties without paying further attention.

SPANKED BY THE MAYOR

As a rule, most elementary school children living in proximity to their school went home for lunch. This was true for me and Wayne Lambert, a school acquaintance.

On one wintry day, we walked home together at lunchtime engaging in horseplay—no snowball fight, just pushing and shoving, attempting to confine each other into a snow-filled ditch. Our roughhousing wasn't aggressive enough that it would cause injury. At least that was what we thought.

We parted company when we first reached Wayne's house. I continued for another three minutes until arriving home.

Upon entering the house, I was met by my mother. Her facial expression immediately aroused my concern. Mom began explaining, "Freddie, Wayne's mother just phoned and said that you were fighting with Wayne and made his nose bleed. The front of his coat is covered in blood. Did you make his nose bleed?"

"No, Mom, we were just playing," I replied. "When I left Wayne, I didn't see any blood and Wayne didn't complain to me." My mother seemed satisfied with my response.

Once lunch was finished, I bundled myself up with winter gear and trudged off to school with no apprehension as to what would happen. Wayne was not to be seen.

Shortly after class commenced, the classroom phone rang. My teacher answered and after hanging up she informed me, "Freddie, please go to the principal's office. He wants to see you."

As a nine-year-old, I felt quite intimidated and apprehensive. My nervousness grew exponentially as I proceeded down the fifty-metre corridor to the office.

Upon my arrival, I was met by Wayne Lambert as well as Mr. Edgar, our principal. It just happened that Mr. Edgar was also the mayor of our city, Sudbury, Ontario. Knowing his stature in the community made the affair doubly intimidating.

Obviously, Mrs. Lambert had lodged a complaint and we were there in the office consequently.

To my relief, Mr. Edgar dealt with us individually in a very terse manner.

He posed a quick question to me, then he picked me up, put me across his knee and gave me two or three whacks on my rump with an open hand. The same process was repeated for Wayne. I can't even remember if Mr. Edgar had even issued a warning after our punishment.

The whole disciplinary affair was such a relief because of its mildness. And it remains memorable to me because who can claim that they were spanked by the mayor of a city?

SCOTTISH FANTASY

As a record store manager in the mid-seventies, I had already acquired a love of music. But classical music was not a category I was completely familiar with.

However, the situation changed remarkably once I met Margaret. Not only did we become live-in companions, but she was in possession of a violin. I had indicated to her that I had the ambition to learn to play the fiddle. Once the instrument was provided, I consulted with a country fiddler friend for lessons.

Richard Mende offered the following recommendation: "I am willing to teach you country fiddle, but my advice is to study classical violin." I took his recommendation and enrolled with a violin teacher.

As a consequence, I began researching the repertoire of classical violin music. In very short order I discovered "Scottish Fantasy," a violin concerto by Max Bruch. To my ear, it brought me enormous pleasure. And the title was unbelievably apropos because Margaret had Scottish heritage. She was my Scottish fantasy.

That piece of music became so much a part of my listening pleasure that we played the recording during our marriage ceremony. It was at this juncture that Margaret, my Scottish fantasy, became my Scottish reality. It was very much a happy event.

The reality aspect became much more evident over the next seven years.

Although we brought two lovely daughters into the world, it became evident over time that we had a compatibility issue. With separation and eventual divorce, Margaret no longer fit either the fantasy or reality category for me.

DUMPSTER DIVING

As an avid urban gardener, I incorporated composting as a worthwhile ingredient in the process.

Over four to five years, I acquired various composters one at a time. My main sources were those discarded at our local recycling centre. I now possess thirteen composters with an average capacity of 100 to 120 litres.

To feed the contents of the composters, good compostable material is required. In addition to grass cuttings and leaves, vegetable and fruit cuttings from home are quite insufficient. So, I concluded that an additional source was required to meet my composting needs. But from where?

While driving around our community, I not only noticed a liberal number of produce stores, but also every location also had dumpsters situated outdoors, usually in the back lane. The light went on—discarded fruit and vegetables could be a potential source.

My initial approach was to talk with the owners/operators to access their dumpsters. But my request was met with resistance. In other cases, these bins were locked and secured during and after business hours.

However, with further investigation, I was able to locate up to three accessible locations. My modus operandi was only to visit these dumpsters during the evening after business closure.

From the outset, I was amazed by the wealth of discovered food waste. You name it: apples, oranges, avocadoes, tomatoes, mangos, plums, nectarines, bananas, dragon fruit, pineapple, grapes, hot peppers, celery, lettuce, various varieties of potatoes, yams, carrots, broccoli, cauliflower, peppers, cucumbers, spinach, cob corn. The quantity and quality varied at any given time but there never was a dearth.

By trial and error, I learned to frequent these sources every other day in order to allow the inventory to build up. This made the visits more productive.

Although not consistent, a serendipitous discovery I made was that a good percentage of the produce waste was perfectly edible. Not only did I salvage fruit and vegetables for our use, but I forwarded a considerable amount to the local food bank.

It was amazing. As an example, bags of sweet potatoes were discarded because one or two were slightly deteriorated. By removing the bad ones and repackaging the rest, they were perfectly suitable for consumption.

Bagged celery and/or chopped stir-fry veggies were without blemishes. Their only sin was an expiry date that coincided with the same day or day before they were being discarded.

Although I was sometimes rewarded with edible food, the vast majority of the produce was deteriorated and unusable for human consumption. But to my army of red wiggler worms housed in the thirteen composters, it was all consumable.

On average, each visit to my dumpster sources generated the equivalent of two full wheel barrels of produce for composting. In turn, the worms thrived and multiplied to the benefit of our garden soil.

FROZEN EARS X 2

Northern Ontario winters could be brutal in the sixties.

While attending high school, I walked to school often. I can remember on more than one occasion having my Brylcreem-saturated hair freeze into a solid stylized iceberg-like form.

And this brings me to a particular wintery Monday morning when the entire school's attention was drawn to one of our fellow students. What made Steve Kaminsky the student focus and butt of our jokes were his ears. They were heavily gauzed, protruding like proverbial cauliflower ears.

This outcome was the result of having camped outdoors the previous weekend with his military reserve group. Kaminsky had suffered frostbite.

Because of the sizable protuberance and the snow-white brightness of the bandages, Steve's ears could be spotted in the corridors from a great distance during class changes.

This situation continued until Thursday of that week when the gauze was removed. He reverted to being almost unnoticed amongst the school population.

However, this normalized situation for Kaminsky was not meant to last.

The weekend came once again, and he participated in another reservist outdoor manoeuvre. School resumed the following Monday, and true to form, we witnessed Kaminsky with a repeat set of gauzed ears. He had frozen them once again.

Needless to say, Kaminsky was the talk of the school again. During class changes, we attentively kept our eyes open for him in order to make light-hearted commentary precipitating laughter at his expense.

Despite Kaminsky's ear coverings being removed during the second episodic week, the student population eagerly anticipated what would happen upon his return after the third weekend.

Disappointingly for us but fortunately for Kaminsky, he returned to school that Monday with his ears unmasked.

DOG OFF-LEASH HEARING

Even after countless confrontations with my neighbour George between 2012 and 2017, he continued to flaunt the dog on-leash bylaw and walk his two dogs off-leash. His defiance of the bylaw continued despite previous warnings and fines by bylaw officers. In reporting his misdemeanours, the animal control officer advised me to take photos.

This is exactly what transpired in early 2017. As Sue and I were driving into our neighbourhood, George was spotted with one dog off-leash. Having my camera at the ready I recorded the situation in a brief video.

As per instructions, I forwarded this incident to the bylaw department. In turn, the offending individual, namely George, was issued a fine. Subsequently, I was informed that he pleaded not guilty and that he wanted to defend himself in a public hearing.

I was asked if Sue and I would attend to corroborate the charge. "Yes," came my reply.

In the interim, I provided a little more detail including the exact address where the incident took place.

On the morning of the hearing, Sue and I arrived before George. When he eventually appeared, the adjudicator placed us at separate tables facing her desk.

After introductory formalities, I was given the opportunity to speak. My presentation briefly confirmed the event recorded in my video: George's dog was off leash.

Then came George's turn. It amounted to a farcical defence. If it had been a court of law, he would have been charged with contempt on two or three occasions.

At the outset, George claimed that he was out of the country at the time of the incident. He presented the adjudicator with a flight ticket indicating that his return date was the day after having been served with the ticket at his residence.

This apparent contradiction aroused the curiosity of the adjudicator. How could a bylaw officer serve a ticket in person to George on a day prior to his return from a vacation out of the country?

The adjudicator asked George, "How long were you away?"

"Two weeks," George replied.

"Then what day did you get back?"

"I don't know," he responded. "You tell me."

His ludicrous comeback caused me to burst out laughing.

A back-and-forth exchange between the two continued for a brief amount of time with no resolution to the timing discrepancy.

Then George was asked to view the video I had provided. There was no doubt about the dog being off-leash as it was defecating at a distance from its owner.

However, in the scene, George's back had been facing the camera. There was absolutely no mistake that this was the George that we had known for a great number of years. Even his habitually worn red winter coat corroborated his identity.

Notwithstanding this evidence, George responded "no" when asked if he recognized this person. "It could have been my brother," came his defence.

Again, this was a preposterous example of George's lack of integrity. The adjudicator demonstrated frustration and what I interpreted as disbelief in his antics.

When the bylaw officer, who served the fine, was asked to confirm the ticket details it became apparent that a discrepancy had occurred. He had issued the location of the off-leash incident as the address of George's residence. This clashed with the address I had provided.

This created a dilemma for the adjudicator. Although the evidence of non-compliance was exceptionally substantiated, she reluctantly deemed the ticket as unenforceable. As a result, George left the hearing chamber, gloating at his dismissal.

A silver lining came as a result of a question Sue posed to the adjudicator: "Can George be photographed any time when there is contact between us?"

"Yes," replied the adjudicator, "as long as you don't stalk him." George was a party to this interchange.

It was less than a week later that George attempted to demonstrate his displeasure with me in a passing situation. His uplifted middle finger quickly changed to a hysterical attempt at a friendly waving motion when he realized that I was photographing him.

DANGEROUS SENIORS

In the early nineties, the cultural and sports centre of Richmond consisted of several buildings. They housed two swimming pools, two ice rinks, a library, a museum, a cultural facility, activity and meeting rooms, and finally a seniors' centre.

The city decided to replace the main building, containing the library, cultural centre, and activity and meeting rooms, due to its age and inefficiencies.

Prior to demolition, the construction site was cordoned with a six-foot height of chain-link fencing. The fence was meant to provide safety to the public during the erection phase. Although the remaining buildings were at a distance, the seniors' centre butted up closest to the fence.

It was at this time that once a week I would transport two to four seniors to the centre to play bingo. As a rule, I would drop them off close to the entrance, drive away and return later to pick them up.

On one occasion my routine changed. Instead of dropping them off, I parked the vehicle and entered the seniors' centre with my companions. Upon entering, we were met by a greeter, a seniors' member. I decided to challenge her.

"I notice there is a sizeable and rather threatening chain-link fence surrounding your centre. Just what makes you seniors so dangerous?"

She did not take the bait. Instead, she answered, "What do you mean?"

I tried to explain that as I approached the seniors' complex, the extent of the fencing was intimidating. I deliberately exaggerated my sense of the threat posed by the ageing occupants.

The greeter finally accepted the challenge. She delightfully bantered with me for the better part of fifteen minutes. My effort to instigate a conversation proved to be very rewarding.

KAYAKING WITH A UKULELE

From the mid-1990s into the early 2000s, Sue and I participated in five extensive ocean kayaking adventures. They typically lasted seven to ten days. We travelled in two single kayaks and never with any other company.

On this trip, Sue decided to bring along her ukulele. She conveniently strapped it by bungee cord to the kayak face immediately in front of her.

This was not unusual for Sue, a music teacher. The ukulele was one of her teaching instruments. When gatherings of family or friends took place around campfires, Sue took immense pleasure in leading sing-a-longs. Her ukulele was ever-present.

Occasionally we would cross paths with other travellers on the water. This occurred on one occasion in Clayoquot Sound, in the vicinity of Tofino, British Columbia.

As we pulled into shore for the night at the base of Catface Mountain, we noticed a sizeable kayaking group. They had already set up camp two hundred to three hundred metres away.

Once we unloaded our gear and set up our tent, we prepared our dinner. The evening was still quite young after completion and clean-up. So, we decided to pay a visit to another group consisting of fourteen members. Sue brought along her ukulele anticipating an opportunity to initiate a sing-along.

Engaging them in conversion proved to be cordial. We discovered they were being toured by an outfitter's organization from the interior of British Columbia.

When five or six members broke off from the main group to join Sue and me, it was at that point that Sue began strumming her instrument and singing. She was in her comfort zone.

Sue attempted to promote participation in the singing but there seemed to be a lukewarm response. Not being discouraged, Sue carried into a second song. Slowly one then a second person drifted away. By the third attempt all guests had disappeared, returning to their campsite.

I felt sorry for Sue. Her intention was honourable. But our new acquaintances demonstrated a lack of enthusiasm for campfire singing. It was not part of their culture.

NINETY-FIVE PERCENT VS. FIVE PERCENT

As a result of our failing marriage, my wife Margaret was demonstrating chronic signs of stress. In consultation with our family doctor, several attempts were made to alleviate her symptoms to no avail.

The required solution was to deal with the cause. That meant that Margaret and I needed to agree to a therapy process. Our GP offered to conduct these sessions.

Initially, Margaret and I met separately with Dr. Faulkner. These were one-on-one sessions meant to familiarize him with our individual interpretations of our incompatibility.

Once these sessions were completed, we were asked to attend a joint consultation.

At the outset of this meeting, Dr. Faulkner posed the same question to both of us: "In percentage terms, how much of the marital breakdown do you feel you are responsible for?" I was asked to respond first.

It took intensive self-reflection for me to determine my answer. "I am willing to assume fifty percent of the responsibility," I replied.

Our GP continued, "And, Margaret, what do you feel is your degree of responsibility?" My wife spontaneously offered, "Fred is responsible for one hundred percent of the marital failure."

Needless to say, I was flabbergasted. I had no idea that her opinion was so skewed.

As for our doctor, I can't recall his reaction to this astounding revelation. The mediation concluded with no resolution.

However, Dr. Faulkner prepared us for the next session suggesting that he would be asking the same question again regarding each of our liabilities. In the interim, we were asked to give the subject a serious reappraisal.

The following week we met again.

Again, the session opened with the promised question directed first to me. "Fred, have you given further thought as to how much you feel you are responsible for your marital divisiveness?"

"Yes," I replied, "I have given it additional reflection and I still am willing to assume fifty percent of the blame."

"Margaret, what have you decided?" challenged Dr. Faulkner.

"I think Fred is responsible for ninety-five percent and I for five percent," came the reply.

This answer was even more mind-boggling than her first one a week earlier. She had given me a magnanimous five percent credit reduction in my liability.

The writing was on the wall. No further consultations were offered by our doctor indicating a concession on his part to the futility of proceeding.

ANARCHY = STATE OF MIND

Since our marital conflict was unresolved, my life with Margaret carried on unsatisfactorily.

Our marriage continued to suffer and in turn, Margaret's stress was accentuated. Sometime during the following year, Dr. Faulkner suggested that we once again attempt a resolution to our dilemma. I was under the mistaken belief that our marriage needed to be kept intact for the sake of our two daughters.

This time our doctor recommended we consult with a psychiatrist specializing in marital difficulties. Both Margaret and I agreed to accept the offer.

My memory is rather vague regarding the experience, except for two facts: there were at least two sessions and the effort ended unsuccessfully.

The doctor attempted to get each of us to give our opinion of our spouse. I'm not sure what Margaret's commentary was of me. It would be safe to say that it wasn't innocuous.

In my case, I responded to the question with, "Margaret is an anarchist."

This answer astounded the psychiatrist. "What do you mean? How could you say that? Margaret isn't destroying things!"

Defending my statement came very easily based on nearly seven years of affiliation with her. "Anarchy is a state of mind. Margaret doesn't need to destroy anything. She does exactly what she wants with total disregard for my opinion."

My resolve on this issue in conjunction with Margaret's attitude must have demonstrated a complete lack of potential resolution. Our doctor appeared disheartened in witnessing our vitriolic conflict.

No further meetings were scheduled. And our separation was processed shortly after.

JOE CLARK REPLY

In 1992 the federal government under the leadership of Prime Minister Brian Mulroney attempted to bring Quebec into a constitutional relationship with the rest of Canada. The process was named the Charlottetown Accord. Despite enormous effort, it failed.

One year later leading up to a federal election, the Progressive Conservative Party was desperate to achieve success. Success with a Quebec inclusion into our federal family would enhance the PC's triumph in the 1993 election.

Joe Clark, our former prime minister, was designated by Brian Mulroney as the ambassador to negotiate a compromise agreement with Quebec. As the November election approached, it was announced that a twenty-eight-clause accord had been reached.

All provinces and territories had participated in and ratified the pact.

As the appointed salesperson, Joe Clark was responsible for convincing Canadians of the benefits of this accord. He traversed the country for a few gruelling months in advance of the election. Public forums were held in as many communities as humanly possible.

One such forum took place in Richmond, British Columbia.

I became aware in advance of this event. As a political junkie and the National Party nominee candidate for the 1993 federal election, I looked enthusiastically to the opportunity to participate.

Having been a veteran of public political forums, I surveyed the meeting room logistics upon entering. The sizeable space was well equipped with seating with two microphones situated in two separate aisles. These were intended for questions from audience members once the main presentation concluded. I strategically sat down in a chair next to one of the microphones.

The building subsequently filled in advance of Joe Clark's arrival. Opposition to the tentative agreement was as vociferous in Richmond as it was across the country.

Joe Clark's entourage included the who's who of Conservative politics including his wife, Maureen McTeer, and the local MP.

Joe's lengthy speech was well-intentioned. He sincerely demonstrated a desire to inform the public fully as to the benefits of the agreement.

Anticipating the conclusion of his presentation, I stood up positioning myself at one microphone in the hope that I would be chosen first to pose my question. My strategy paid off when Mr. Clark allowed me to speak first.

Having studied the agreement's twenty-eight clauses in advance, I concluded that there were two major flaws. "Mr. Clark," I asked, "why would you and the other parties agree to Clause 26 in which Quebec would be given twenty-five percent of all parliamentary seats into perpetuity? This is completely undemocratic. The decision lacks common sense. And Mr. Clark, how could you agree to such an illogical decision?"

After I posed my questions, Joe Clark gave an inordinate twelve-minute answer. The gist of which was this: because it had been so difficult to previously bring Quebec into the Canadian repatriation of 1984 when Quebec agreed to the twenty-eight clauses unanimity erupted. This momentous decision was reached in the wee hours of the morning after long and strenuous deliberations. Perhaps exhaustion precipitated the flawed consensus.

To gain full benefit from the exposure, I remained standing for the entire extended reply.

So that was my invaluable opportunity in the federal political arena for which I am forever thankful.

VANITY EXTRAORDINAIRE

For a period in the late sixties, I was befriended by Pat.

It didn't take long to discover that Pat was a classic extrovert. He was a nonstop talker and always the life of the party. In retrospect, he may have had bipolar disorder because when he was on a high it was impossible to dislodge him from his antics.

Along with his extraordinary ability to entertain others, Pat had killer looks. He was extremely handsome. With the combination of his attractive physical features and his winsome personality, women were irresistibly attracted to him. He always had a way with women.

So, it seemed to me that Pat was destined for a lifetime of bachelorhood. He was too much of a playboy.

We went our separate ways and lost contact with each other.

Six years later I heard through the grapevine that Pat was about to be married. This came as a shock to me. Knowing Pat, I couldn't fathom him ever tying the knot. I was desperate to know the rationale behind this decision.

Sure enough, I crossed paths with him not too long after my discovery. "Pat," I asked, "is it true that you're getting married?"

"Oh, yeah," he replied, "her name is Marian Tokaryk."

I continued, "And what made you decide to finally get married?"

"She'll be my income tax write-off for the year," was his excuse.

I didn't pursue whether questions of love, compatibility or any other necessary bonding issues existed in his decision-making. Considering who Pat was, it would have been a fruitless endeavour.

DR. ROGER FISHER'S ADVICE

Because of the 1995 Quebec Sovereignty vote in which sovereignty was narrowly defeated, the majority of Canadians outside Quebec were shocked out of their complacency.

In British Columbia, the concern was equal in intensity. And for that reason, the Law Society of British Columbia decided to host a one-day conference on the UBC campus in 1996.

The forum topic was "How to Prevent a Quebec Cessation." The invited panel of fifteen guests were some of the foremost politicians and legal and constitutional experts in Canada. The event was divided into morning and afternoon sessions with a lunch hour in between. A keynote speaker was invited to make a brief fifteen-minute presentation.

We were honoured with Dr. Roger Fisher as the presenter. Dr. Fisher's credentials were as follows: lawyer, international mediator, member of Harvard University faculty and author of *Getting to Yes*. It was anticipated that his expertise in negotiating settlements between nations could assist Canada with its internal divisiveness.

A Canadian by birth, Roger indicated solving the issue of sovereignty was so important that he was donating the time and cost of his appearance.

Of course, the fifteen minutes he was allocated to speak was vastly inadequate. When he concluded, most attendees rushed back into the auditorium. However, eight to ten people remained behind, me included. Questions were posed to Mr. Fisher in a scrum setting. Queries varied from Cuba–US relations to the 1990 Oka Crises. Roger's responses were invaluable. The session proved to be momentous for me, a once-in-a-lifetime experience.

And to our surprise, Dr. Fisher offered one last piece of advice before we parted company: "Now you have to remember that despite my expertise those that scream the loudest and maintain their position the longest usually get their way."

I concluded that his statement was a sad reflection on humanity.

HAIR TOO LONG

During the school year 1967–68, I attended the University of Waterloo. As an engineering student enrolled in the co-op program, practical work experience was encouraged during non-academic intervals.

The program enlisted industrial companies to hire students. Fortunately, the chief technical recruiter for INCO interviewed me for a 1968 summer position. I was hired.

This was a prestigious opportunity as I was considered a professional-in-training with a salaried position. In contrast, I had worked for INCO as an hourly paid labourer the previous year.

On completion of this work term, I was asked to submit a report to my manager in the engineering department. Not having heard any feedback, I assumed all was well with my employment contribution.

Fast forward to the following year when I returned home in the hope of securing employment once again in the engineering department.

When I contacted the department, I specifically asked for the same interviewer as the previous year. I felt that I had built a rapport, albeit briefly with the head of the technical department.

To my disappointment, I was informed by the assistant technical director that his superior was out of town. However, he informed me that he was willing to interview me for the position.

A date was established. The interview took place with no noticeable sticking points. My impression was that everything went well. At the conclusion of the meeting, I was told that I would be contacted in one week.

I waited out the seven days with no response from the interviewer.

Patiently, I spent the better part of another week in anticipation. My patience ran out before the second week ended.

I put in a direct call to the interviewer and asked if he had decided. He politely put me on hold as he explained that he wanted to refer to my file.

When he returned to the phone, he informed me, "We will not be hiring you this time as your hair is too long." I was devastated. What a ridiculous excuse, I thought. "However," he added, "you can apply to the labour department."

My hair had certainly grown longer in the interim of one year, but it was barely over the top part of my ear. This period for hair growth was well before the hippie-length days. It was a simple case of discrimination. I didn't pursue an appeal.

YOU ARE YOUR OWN GOD

As someone who excelled at public speaking, Dr. Ferdie Chen was an inspirational role model for me.

I first met Dr. Chen in a Toastmasters' Speakers club. Within the Toastmasters International Organization, he was the first to receive the Professional Speakers designation. This was achieved notwithstanding the fact that English was not his mother tongue. In fact, it was his fifth language.

Ferdie, as he was respectfully called, was a man with many varied interests, one of which was world religions.

Not only did Ferdie participate in weekly Toastmasters meetings by demonstrating his speaking skills, but he also made presentations in public forums. On more than one occasion he would invite club members to attend his speaking engagement.

On my first occurrence of hearing Dr. Chen speak outside our club, I was unaware of what his speech topic would be. It turned out to be "World Religions."

His presentation was not only proficient, but I was also impressed with his extensive knowledge of the subject matter.

After the conclusion of his speech, I approached him to offer my congratulations. Upon greeting me he asked, "What did you think?"

"I enjoyed your delivery, but I can't agree with the content of your speech," came my response.

With no malice in his voice, Dr. Chen replied, "Then you are your own God."

I thought to myself, "What a wonderful comeback." It suited me perfectly since I was a practising atheist. His statement did not empower me with the belief of being a power unto myself.

Instead, he gave me the confidence to realize I could make my own decisions without the need for a supernatural entity.

On another occasion, Dr. Chen invited us to his presentation called, "Need for Human Harmony."

As usual, Ferdie's delivery was flawless. However, when he made an accusation that Serbia was the cause of the Serbian/Kosovo conflict all hell broke loose.

An audience member immediately took offence to his statement. She introduced herself as Serbian and began to vehemently challenge Dr. Chen. This in turn drew other audience members into the debate. The heated discussion lasted no more than five minutes.

I did not participate in the verbal melee but benefitted as an objective observer. Not once did Dr. Chen enter the give-and-take of the debate. He made no attempt to defend his statement. He simply remained silent at the lectern.

Finally, when the emotional and verbal contributions were exhausted, the focus returned to Dr. Chen.

In a very nonchalant manner, he informed the audience, "That concludes my presentation."

It was a jaw-dropping moment for me for two reasons: his choice not to engage in a very heated argumentative environment and his formidable subtle conclusion to the event.

It was a lesson well learned.

SHEEP HUNTING HIKE

After a lengthy camper trip through Northern British Columbia, the Yukon, Alaska, and the Northwest Territories, returning through British Columbia, Sue and I settled into a campsite in the Northeast Rockies of British Columbia.

A spectacular lake bordered us on one side and a highway on the opposite side acted as a partition to a very steep access to the Rocky Mountains.

With the benefit of a travel guide, we learned that a population of wild Dahl sheep habituated the area. Locating these sheep became our goal the following morning.

With more than glorious weather conditions, we set off the next morning for an arduous trek up steep terrain.

Although we were in great physical condition, the ascent required us to rest at five-minute intervals. All the while we accessed 360 degrees of the surroundings. Our goal was to locate the sheep. However, our continued climb with the benefit of binoculars produced negative results. No sheep were to be seen.

We finally realized that our effort was proving to be fruitless. Although the surrounding view was spectacular, we decided to descend in futility.

But we did not give up on our quest during our downward return. We continued to peruse the vast landscape for our elusive Dahls.

We finally arrived at the highway two and a half hours from our initial departure. With a leisurely walk of some two hundred meters to our campsite, we rounded a corner and to our amazement stumbled onto a flock of Dahl sheep grazing on road salt alongside the highway. We were astonished.

We couldn't believe the irony. Two and a half hours of demanding effort spent searching for these animals and there they were casually licking salt no more than one hundred metres from our campsite.

What utter frustration!

MOROCCAN POLICE BRIBE

A thirty-day house exchange tour of Morocco proved to be an exercise in tolerance for Sue and me.

Not only were there language and cultural barriers, Sue and I experienced numerous challenges while driving along the highway system. Notwithstanding city traffic congestion, donkey cart backups and animal market impositions, the greatest dilemma was dealing with highway police enforcement.

Police checkpoints seemed to exist everywhere, including entering and exiting cities. In quick order, we realized that issuing traffic tickets was a make-work policy for the country.

The most egregious example took place when we were descending a gentle mountainside highway into a small isolated townsite. The roadway, approximately one kilometre in length, curved multiple times. Roadside signs indicated that passing was prohibited.

Commencing the descent, we encountered a large slow-moving truck travelling in the same direction. Initially, I exercised caution and patience. The truck was maintaining a pace well under the speed limit, and although tempting, I resisted the idea of passing it.

With the benefit of clear views and a lack of approaching vehicle traffic, I finally relented. I decided passing the truck was necessary. There were no danger signs whatsoever.

Once I completed the pass, it appeared to be clear sailing into the village below. Just as we entered the community, two motorcycle cops stepped out onto the road. They signalled us to pull over.

Somehow, they managed to communicate that they had observed us passing the truck. Both police officers were rather impressive in their dress and gentle mannerisms. Being youthful and bedecked with sunglasses gave us the impression of friendliness.

However, our attitude towards them reversed when they demanded five hundred Moroccan dirhams. After two previous police speeding fines, I feigned utter frustration with this new attempt at bribery. No formal paperwork was presented. It appeared to be an arbitrary amount.

Having French as a mutual language, I was able to communicate my frustration.

The conversation was quite jovial when one of the officers indicated that he wanted to try on my sunglasses. These were quite exotic to them, therefore the appeal.

I handed them to the first officer. Once positioned on his face, he immediately simulated the revving of his motorcycle with a "vroom, vroom, vroom." This brought a round of laughter from all of us.

Then the second officer demanded the sunglasses to try on. The scenario repeated itself with a "vroom, vroom, vroom."

All the while negotiations carried on in this comical encounter. It occurred to me that the sunglasses could have been utilized as a bargaining chip. But I sensed that one pair of sunglasses for two police officers would not be adequate.

In the end, we negotiated a half-price 250-dirham settlement. We departed on good terms. Being amused by the encounter created a sense of satisfaction even though a financial penalty was extorted.

HIGH-PRESSURE CARPET SALE

While spending a few days in Fez, Morocco, we were offered the opportunity of a guided tour of the city's medina.

I was reluctant to visit the city's ancient quarter. I had toured it for nine days, forty-five years previously. The old part of Fez with its million occupants can be best described as a labyrinth. Becoming disoriented within a minute of entry is not an exaggeration.

So, on second thought, Sue agreed to a half-day guided tour. Our female guide arrived at the appointed morning time and off we went. She would be the determinant of our itinerary. To our great satisfaction, we visited ample historical, religious, and traditional craft-making locations. Then we were blindsided with an unsolicited visit to a Moroccan carpet shop.

We learned later that this was a compulsory stop as part of a Moroccan guide/carpet sales ploy. The guide would not only deliver the tourist to the merchant but would remain completely detached from the process. The guide was not obligated to work on behalf of the client/tourist. Instead, the client would be handed over on a platter to the carpet sale staff.

On this occasion, we experienced a vendor who was extremely aggressive and manipulative. He deliberately separated Sue from me in the sales room. The strategy was to prevent us from communicating with each other. We entered with absolutely no intention of buying a carpet.

The slick salesperson directed almost all his attention in my direction. The assumption was that I, being the male, would control the finances. His deliberate sales tactic was not a case of "if" but "how much."

The merchant beckoned staff to bring in carpets for us to view, one after another after another. He requested our opinion on each item to determine if we were pleased with it or not. This process repeated itself multiple times under the direction of the carpet ringleader. His motive was to sell not just one unit but three carpets.

"Which ones do you like?" was repeated over and over until he finally managed to draw from us a choice of three favourites. Once that was achieved, he sat down to calculate the cumulative price.

When the price was announced he asked, "What are you willing to pay?"

Again, the salesmanship was directed to me and not to Sue. I was put on the hot seat, especially because a carpet purchase was not wanted.

My reply to his challenge was "half price." This was based on my previous experience forty-five years earlier when I negotiated a fifty percent reduction on three carpets over a seven-day period.

The merchant reacted immediately with, "That's impossible. I can't sell for that price. What can you pay?" I attempted to communicate with Sue. It was a case of shrugging our shoulders realizing that we were not in the driver's seat.

Our guide sat beside Sue offering no commentary or support as she was an accessory to the scheme.

Once the price was agreed to, I was led immediately into the financial transaction room. A bill of sale was written up and a credit card payment was to be processed. The first attempt failed, and I wishfully hoped that the process would fail completely. It would have been no loss as far as I was concerned. Unfortunately, the second attempt succeeded.

We walked away with mixed emotions. We had acquired unique handmade Moroccan carpets that we had had no intention of buying. Hopefully, we learned a lesson.

As it turned out, this experience did prepare us for a later situation in Marrakech when another Moroccan individual attempted to steer us into a carpet shop. We balked as soon as we realized the familiar ploy.

A CUT BELOW THE REST

On a visit to a friend's Christmas tree farm, I brought along an antique crosscut saw. My intention was to do the cutting by hand even though I owned a chainsaw.

I first spent time traversing the tree lot inspecting for the perfect tree. I located one and just as I was about to cut it down, Russ, the owner arrived. He offered to cut the tree with his trusty chainsaw. The situation was rather uncomfortable. His intention was generous, but I had planned to do it my way. He kindly relented. I then spent a minimal amount of sawing through a six-inch diameter stalk.

Once it was felled small branches at the base level required removal. Russ again offered to do the job. I agreed that he should.

He revved up his chainsaw. When it was placed against the first half-inch-diameter branch, no cutting action occurred. He applied more pressure with little improved cutting effect. He then shut off the chainsaw and inspected it. To everyone's amazement and Russ's embarrassment, the chain had been put on backwards.

Thus, no cutting ability.

I thought of the "Lumberjack Song" made famous by the comedy troupe Monty Python's Flying Circus. Their promotion of the quintessential Canadian lumberjack image failed in this case.

MOROCCAN REAR-ENDER

On the second last day of our five-week-long Moroccan road trip, Sue and I were travelling through a rural section.

As we entered the central part of a small, isolated town we encountered robust market activity. The main street was clogged with carts drawn by donkeys.

This forced us to reduce our speed to a snail's pace. Our utmost caution was required to avoid not only the donkey carts but also buyers and sellers crisscrossing the street.

Within five minutes of entering this melee, our vehicle suddenly lurched forward. Another vehicle rear-ended us at what appeared to be no more than twenty kilometres per hour.

The effect was minimal on us physically although we did sustain some damage to the trunk. The impact had popped the trunk open, and it was now unable to close properly.

The immediate aftermath was discombobulating. It was a foreign country, a foreign culture, and a foreign language. Within ten seconds the hand of a beggar was extended through my open window, seeking a contribution. Others in turn began giving us instructions as to what to do. Turn the car around. Follow another vehicle. Turn right on the next street. Keep following the lead vehicle. All of this was communicated in a combination of Arabic and sign language. We were at the mercy of these people, not having the faintest idea of what was taking place.

Within five minutes we arrived at an auto repair shop. Instructions were given by persons unknown to the occupants of the business to come out and inspect our vehicle.

In short order, employees began scurrying back and forth, attempting to repair the trunk of our car. The main dilemma was the inability of the trunk to close properly and lock. While this whole process ensued, we had no knowledge as to the "what and why." The language barrier prevented adequate communication. No one spoke or understood English. And we did not speak Arabic.

However, somehow, we impressed upon the attending workers that we also spoke French. It was then that a French-speaking individual was identified in an adjacent business. After he was sequestered, we learned that the owner of the offending vehicle had rushed to have our vehicle repaired.

After two hours of hammering the trunk into shape, success was achieved. The trunk managed to close and remain so. Minor physical damage was visible.

So, off we went. Our destination was Casablanca.

We met the car rental agent early on the morning of our departure. Once the damage was brought to his attention, he requested our police report. We had none. It was then that we learned the purpose of the panicked vehicle repair was motivated by the other driver's need to avoid police scrutiny.

Another lesson learned.

DECEPTIVE SOUNDS

While travelling in the wilds of the Yukon, we often ventured on hikes.

On one occasion as we were about to enter a territorial park, we stopped to read the signage. What struck us immediately was the warning: "High Risk of Grizzly Bears."

With the benefit of having our camper van nearby we extracted metal pots and spoons. These were going to be utilized as preventative measures to ward off grizzly bears.

As we clanged our way up the mountainside, we made no contact with either grizzly or human beings. The remoteness and the spectacular scenery made the strenuous effort worthwhile.

After a one or two-hour ascent we began our return, banging our saucepans once again. We were taking no chances. Eventually, we met up with a German tourist. Having heard our sound effects, he commented that he had spent time in Thailand and his immediate thought was that he was being approached by Buddhist Monks chiming their instruments.

MOROCCAN HIGHWAY CON ARTISTS

The Moroccan highway network was quite impressive. This also applied to most isolated areas of Morocco.

We crisscrossed most of the country except for the Northeast and Southwest extremes.

On one of our transits across the High Atlas, we were flagged down on a very isolated portion of the mountain highway. Foolishly we stopped, anticipating the driver needed assistance. It could have been a trap to mug us.

However, the lone male occupant explained in perfect English that he was having car trouble, namely oil issues. He presented us with an address written on a piece of paper, explaining that his friends lived there. "Could you stop and let them know I need help?" he asked.

The request seemed innocuous enough. The location was in a small town twenty kilometres down the road, so we proceeded there. Once entering the town, we slowly scanned street addresses. It was in the mid-business district that we found our goal. It was a small business catering to tourists. Its inventory consisted of Moroccan crafts and trinkets.

After parking our vehicle, we approached the entrance. A Moroccan male greeted us. Once we explained the situation, he and another male employee welcomed us with inordinate exuberance. They ushered us inside, offering us traditional Moroccan mint tea.

We were brought upstairs into a hospitality room. While the tea was brewed, they asked us questions in perfect English. In addition, they promoted the sale of the multitude of goods that surrounded us. It was then that I realized the entire plot.

We had unsuspectingly been directed to a business where we were expected to purchase their wares. It was quite ingenious.

Tea was served and the atmosphere was quite hospitable. No heavy-pressure sales tactics were used. We deflected each of their attempts. Yes, we had already purchased many of the items they promoted: carpets, leather, ceramics, and clothing.

This deflated their sales strategy. We departed on friendly terms. It was another lesson learned.

FEZ-LESS MUSICAL ENSEMBLE

In the latter days of our Moroccan tour, we ended up in the Atlantic port city of Essaouira.

It turned out to be an attractive location for several reasons: architecture, ambience, extensive market area, and seafood selection. To our delight, we arrived at the beginning of the Atlantic Andalusian Festival.

The three-day event consisted of music, dance performances and lectures, all of which focused on the historical bond between the Iberian Peninsula and North Africa. And what made it especially attractive was the fact that entry was free to all the events—first come, first served of course.

The first event we attended was an over-the-top energetic performance of traditional music. Led by a flamboyant violinist, the ensemble consisted of ten to twelve musicians. Most of the instruments were traditional string instruments. From time to time, solo or duet vocalists performed.

An eye-catching aspect of the ensemble was a cluster of four musicians dressed in their traditional fez head coverings. We enjoyed this unique visual and audible opportunity. The full-house performance venue rocked with enthusiasm. Sue and I revelled in experiencing this rare opportunity.

With the festival schedule in hand, we attended a second performance the following day. Again, the venue was filled. The audience members seemed to be starved for this cultural revival.

It was not long into the performance that I noticed the ensemble had been altered. The four fez-covered musicians of the previous day were absent.

From my observation, I thought their absence was a visual loss.

I voiced my concern to Sue, seated beside me: "This is a fez-less orchestra."

Her reaction was immediate. She burst out laughing, causing me to join her with the same intensity. It became a dilemma. We couldn't control ourselves. At the same time, we were cognizant of the disturbance we were creating for the surrounding patrons. It was a shoulder-to-shoulder packed house.

Why my comment precipitated a knee-jerk outburst of laughter we will never know.

A MATTER OF PERSPECTIVE

On two occasions I have had the benefit of witnessing talks given on the topic of the need for human harmony in times of disharmony.

The first occurred in the late 1990s. The speaker—Dr. David Suzuki.

Although David's main theme was environmental concerns, he did deviate during the question-and-answer period.

The question posed was, "How do you prevent nations' leaders from waging wars in times of confrontation?" David's response was well-intentioned but flawed.

"The solution is to appeal to the leaders based on protecting their own offspring and grandchildren from the devastation of wars. Nothing is more precious than your own blood."

At that moment I raised my hand in the hope that I could offer a countering argument. Fortunately, David acknowledged me.

"Dr. Suzuki," I offered, "your solution does not work. Just a short time ago the Iran–Iraq War demonstrated the futility of your proposal. Both leaders of those nations conscripted children as young as twelve years old. They were exploited to fight a war with the promise of eternal heavenly bliss. Obviously, there was no allegiance to the youth of each nation."

The discussion ended there with no further response from Dr. Suzuki.

The second scenario occurred in a public presentation during the Atlantic Andalusian Festival in Essaouira in 2017.

The talk was given by a British academic of Israeli descent. The topic: "The Need for Harmony in the World."

His speaking skills were near flawless. I was very impressed with the clarity and persuasiveness of his argument. The full-house audience was captivated by the nature of his cause. His passion was very convincing. However, I felt that his argument was idealistic.

Following the talk, Sue and I milled around the balcony overlooking the main floor. It wasn't long before we brushed aside the presenter. He was going in the opposite direction to ours. When we were directly shoulder to shoulder, I took the opportunity to engage him in a conversation.

"May I compliment you on your speech. I was very impressed." He acknowledged my kind words. But I pursued my commentary further, "Although I respect your point of view, I feel it is naïve because harmony amongst humans does not work. There are countless examples. Humans do not have the genetic code to resolve issues peacefully. It is my opinion that what is required for the human species to achieve harmony is a need for genetic engineering. The hostility gene must be eliminated."

"Oh, no, no. I don't accept your perspective," was his immediate response. Almost simultaneously he rushed off leaving me abandoned.

I was no less respectful of this gentleman. I was thankful that he gave me the time to voice my opinion.

WILD BOAR

On our most recent trip to Spain, we arranged a house exchange in the Girona countryside. It was a mutual exchange with our home in Canada and necessitated several communications with the owner in advance. In addition to the crucial details, such as address, house access and cat-sitting chores, the owner offered a cautionary request: "Please keep the property gate always closed. The area is overpopulated with wild boars. If they gain access to my property, all the vegetation will be uprooted and eaten." Naturally, we planned to follow his directions.

Within a few days of our arrival, we spotted our first wild boar. It crossed the highway fifty metres in front of our vehicle. Having previous farm experience, I estimated the weight of the boar between three hundred and four hundred pounds. It was sizeable.

As we drove on subsequent days, I noticed that Sue was being quite persistent in checking the roadside terrain. This finally aroused my curiosity. "Sue, what are you looking for?" I asked.

"I'm looking for wild boars," she replied.

"You don't have to do that; you're sitting beside one," I replied.

My commentary was followed by a loud groan.

MICROWAVE

As we are all aware, every modern household seems to be outfitted with at least one kitchen microwave. They have become ubiquitous.

This situation even applies to secondary suites and recreational properties. In fact, there's a microwave in my wife's cottage.

We spend a fair number of weekends there. With a rather small kitchen area, the use of the microwave becomes a challenge. Opening and closing its door can infringe on the other person's space.

On one occasion, I opened the microwave by opening the door ninety percent to retrieve a coffee mug. This coincided with Sue being directly on the opposite side of the door. I happened to peer through the glass portion at the same time. Sure enough, there was Sue with her nose pressed against the glass. She was visible to me and vice versa.

Spontaneously I raised my hand to the glass and gave her a deliberate micro-wave in slow motion.

Sue burst out laughing. It was one of my better attempts at humour. Success is never guaranteed. It's always a case of trial and error.

AIRBNB

Everyone has become aware of the phenomenon known as Airbnb.

As a relatively recent addition to the world of travel accommodation, Airbnbs have become ubiquitous. However, it can be argued that they are not the original. Let me explain.

My wife and I were introduced to mason bees a few years ago. Our beekeeping experience over approximately ten years has been both enjoyable and educational.

Because mason bees don't sting, closeup observation is easily achievable. In fact, the whole process is very intriguing. Anticipating their mating habits, watching their continuous flying pattern to and fro to lay eggs and then depositing pollen makes the experience thrilling.

It was only during the most recent summer that I came to the conclusion that beehives are the original and only true "air bee and bees."

SPEEDO AND CHOCOLATE

Years prior to meeting Sue I swam regularly in indoor and outdoor pools.

My focus was to remain physically active. Swimming pool lengths necessitated my need for streamlined swimming apparel: the Speedo.

My swimming activity continued in the early days of our relationship. However, Sue's two teenage sons cringed at every opportunity at my appearance in a Speedo.

For the sake of providing the preliminary ingredients to the conclusion of this story, it is important to know that chocolate also became a bone of contention. Following a Christmas/ New Year's vacation, Sue and I returned to discover that our reserve of chocolates had disappeared.

When the stepsons were confronted, "You shouldn't have left them by the phone" was their excuse."

Fast forward several years. When on a lengthy trip to Australia, a visit to Sydney's Bondi Beach precipitated a thought. "Why don't I put on my Speedo, stick a piece of chocolate in my mouth, stand on the beach, and have Sue take a photo of me?"

My motive was to email the resulting photo to Chris and Michael.

Sure enough, Sue did take the photo at 6:30 a.m. by the way. It was sent with the covering comment. "I hope you appreciate two of your favourite things, Speedos and chocolates."

Only one response materialized. "I see that no one else was on the beach." Obviously implying that my appearance deterred others.

In turn, my reply read, "I am looking to purchase Official Australian Team Speedos for both of you. My recollection is that your sizes are extra small."

SPEEDO AND CHOCOLATE REVISITED

Ten years after I sent my stepsons, Chris and Mike, the photo of me in my Speedo with a piece of chocolate in my mouth, I thought, "Why don't I resend them that photo?"

And so, I did under the heading, "Momentous Anniversary."

"This is the tenth anniversary of the photogenic pose on Bondi Beach, Australia," I wrote. "I am sure you will savour the view again since, as I recall, you appreciated the original. I can even recall the sensation of the chocolate melting in my mouth."

The responses were slow in coming. But the comments are to be treasured: "Still cringeworthy after all these years," wrote Mike. "Fantastic," wrote Chris. "My new screenshot."

I can't wait till the next significant anniversary.

ASSAULT OF A PRIME MINISTER

In early November 1960, I was thirteen years old.

My uncle Metro invited me to join him in a demonstration at a union hall located on the outskirts of Sudbury, Ontario. John Diefenbaker, prime minister of Canada, was to make a speaking appearance there.

The protesters, members of the Mine Mill Union, were demonstrating their grievance against the United Steelworkers union, which had raided the MMU. The presence of Mr. Diefenbaker at the hall offered the protesters a high-profile opportunity to voice their discontentment.

Protest members began arriving two hours in advance of the speaking engagement. With placards in hand, they formed a circle in the sizeable gravel parking lot. As more arrived the circle expanded, and members rotated slowly in a clockwise fashion.

I did not participate but stood back on a small bluff overlooking the event.

Approximately thirty minutes prior to the appointed meeting, a black Cadillac limousine arrived.

It slowly entered the parking lot. At the same time, the hundred or so protesters made an opening in their circle allowing the vehicle to enter. Once entered, the limousine became surrounded by the tightening of the circle.

When the chauffeur could not safely proceed any farther, the vehicle stopped.

At that point, a rear door opened, and Mr. Diefenbaker stepped out to confront the protesters. His wife Olive and the chauffeur remained inside the vehicle.

I quickly became agitated. As a young teenager, I was deeply disturbed at the possibility of violence towards a person of such stature, the prime minister of Canada. Remarkably, no police escort or protection was present.

Shortly after exiting the limousine, words were exchanged between Mr. Diefenbaker and the protesters. Simultaneously I observed our prime minister being whacked on the head several times with placards.

My recollection is that he walked the remaining thirty metres into the union hall without any further assault. The chauffeured vehicle followed.

Having witnessed this event was quite traumatizing for me. I couldn't fathom the disrespect shown towards someone who deserved reverence. At the same time, I admired Mr. Diefenbaker for his courage.

The affair concluded with tomatoes being thrown at the building's exterior windows and police arriving well before the completion of the speech.

As an epilogue, two or three protesters were eventually arrested and found guilty of assault one year later.

TWO OF MY FAVOURITES

For several years, the Pawluk family conducted an annual gathering in Stratford, Ontario. The last occasion was in 2019, before COVID disrupted the following years of 2020 and 2021.

Stratford, Ontario, was the logical location since it was central to various family members. Firstly, it was the hometown of my daughter Emma and her family. My daughter Katie and her four children would travel from Brooklyn, New York. My sisters, Margaret and Caroline, would drive from Sudbury, Ontario, and my wife and I would fly from Richmond, British Columbia.

The date of the family affair always took place in the first week of July, and for good reasons: It was an opportunity to celebrate Canada Day on July 1, our grandson Avery's birthday on July 3, American Independence Day on July 4, my birthday on July 6, and our grandson Andrew's birthday on July 7.

For the 2019 festivity, Sue and I arrived on the evening of July 3 just in time to celebrate Avery's birthday. A barbeque was being hosted at the home of my ex-wife Margaret. Fortunately, I have remained on good terms with her, and we were welcomed.

With the meal in progress, I spontaneously announced my pleasure. "I am so happy to be here. I have my five treasured grandchildren, my two favourite daughters, my two favourite sisters and my two favourite wives!"

Of course, my presumptuousness was met first with astonishment and then with hearty laughter.

I am happy to report no ill will was generated between my ex and me. A sense of humour can overcome great difficulties of the past.

FIRE ON FIVE

January 30, 1984, began as a typical day. My first daily responsibility was to pick up my daughter Katie and drive her to school. Her mother accompanied us as our shared vehicle was to be transferred to her for the day.

We travelled our usual route beginning with a long stretch along No. 5 Road. As we proceeded in a southerly direction, I noticed a stream of smoke rising into the sky in advance of our location. As we continued, it became apparent that smoke was emanating from a house on the left-hand side of the roadway.

I slowed down considerably to assess the situation, eventually stopping on the side of the road opposite the building in distress. Smoke was billowing from the upper southerly portion, but the most remarkable aspect of the scene was the lack of any human activity.

In my mind, the situation necessitated an immediate response. I parked our vehicle, ran across the road, and banged on a ground-floor door. I assumed this was the entrance to the fire source.

No response came. I then began kicking in the door with success. My shouting, hoping for a response, was futile.

I immediately moved on to the next doorway to my left. I repeated the same procedure, banging, kicking in the door, and then shouting. This entrance led to a long staircase and a second-floor residence. I yelled, "Fire!" multiple times.

Within ten to fifteen seconds a nude man appeared at the top of the staircase. He was a very disoriented individual. He disappeared just as quickly into the area from which he appeared. His action totally mystified me. However, he reappeared shortly after with a female clutching a child. All three were wrapped in sheets. I coaxed them downstairs to the support of other awakened tenants. At the same time, I asked the male if others were present in the same unit. He replied in the affirmative, pointing in the opposite direction of the apartment.

I then asked for and received a wet cloth to cover my mouth and nostrils. I returned, and climbed the staircase, shouting and hoping to elicit a response. The upper three-quarters of the hallway was now filled with smoke. Sparks were falling from the ceiling light fixture. Still no response.

Without success, I returned downstairs to my frantic wife, a crowd of onlookers, and the sound of sirens approaching. With what appeared to be a situation gaining control, I returned to the vehicle and drove my daughter to school.

It was the following day that the RCMP interviewed me regarding my involvement and observations. I was informed that a twelve-year-old girl had started a fire with matches. She perished as well as a thirty-year-old guest from smoke inhalation. In addition, I had awakened two other adults who escaped through a secondary rear exit.

According to the authorities, this tragedy was preventable if smoke alarms had been present. As a postscript, I was credited with saving the lives of five individuals.

GRANDKIDS' COMMENTS

With family arriving from Brooklyn, New York, I needed to provide them with transport from the Vancouver Airport to our home.

I arrived with the family van, parked, and greeted them at the terminal.

With the size of the family and accompanying luggage, a taxi was required as well. When we all reconvened at home, I was informed by my daughter that after seeing me again one of my grandsons, Avery, age four, remarked that I, the grandfather, was "a very old man."

***

Gardening was a practice that we tried to instil in our grandchildren at the earliest possible age. We purchased children's garden tools and equipment to have them participate.

On one occasion, our grandsons Sammy and Oliver scooped up shovels full of soil to be deposited in the kids' wheelbarrow. When it was heaping full, Sammy, age six, asked, "Grandpa, do you think you can lift the wheelbarrow and put it on the grass? Then can you push it to the other end of the garden and put it back in the garden?"

"Yes, I can, Sammy."

Once I had lifted the wheelbarrow and placed it on the grass, Sammy commented, "Grandpa, are you ever strong for an old man."

I burst out laughing.

***

As a professional house painter, my work attire would never have been considered tidy. I had unlimited opportunities for dirt and paint to accumulate on my painter's clothes.

This was the condition of my clothes when I returned home from work at the time of a family dinner. Knowing that my grandchildren were in attendance, I decided to ring the front entrance doorbell.

Matthew, age five, swung the front door open, looked at me and volunteered, "Are you ever dirty."

***

On a visit to my family in Brooklyn, New York, I had the opportunity to walk two of my grandsons to the subway en route to their school.

The fifteen-minute walk required multiple street crossings. It was always our practice to hold hands, stop, and look both ways before crossing.

As we waited patiently at one intersection until the traffic passed, Avery, age six, blurted out, "Get off the road, Grandpa."

He startled me. "What do mean, Avery?"

"Your shadow is on the road," he replied. "You will get run over."

I was impressed with his insightful observation.

***

We became aware of my grandson Sammy's precociousness when he was at the early age of three. This was the era of uttering "why" to every possible circumstance. It brought hilarity to us, his grandparents, especially.

Often Grandma Sue would react by commenting, "You crack me up."

And Sammy would come back immediately saying, "I'm not an egg."

Sue and I, as proud grandparents, were looking forward to attending hockey games. We were informed that Sammy and Oliver were playing in two separate games on a Saturday afternoon.

Shortly after arriving at the rink, we were able to observe Sammy playing on the ice. However, I noticed Oliver running around in his street clothes. We had expected Oliver to be playing hockey as well.

I beckoned Oliver and asked, "Aren't you playing hockey?"

"No," he confided, "I just lie on the ice and cry." This came as a complete surprise.

Ironically, seven years later, Sammy no longer plays hockey and Oliver is an outstanding defenceman on a championship team.

***

A remarkable observation and unsolicited comment from Andrew, our five-year-old grandson, was that "birds laugh out loud." It blew me away.

***

Our grandson Sammy, age eleven, approached his grandma Sue at a family gathering.

"Why don't you live with Poppa?"

"Because we are divorced" replied Sue. "We didn't get along."

Obviously, this didn't satisfy Sammy as he floored everyone with the following question: "What was the issue?"

Sue and I spontaneously burst out laughing as did the others within hearing range.

No answer was forthcoming on Sue's part.

***

My granddaughter Aretha was introduced to banking at the very early age of five. Her mother had decided that it was a worthwhile experience.

While establishing the account with a bank teller, Aretha was asked, "Would you like to use an ATM?"

"Yes," Aretha replied.

"Then you will need a pin," countered the teller. "Will you be able to remember your pin?"

"Of course," Aretha volunteered, "I'm a very smart girl."

***

Andrew, my grandson, was on the cusp of turning four. On the day before his fourth birthday, he announced, "This is the last day that I am three. A few days after celebrating his fourth birthday, he asked, "Am I still four?"

***

Felix, my oldest grandson, was in the habit of climbing trees in his thirteenth year. The opportunity usually occurred when visiting his aunt Emma. Her property was lined with trees. One tree taller and larger than the rest attracted his attention.

While the family gathered in the backyard, Felix and his brother Avery scrambled amongst the branches at a height of about three metres.

Suddenly we heard a piercing vocal outburst signifying intense pain. Felix had fallen from a branch that had given way. Within seconds we gathered around attempting to soothe his pain while emergency vehicles were called. Felix had broken his right tibia and fibula.

As Felix lay on the ground, I noticed the concerned look on the face of the youngest brother, Freddie, age six. "What are you thinking Freddie?" I asked.

"At least he still exists," he replied.

To me, it was an interesting turn of phrase. Felix eventually mended successfully from the freak accident.

***

At the end of the 2019 school year, the Pawluk family gathered in Stratford, Ontario. Four of the school-aged grandchildren arrived from the US. Shortly after my arrival, I wanted to question them about their year-end report cards. Aretha, age seven, happened to be first.

"Aretha," I asked, "How were your school marks?"

"The best in the family!" elicited Aretha.

I was taken aback. "What do you mean?" I responded.

"I beat all of my brothers."

On checking with her mother, she corroborated that Aretha had outperformed everyone in the family.

***

Having just enjoyed a wonderful outdoor family dinner, my grandson Andrew, newly four, turned his attention to me. "Gigi [Grandpa]," he announced, "you're handsome."

This spontaneous and unsolicited comment came as a surprise to all present.

I will treasure that remark forever.

***

During a facetime session with our twin grandchildren, Aretha and Freddie, I noticed Aretha engrossed in a book. She was oblivious to my attempt to include her in our conversation. When I eventually gained her attention, I asked "Aretha, can you read?"

"Yes, I can, but Freddie can't," came her response.

At that point, Freddie raised two fingers in the air declaring, "I can read two words."

420

EPILOGUE

The entire process of first recalling the stories, then jotting them down in two or three words, and eventually fleshing them out over a ten-year span has been extremely rewarding. Never did I think that a marketable book would evolve.

My recollections were meant for personal satisfaction, to be shared with family and friends. Now that the process has concluded I hope I have passed the audition.

But just in case, an additional thirty thousand to forty thousand words have been archived for a potential continuation of my memoir . . . and as every day passes more anecdotes accumulate in a life of laughter and lessons.

CPSIA information can be obtained
at www.ICGtesting.com
Printed in the USA
LVHW052248090523
746584LV00017B/179